CHURCHILL'S PEACETIME MINISTRY, 1951–55

Also by Henry Pelling

WINSTON CHURCHILL
THE LABOUR GOVERNMENTS, 1945–51
A SHORT HISTORY OF THE LABOUR PARTY
A HISTORY OF BRITISH TRADE UNIONISM
BRITAIN AND THE MARSHALL PLAN
BRITAIN AND THE SECOND WORLD WAR
THE ORIGINS OF THE LABOUR PARTY
THE CHALLENGE OF SOCIALISM
THE BRITISH COMMUNIST PARTY
AMERICA AND THE BRITISH LEFT
AMERICAN LABOR
LABOUR AND POLITICS, 1900–1906 (*with Frank Bealey*)
THE SOCIAL GEOGRAPHY OF BRITISH ELECTIONS, 1895–1910
POPULAR POLITICS AND SOCIETY IN LATE VICTORIAN BRITAIN

Churchill's Peacetime Ministry, 1951–55

Henry Pelling
Fellow of St John's College
University of Cambridge

First published in Great Britain 1997 by
MACMILLAN PRESS LTD
Houndmills, Basingstoke, Hampshire RG21 6XS
and London
Companies and representatives
throughout the world

A catalogue record for this book is available
from the British Library.

ISBN 0–333–55597–X hardcover
ISBN 0–333–67709–9 paperback

First published in the United States of America 1997 by
ST. MARTIN'S PRESS, INC.,
Scholarly and Reference Division,
175 Fifth Avenue,
New York, N.Y. 10010

ISBN 0–312–16271–5

Library of Congress Cataloging-in-Publication Data
Pelling, Henry.
Churchill's peacetime ministry, 1951–55 / Henry Pelling.
p.   cm.
Includes bibliographical references and index.
ISBN 0–312–16271–5 (cloth)
1. Great Britain—Politics and government—1945–1964.
2. Churchill, Winston, Sir, 1874–1965.   I. Title.
DA592.P45   1996
941.085'5—dc20   96–2994
                                                              CIP

© Henry Pelling 1997

10   9   8   7   6   5   4   3   2   1
06   05   04   03   02   01   00   99   98   97

Printed and bound in Great Britain by
Antony Rowe Ltd, Chippenham, Wiltshire

Contents

List of Plates

Preface

This book covers the three-and-a-half years of Winston Churchill's second premiership, 1951–55. It thus deals with the same period as the notable and fuller study by Dr Anthony Seldon, *Churchill's Indian Summer* (1981). Its claim to novelty lies in its use of the Cabinet Minutes and Papers now available at the Public Record Office at Kew, of the Prime Minister's papers at the same location, and of the private papers of more Cabinet Ministers, especially those of Anthony Eden now at Birmingham University Library.

I am particularly grateful to Lady Avon for allowing me access to the Eden Papers before they were formally declared open, and to Dr Benedicz, the Birmingham University Archivist. Mr Graham Stewart of my own college helped me with research assistance in the final stages. Mrs Jane Rogers patiently undertook the retyping of the final version. Mr Damien Browne, also of St John's College, kindly read the proofs. Any errors that remain are my own responsibility.

St John's College   H.M.P.
Cambridge

1 The Labour Interlude

When Churchill and the Conservative Party were defeated in the 1945 General Election, the verdict of the electors was so decisive that the Prime Minister concluded that he 'did not wish to remain even for an hour responsible for their affairs'.[1] He therefore resigned office on the evening of the declaration of the results, 26 July, and advised the King to send for Clement Attlee, the Labour leader. But those Conservatives who were elected to Parliament realised that had it not been for Churchill's leadership their defeat would have been even more severe. When the Commons reassembled on 1 August, therefore, they greeted him by singing 'For He's a Jolly Good Fellow'. And Churchill himself, although already over seventy years old, signified his willingness to continue as party leader by buying a house in Kensington, 28 Hyde Park Gate, to supplement his country residence at Chartwell, near Westerham in Kent.

As the party was out of office, however, Churchill saw no need for regular attendance at the House of Commons. He sympathised with many of the early measures of the Government, including the state control of the Bank of England, and Ernest Bevin's blunt confrontation of the Soviet leaders at Foreign Ministers' meetings. He formed a Shadow Cabinet of some fifteen members, but they were not allotted specific responsibilities in the fashion which has since become customary.[2] The Shadow Cabinet met weekly on Wednesdays at 6 p.m. when the House was sitting. It included three peers – Lord Woolton, the wealthy man of commerce who had served as Minister of Food during the war, and had only joined the Conservative Party after the 1945 election; Lord Cranbourne, who used his courtesy title as eldest son of the Marquess of Salisbury, but who had joined the Lords in 1941 as Lord Cecil of Essendon; and Churchill's scientific adviser, Lord Cherwell, who held the chair of Experimental Philosophy (Physics) at Oxford. The Commons members were led by Anthony Eden, the wartime Foreign Secretary, whom Churchill regarded as his Deputy; the 'two Olivers' – Oliver Stanley, a younger son of the Earl of Derby, who had been Colonial Secretary for three years, and Oliver Lyttelton, another businessman who had been the wartime Minister of Production. Others on the Front Bench included R.A. Butler, the wartime Minister of Education; Harold Macmillan, who had been Minister of State in the Mediterranean; Harry Crookshank, who had held only minor office but was respected as a debater; Sir David Maxwell Fyfe, a former Attorney-General; and James Stuart, who had been Government Chief Whip for four years and now became Opposition Chief Whip. Members of the Shadow Cabinet were also invited by Churchill to join him at a fortnightly lunch at the Savoy Hotel when he was in London.[3]

At first the Opposition had difficulty in getting into its stride. The backbenchers wanted a more vigorous attack on Labour domestic policy than its leaders seemed capable of mounting, and this concern manifested itself at a meeting of the 1922 Committee (the Conservative backbenchers) on 19 November 1945, when Churchill had to promise that either he or Eden would be present for major debates.[4] Shortly afterwards the Opposition tabled a censure motion on the Government, and on 28 November Churchill delivered a vigorous speech to the Central Council of the Conservative Party deploring the fact that 'the Socialists' were encouraging the 'gloomy State vultures of nationalisation' to 'hover above our basic industries.'

Nevertheless, Churchill had no intention of spending all his time at Westminster. Early in the New Year (1946) he went off on a prolonged visit to the United States – first to have a rest in the sun in Florida, and then, early in March, to address an audience at Fulton, Missouri, on international affairs. His speech, introduced by President Truman, caused a sensation because of his blunt attack on Soviet policy in Eastern Europe: 'From Stettin in the Baltic to Trieste in the Adriatic, an iron curtain has descended across the Continent... This is certainly not the liberated Europe we fought to build up. Nor is it one that contains the essentials of permanent peace.' He then called for the unity of the 'Western Democracies' and especially 'the whole strength of the English-speaking world and all its connections.'[5] The reactions to the speech were at first critical, both in the United States and in Britain, but after a few months its general theme won more and more approval, and it was accepted as prophetic.

On his return to England in late March Churchill at once began to recruit a team of experts to help him write his war memoirs. He had resolved to sell them to the highest bidder, and thereby to build up a fund for the future maintenance of his family. He wrote to Anthony Eden formally to ask him to be Deputy Leader of the Opposition in the Commons.[6] Churchill in fact wanted Eden to take the salary of the Leader of the Opposition, but Eden felt he could not do so while also serving as a director of public companies – a role which he had assumed in order to provide himself with an income, but which he had come to enjoy.[7]

Eden also prevailed over Churchill in the choice of a new Chairman for the extra-parliamentary Conservative Party. Churchill favoured Harold Macmillan, but Eden preferred Lord Woolton.[8] Woolton's appointment was announced on 1 July 1946, and he took over the Central Office in September.[9] There were not a few, also, who thought that Conservative policy needed re-stating. Among these was Eden, who at the Party Conference in October called for a 'property-owning democracy'. Although Churchill was sceptical of any programme of policies, commenting 'It is dangerous to pre-scribe until you are called in,'[10] he agreed to the establishment of an Industrial Policy Committee, under the chairmanship of R.A. Butler, who had become head of the party's Research Department. The Committee included, besides Butler, the Olivers (Stanley and Lyttelton), Macmillan and Maxwell Fyfe, as well as four backbenchers.

The result of the Committee's work was the *Industrial Charter*, which called for private enterprise and incentive, and opposed nationalisation on principle. Some Conservatives were shocked, though, that it accepted several of the Labour Government's measures, including the public ownership of the Bank of England, the coal industry and the railways. On the other hand, it demanded the privatisation of road haulage and expressed strong opposition to the Government's im-pending nationalisation of the iron and steel industry, which was profitable and enjoyed good labour relations. The state-ment was tacitly accepted by Churchill, published in May 1947, and, in spite of some right-wing criticism, overwhelmingly ap-proved at the Brighton Party Conference in October that year.[11]

Until this date the party was making little recovery in the country. Churchill's apparent indifference to the situation and his concentration upon his war memoirs caused a revolt in the Shadow Cabinet. James Stuart has recorded how early in 1947 he and other colleagues met at Harry Crookshank's house in Pont Street, Belgravia, and deputed him (Stuart) to call on Churchill and urge him to retire. Stuart wrote that Churchill, who had evidently heard other suggestions to the same effect, 'reacted violently, banging the floor with his stick and implying that I too had joined those who were plotting to displace him.'[12]

In the course of 1947, however, the Labour Government ran into increasing difficulties, many of them of its own making. Few Conservatives believed that the fuel crisis during the harsh winter months was due to an 'Act of God'; they were inclined to blame, as Lord Swinton put it, 'the inactivity of Emanuel' (the Minister of Fuel and Power was Emanuel Shinwell).[13] In August the Government was again in trouble: the convertibility of the pound which had been insisted on by the Americans as a condition of a substantial loan had to be suspended, and further economies were forced upon the country, including the abolition of the basic petrol ration. This was the Conservative Party's opportunity. Woolton issued an appeal for a central fund of £1,000,000, a sum which he succeeded in raising within a few months, and party membership, which was well over a million by the end of 1947, was almost doubled by mid-1948.[14]

Churchill's personal interests continued to be in the sphere of external relations. Although he sympathised with the main lines of Ernest Bevin's foreign policy, he deplored the Labour Government's disengagement from India, and warmly supported the Zionist cause in Palestine. On neither of these issues, however, was he whole-heartedly backed by members of his own parliamentary party. If he was somewhat more successful in securing their support in his campaign for the unification of Europe, that was perhaps because few of them realised what it might imply for Britain.

It was in a speech at Zurich in September 1946 that Churchill first called for 'a kind of United States of Europe', and urged as a first step a 'partnership' of France and Germany.[15] To further this end, he formed in Britain a nonpartisan 'Committee for a United Europe', and similar bodies were established in other Western European countries. On the Continent, Socialists joined as eagerly as Conservatives and Liberals, but in Britain, largely owing to Bevin's opposition, the Labour Party refused to participate. In spite of this setback, the movement held a Congress at The Hague in May 1948, and several Labour MPs attended, as well as Churchill himself and a distinguished host of Continental leaders. In his speech at the Congress, Churchill pointed out that since he spoke at Zurich, General Marshall, the American Secretary of State, had initiated the European Recovery Plan, popularly known as 'the Marshall Plan', and had acknowledged his debt to Churchill's ideas. Churchill also welcomed to the Congress a German delegation which included Dr Konrad Adenauer, later the leader of the West German Government.[16]

Back in England, and in accordance with the decisions of the Hague Congress, Churchill together with colleagues in what was now called the British section of the 'United Europe Movement' visited No. 10 Downing Street in a deputation to urge Attlee and Bevin to accept the idea of a 'European Assembly'. Under pressure from the other countries of Western Europe as well as the United States on this point, Bevin in January 1949 accepted the idea of a 'Council of Europe' with consultative powers, comprising a Committee of Ministers appointed by Governments and an Assembly representing Parliaments.[17] The first meeting of the Assembly was held at Strasbourg in August 1949, and although Eden was a conspicuous absentee, the British Conservatives who attended included Churchill himself and two of his other front-benchers, Maxwell Fyfe and Harold Macmillan.[18] In a speech on 17 August, Churchill called out 'Where are the Germans?' He urged that they should forthwith join the deliberations. Arrangements were made to ensure that they would be invited to the next meeting of the Assembly in 1950.[19]

Meanwhile, as the next General Election approached, the Conservative Party at home had been getting restive, especially at their conspicuous failure to win any seats at by-elections. A marginal seat which became vacant at Hammersmith South was contested vigorously in February 1949, but in spite of a swing to the Conservatives the Labour candidate was again the victor. Actually, the swing if reflected nationally would have been quite sufficient to return a Conservative Government.[20] But the failure to capture the seat caused the 1922 Committee to hold a post-mortem early in March, and Churchill came in for no little criticism. However, after a long debate he succeeded in pacifying the backbenchers, promising them a general statement of policy in the near future and a commitment to concentrate his own efforts thereafter on electioneering.[21]

The new statement of Conservative policy, *The Right Road for Britain,* was published in July 1949 with an introduction by Churchill, who also outlined it in a speech at Wolverhampton. Once again, as in the *Industrial Charter,* there was an acceptance of the main achievements of the Labour Government, both as regards social services and nationalisation, though the industries already nationalised were to be reorganised and decentralised. The statement also called for the reform of the House of Lords and the restoration of university representation. It was approved with only eight dissentients at the party conference at Earl's Court in October.[22]

Early in January 1950 Attlee announced the dissolution of Parliament. The General Election was to take place on 23 February, and Churchill, who had gone for a working holiday to Madeira, flew back to take charge of the Conservative Party campaign. In an election broadcast on 21 January, he took care not to denounce his opponents as bluntly as he had done in 1945, and declared that 'the Conservative and National Liberal Parties regard the prevention of mass unemployment as the most solemn duty of government.' Churchill's keenness to enlist the Liberal vote on his side was resented by the leader of the independent Liberal Party, Clement Davies, who sent Churchill a letter of protest. Davies, however, was personally on very weak ground, as Churchill immediately pointed out:

> As you were yourself for eleven years a National Liberal and in that capacity supported the Governments of Mr Baldwin and Mr Chamberlain I shall not presume to correct your knowledge of the moral, intellectual and legal aspects of adding a prefix or a suffix to the honoured name of Liberal.[23]

The Conservative manifesto for the election, *This is the Road,* was published on 24 January. It echoed all the themes of the

1949 statement, *The Right Road for Britain,* but with a little more emphasis on the problems caused by the dollar gap which had led to devaluation of the pound in the previous September. As the Act nationalising the iron and steel industry had been passed but not yet brought into force, the Conservative manifesto promised to repeal it and also to restore the road haulage industry to private ownership. Other nationalised industries would be decentralised and subjected to 'periodic review...by Parliament'. The attitude to trade unions was cautious: they were to be encouraged, and consulted so as to secure 'a full and friendly settlement of the questions of contracting out and compulsory unionism'. A 'Workers' Charter' would guarantee employees' rights *vis-à-vis* employers. The House of Lords would be reformed and university constituencies restored.[24]

Churchill followed his practice of earlier years in addressing large meetings in the country, at Leeds, at Cardiff, at Devonport (where his own son Randolph was standing) and at Edinburgh. Speaking at Edinburgh about the outlook in international affairs, he said: 'It is not easy to see how things could be worsened by a parley at the summit.' This was, as his principal biographer has pointed out, the first use of the term 'summit' for a meeting of heads of government.[25] Churchill's final excursion outside the London area was to address a big meeting at Manchester on 20 February.

The outcome of the election was at first very uncertain. The count took place in only 266 constituencies on the night of polling, and of these Labour won 163. When next day's results began to come in, however, the gap between the parties began to close, and briefly in the afternoon the Conservatives and Liberals together equalled the Labour total.[26] In the end the result gave Labour a narrow majority over all other parties of six seats. Labour had 315, the Conservatives 298 and the Liberals nine. Although there had been a considerable swing from Labour to the Conservatives, the most crushing defeat had been suffered by the Liberals, who had put up 495 candidates, had a net loss of three seats out of twelve and lost 319 deposits.[27] Randolph Churchill failed to win Devonport but his two brothers-in-law, Duncan Sandys, the husband of Diana Churchill, and Christopher Soames, who had married Mary Churchill in 1947, both won their contests.

When Parliament reassembled in March, Churchill argued at once that the Government now had no right to proceed to further measures of nationalisation. He also maintained that the injustice done to 2,600,000 Liberal voters made a case for a Select Committee on Electoral Reform. He held emphatically that the Labour Government had no mandate for the continuation of its policy of nationalisation. Nevertheless, Attlee and his colleagues, although recognising that fresh legislation for this purpose was out of the question, had no intention of abandoning the Iron and Steel Act which was already on the statute book though not yet in operation. The Opposition offered two amendments to the King's Speech, but it was clear that they were not anxious to bring the Government down at once, for the amendments were defeated by majorities of 14 and 25 – the Liberals voting first with the Opposition and then with the Government.[28] The fact was that the Conservatives did not wish to take responsibility for the 1950 Budget, which passed through the House relatively easily, and Churchill did not object to a normal summer recess, although the invasion of South Korea had taken place in late June and a British contribution to the United Nations forces was soon on its way there. For the time being Churchill kept his eyes upon Europe, and in August at another meeting of the European Assembly he called for a European army 'with a unified command, and in which we should all bear a worthy and honourable part.'[29]

When Parliament was recalled in September in order to pass a National Service Bill (increasing the length of service from 18 months to two years) the Conservative leadership decided to make a challenge to the Government on the issue of iron and steel nationalisation, which the Government was now bringing into operation. The motion was defeated by six votes. But apart from this, the Opposition preferred to bide their time. Indeed, throughout 1950, as Professor Hoffman has put it:

> The Conservative Opposition...refrained from using the full potential of its imposing parliamentary position to try to topple the Labour Government from power.[30]

The extra-parliamentary party was more restive, and in October, when the Party Conference met at Blackpool, the delegates demanded, and Woolton on behalf of the Shadow Cabinet accepted, a commitment to build 300,000 new houses a year. Churchill in his closing speech accepted this as the party's main domestic priority 'in time of peace' and appealed to the delegates for 'one more heave' to remove Labour from power.[31]

Churchill's hopes were realised in 1951, when the Conservatives took a clear lead in the opinion polls. This was due in large part to the inflation caused by the Korean War: the price of raw materials rose rapidly, and the Labour Government actually established a Ministry of Materials under a Cabinet Minister, Richard Stokes. Politically, the Conservatives in Parliament became more vigorous in their attempts to unseat the Government. By putting down 'prayers' to annul statutory orders, they forced the Government to keep its MPs in the House until the small hours of the morning. As Robert Boothby put it, it was their object 'to make the Government sit up day and night and grind away until they get absolutely hysterical.'[32] However. the Government found a solution to the problem by moving the adjournment of the House at ten o'clock. Nevertheless, there were prolonged debates on clauses of the Finance Bill, and when the vote was expected to be close, MPs were brought in from hospitals, in some cases on stretchers.

Meanwhile, the Labour leadership was seriously weakened early in 1951 by the enforced resignation owing to ill-health first of Ernest Bevin, the Foreign Secretary, and then of Sir Stafford Cripps, the Chancellor of the Exchequer. Bevin was succeeded by Herbert Morrison, who proved to be out of his depth at the Foreign Office; and Hugh Gaitskell, who was appointed Chancellor at the age of 44, was a man of technical ability but political inexperience – as his mentor Hugh Dalton put it in his diary, he had no 'Public Face in the Labour Movement in the country.'[33] Gaitskell's 1951 Budget imposed charges on National Health dentures and spectacles, to help pay for the enlarged rearmament programme, and this provoked a revolt by Aneurin Bevin and Harold Wilson, who both resigned their Cabinet posts.

Meanwhile, in November 1950, so-called 'volunteers' from China had intervened in the Korean War and swept the United Nations forces back from near the Manchurian border to a line well south of the 38th parallel, which since 1945 had divided the two zones of occupation. In the spring of 1951 President Truman boldly dismissed his Far Eastern Commander-in-Chief, General Douglas MacArthur, who wanted to carry the war into China, and replaced him with General Matthew Ridgway, who as Army Commander had already won back the ground lost south of the 38th Parallel. In July armistice negotiations began between the two sides, although the fighting continued at a reduced tempo.[34]

On the main issues of the Korean War, and the participation of British troops on the United Nations side under American command, there was no difference between the main parties in Britain. But when the Persian government nationalised the Anglo-Iranian Oil Company in the spring, the issue aroused much conflict in Parliament. Early in July the Labour Government secured an injunction from the International Court at The Hague, and in August Attlee sent Richard Stokes, the Lord Privy Seal (and Minister of Materials), to Teheran to see if he could negotiate a settlement. But the Persian Government under Dr Mossadeq was inflexible, and early in October the British technicians at the refinery at Abadan were forced to abandon their posts. Churchill commented on this: 'Now that it is known that we will not in any circumstances offer physical resistance to violence and aggression...we must expect that Egypt will treat us more roughly still.' Herbert Morrison challenged Churchill to say whether he was advocating war with Persia, but Eden replied on his behalf: 'It was nonsense to pretend that there was no alternative between the total abandonment of Abadan and war, or to suggest that if the Tories had been in power there would have been a war.'[35]

Although Labour was trailing in the opinion polls, Attlee decided to call a General Election in October. He realised that the Government could only lose still further ground, faced as it was by a worsening financial situation due to the loss of Persian oil and the increase in prices caused by the Korean War. Both the two major parties had been courting the Liberals, but the latter stubbornly maintained their independence, yet by reducing the total number of their candidates to 109 they in fact helped the Conservatives. In addition, three of the sitting Liberal MPs were left unopposed by the

Conservatives, as also (at Churchill's insistence) was their candidate in the Colne Valley, his old friend Lady Violet Bonham-Carter.

The Labour Party made a remarkable recovery during the election campaign, and it is difficult not to ascribe this in large part to the 'war-monger' charge. The more the Conservatives sought to deny it the more it came to the attention of the electorate. On polling day (25 October), the *Daily Mirror*, which as in 1950 was the leading supporter of the Labour Party in the popular press, published on its front page an illustration of a revolver with the headlines 'Whose Finger? Today Your Finger is on the Trigger.' This led to a libel action by Churchill, eventually settled out of court by an apology and a donation to charity by the *Mirror*.

In sum, the electoral swing to the Conservatives was only an extra 1.1 per cent, whereas in 1950 it had been 3.3 per cent. But this was enough to give them an overall majority of 17 seats. They returned 321 strong, the Labour Party won 295 seats, the Liberals were reduced to six (Lady Violet Bonham-Carter was not elected, although Churchill went to speak for her), and there were two Irish Nationalists and one Irish Labour. Only 28 seats changed hands, and the Labour Party actually received more votes than the Conservatives – in fact the largest number it has ever received to this day – but too many of them were 'wasted' by piling up excessive majorities in mining constituencies.[36] In the early evening of Friday 26 October, as soon as he knew that Labour had lost its overall majority, Attlee went to Buckingham Palace to offer his resignation. A few minutes later the King invited Churchill to visit him at the Palace, and at 6 p.m. asked him to form a Government in place of Attlee's. Churchill readily agreed, and drove back to 28 Hyde Park Gate to begin his Cabinet making.

2 Cabinet Making

As we have seen, that Friday evening Churchill readily accepted the royal invitation to form a Government.[1] He was within five weeks of his seventy-seventh birthday, but he was still six years younger than Gladstone when the latter last took office. He at once told the King that he would like to make Field Marshal Lord Alexander his Minister of Defence; the King approved this idea, although it would take some time for Alexander to be relieved of his existing post as Governor-General of Canada. Meanwhile he proposed to hold the post of Minister of Defence himself, but for the rest he acted quickly to assemble a first group of leading Ministers.

That evening he consulted first of all with Anthony Eden, who dined with him, and then afterwards with Sir Edward Bridges, the Permanent Head of the Treasury, and Sir Norman Brook, the Cabinet Secretary. A short list of leading appointments was drawn up, all of them being men who had been prominent in the wartime Coalition Government. Eden himself was to be Deputy Prime Minister, Foreign Secretary and Leader of the House of Commons. There were two rival contenders for the post of Chancellor of the Exchequer – Oliver Lyttelton, who had led the Commons battle against the last two Labour Finance Bills, and R.A. Butler, the Head of the Conservative Research Department. Reluctantly, Churchill concluded that Lyttelton's Parliamentary skills were not quite equal to the task. So Butler was sent for that evening and offered the Treasury – but with some strings attached. Churchill told him that it did not matter that he did not know any economics; he was going to appoint 'the greatest economist since Jesus Christ' to assist him. This turned out to be Sir Arthur Salter, who after a long career mostly in shipping control was at the age of 71 to become Minister of State for Economic Affairs.[2]

When Churchill sent for Lyttelton the latter was naturally disappointed not to be offered the Chancellorship. Instead, the Prime Minister offered him the post of Minister for Materials and Rearmament. This was somewhat similar to the task he had undertaken during the war as Minister of

Production, but Lyttelton did not think it would be of equal importance in peacetime. Nevertheless he went away thinking that he had accepted this post, although he told Churchill that he would sooner be Colonial Secretary, as his father had been early in the century. It seems that Churchill wanted to reserve the Colonial Secretaryship for his wartime Minister of Information and long-time colleague Brendan Bracken, but Bracken was suffering from such severe sinusitis that he felt obliged to refuse any office. Churchill was then able to telephone Lyttelton with the good news that he could have the Colonial Office after all.[3]

The two immediate appointments in the Lords were those of Lord Woolton, the Chairman of the Party, who was to become Lord President of the Council as he had been in the Caretaker Government, and have a superintending role over Food and Agriculture; and Lord Salisbury, who was to be Lord Privy Seal, to assist Eden in foreign affairs, and to be Leader of the House of Lords. It was late at night when Churchill telephoned his wartime military aide, Lord Ismay, and asked him to call on him at once. Ismay had been asleep for an hour, but he put his head under the cold tap, dressed hurriedly, and reported to 28 Hyde Park Gate, to find himself invited to be Secretary of State for Commonwealth Relations. 'I thought that the cold tap had failed to do its work and that I was still dreaming,' wrote Ismay in his memoirs.[4] In practice his role was largely to help Churchill master the defence portfolio which he had temporarily assumed.

Cabinet making continued on Saturday. That afternoon Sir David Maxwell Fyfe, who had been Attorney-General in the Caretaker Government, saw the Prime Minister, hoping that his ambition to be Lord Chancellor would be satisfied. But Churchill told him that as yet he could not be spared from the Commons, and asked him to become Home Secretary and also (to fulfil an election promise) Minister for Welsh Affairs.[5] Meanwhile Churchill had seen Walter Monckton, who had been Solicitor-General in the Caretaker Government of 1945 without a seat in the Commons and had only been an MP for a few months (he had taken Oliver Stanley's seat on the latter's untimely death). Monckton expected to be asked to be Attorney-General, and was taken aback to be offered the Ministry of Labour – so much so that he could hardly find words to explain his reluctance; his brief was, in effect, to keep the unions friendly to the Government. Monckton was known to Churchill above all for his skill as a negotiator during the Abdication Crisis of 1936, when he managed to represent King Edward VIII without alienating the other parties.[6] Another prominent figure to be offered a post at this time was Sir John Anderson, an ex-civil servant not formally a member of the Conservative Party, but nevertheless an ex-Chancellor of the Exchequer in wartime and since then an occasional participant in the meetings of the Shadow Cabinet: Churchill invited him to be Chancellor of the Duchy of Lancaster with responsibility for the Ministry of Materials. But Anderson refused the office, taking the line that he could not afford the drop in salary, but also thinking that he should have been offered a more senior post.[7]

That afternoon the first eight Ministers in Churchill's Cabinet went to Buckingham Palace to take the oath of office. There had previously been a flurry of telephoning over Eden's appointment as Deputy Prime Minister. Both Sir Norman Brook and the King's Secretary, Sir Alan Lascelles, had remarked that this would infringe the King's prerogative of appointing Prime Ministers, and therefore objected to it. But Eden insisted on being given the title, and Churchill accepted his view.[8]

Churchill saw the three Service Chiefs, headed by Admiral Lord Fraser, that day, and Eden went to the Foreign Office to meet Sir William Strang, the Permanent Under-Secretary, and other senior officials. Ismay went to the Commonwealth Relations Office, and Butler was given a late lunch at the Athenaeum by Sir Edward Bridges to meet William Armstrong (who was to be his Private Secretary) and to receive a preliminary account of the parlous state of the economy.[9] Meanwhile Churchill was anxious to bring the Liberal Party into the Government so as to improve his Commons majority. He invited Clement Davies to call upon him at Hyde Park Gate and put this proposition to him. Davies promised to think it over and also accepted an invitation to lunch with the Prime Minister at Chartwell next day.

Churchill also decided to summon to his assistance again his wartime Private Secretary John Colville, who was now First Secretary at the British Embassy at Lisbon. He discovered that

Colville was on leave in England, succeeded in finding him at the races in Newmarket, and summoned him to London to be his Principal Private Secretary. Colville agreed, and hurried back to London. He found that Attlee had lately appointed a Prime Minister's Principal Private Secretary, David Pitblado. It was agreed that he and Pitblado should share the office.[10]

If at least one of Churchill's old colleagues, Lord Ismay, had been surprised to be summoned to the Cabinet, others were waiting somewhat impatiently at their telephones. One of the latter was Harold Macmillan, who was asked only on Sunday morning to visit Churchill at Chartwell. Meanwhile Clement Davies lunched with the new Prime Minister, and received the offer of the Ministry of Education in the Cabinet – a post likely to appeal to any Welshman. Davies was tempted, but said he would have to consult his colleagues before accepting. Macmillan arrived at 3 p.m., and was invited to take on the commitment to build 300,000 houses a year: 'What an assignment!' he commented in his diary.[11] After some discussion with Bridges and Brook, who were also there, it was decided that his department, known under the Labour Government as the Ministry of Local Government and Planning, should be renamed the Ministry of Housing and Local Government. Macmillan asked for Ernest Marples, who had experience of the industry, to be appointed his Parliamentary Secretary, and this was agreed.

Harry Crookshank, one of the best Parliamentarians on the Conservative side, then arrived and was offered the post of Minister of Health. He probably expected a different and more senior post, but as Eden had discovered that the task of Foreign Secretary was heavier than he expected – owing to all the international organisations now in existence – and asked for relief, it was agreed that Crookshank should take on the Leadership of the House in his place. Crookshank and Patrick Buchan-Hepburn, who was to be Chief Whip, then settled down to advise Churchill on junior appointments, for the Prime Minister hardly knew the members of the parliamentary party. There was also the Speakership to be considered, as Colonel Clifton Brown had retired at the General Election. That day Churchill wrote to Attlee suggesting either W.S. Morrison, a Conservative ex-Minister, or Hopkin Morris, a Liberal.[12]

That evening an official statement from Liberal Party Headquarters said that Clement Davies had refused office in the Government, but that 'the Liberal Party is deeply concerned at the possible effect of the narrow majority in the House of Commons resulting from the General Election...In these circumstances it will...give to the Government support for measures clearly conceived in the interests of the country as a whole.'[13]

Churchill remained at Chartwell on Monday, 30 October, partly at least because the Attlees had not yet vacated No. 10 Downing Street. (They departed on Wednesday for Cherry Cottage, the home that Attlee had bought in the Cotswolds near Chequers.) The new Prime Minister was visited by Butler, the new Chancellor, and Sir Edward Bridges, who wished to discuss immediate economic measures. Churchill also summoned Selwyn Lloyd, one of the 1945 intake of Conservative MPs, whom Eden had asked for as his Minister of State. As Selwyn Lloyd's work so far had been largely devoted to finance, he was taken aback by this invitation to the Foreign Office, and told the Prime Minister that he had not been abroad in peacetime, that he did not like foreigners and that he knew no foreign languages. 'Young man,' said Churchill, 'these all seem to be positive advantages.'[14] Another visitor to Chartwell was Sir Peter Bennett, a Midlands industrialist who was to be Monckton's Parliamentary Secretary at the Ministry of Labour.

On Tuesday Churchill was back again in London, to complete his Cabinet and to hold its meeting at No. 10 Downing Street. He had to appoint a Lord Chancellor, but his first choice, Lord Asquith of Bishopstone, had refused his invitation on the grounds of ill-health. Churchill's choice of a son of the Liberal Prime Minister under whom he himself had served for over six years was thus thwarted.[15] His second choice, largely on Salisbury's advice, was Lord Simonds, like Asquith a Lord of Appeal, and a man who had played no previous part in politics.[16] James Stuart, the former Chief Whip, was to be Secretary of State for Scotland, and the Cabinet was completed with the appointment of Lord Cherwell, Churchill's long-standing scientific adviser, as Paymaster-General, with a responsibility for science including atomic energy.

With a Ministry of Defence already in existence, Churchill followed Attlee's practice of placing his three Service Ministers outside the Cabinet. But at a time when conscription was still in force, the posts were important ones. He initially proposed to appoint his own son-in-law, Duncan Sandys, as Secretary of State for War, but Clementine Churchill advised him against it, pointing out that it would be embarrassing to have Sandys working immediately under his orders as Minister of Defence: 'If anything were to go wrong it would be delicate and tricky – first of all having to defend your own son-in-law and later if by chance he made a mistake having to dismiss him.'[17] So Churchill made him Minister of Supply instead, and the three Service Ministers were Brigadier Antony Head for the War Office, J.P.L. Thomas, a former Parliamentary Private Secretary to Anthony Eden, for the Admiralty and Lord De L'Isle and Dudley for the Royal Air Force. The claims of the latter for high office were much enhanced in Churchill's eyes by the fact that he had won the Victoria Cross in 1944.

Another post that Churchill filled that day was that of Financial Secretary to the Treasury. His choice for this post was John Boyd-Carpenter, who has provided an amusing account of his encounter with the new Prime Minister. When offered the post, he accepted at once, but was invited to sit down again and listen to a long account of Churchill's own experience of financial office: '"I was", he said, "Chancellor of the Exchequer for five years, but, you know, I never understood it."' The interview lasted a full half-hour, although other MPs who had been summoned were waiting outside. In one case – Nigel Birch – the Prime Minister forgot what post he wished to appoint him to, and after an agreeable conversation sent him away still mystified. He had to be telephoned later to be told he was to be Parliamentary Under-Secretary for Air.[18] Many were never to receive the call, in one case owing to his absence from home: this was Walter Elliot, a senior ex-Minister who was initially to be Minister of Education. In his absence the post went to Florence Horsbrugh, who described Churchill's Hyde Park Gate home as looking at the time 'like a domestic servants' agency'.[19] Miss Horsbrugh was the more senior of the only two women appointed to posts in the Government, the other being Pat Hornsby-Smith, who became Parliamentary Secretary at the Ministry of Health.

The first meeting of the Cabinet took place at No. 10 Downing Street that afternoon. The only absentee was Cherwell, but he and two of those who were present, Simonds and Peter Thorneycroft, a backbencher promoted to be President of the Board of Trade, were so far only 'designate' as their names had not yet been submitted to the King. A Cabinet of sixteen in all was a reduction of two on Attlee's final total, the change being effected by Churchill himself taking the Defence portfolio and the Minister of Education being left out. Six members were in the Lords, as against four of Attlee's Cabinet, and of the six, three (Woolton, Leathers and Cherwell) were 'co-ordinating' Ministers, that is to say, responsible for groups of Departments. *The Times,* reporting this, described it as 'an arrangement with many advantages',[20] but in a few days' time other sections of the press were expressing doubts: *The Economist* commented:

> It is a pity that in all these first experiments the co-ordinating Minister is a peer, who will not be able himself to expound general policy to the Commons.[21]

On 11 November *The Sunday Times* asked:

> What is the extent of the power and responsibility of the 'Overlords' – as we understand Whitehall has already dubbed them? Departmental Ministers must answer, both to the country and to Parliament, for the conduct of their Departments.

At the first Cabinet meeting on 30 October Churchill was able to secure agreement on a number of immediate issues of policy. It was decided to retain the choice of W.S. Morrison for the Speakership in spite of the Labour Party's change of mind – they now wanted Major James Milner, the former Deputy Speaker and a member of the Labour Party, but Churchill explained that he had already offered the post to Morrison after having obtained Attlee's assent. It was agreed that the King's Speech should declare the Government's intention to repeal the Labour Government's Iron and Steel Nationalisation Act, to restore the university franchise and to allow more scope for private road hauliers – all of these having been promised in the election manifesto. But the university franchise was not to operate until the next election, nor was it to 'perpetuate the old system of dual voting'. This meant that those qualifying would have to choose between voting in the university constituency or in a locality. Two committees, both chaired by Crookshank, were appointed, one to draft the King's Speech and the other to decide whether legislation could be carried before Christmas 'to implement the Government's pledge to restore the iron and steel industry to free enterprise.'

Butler then circulated to the Cabinet Bridges' note about the critical economic situation, which as he pointed out Attlee and his colleagues had done nothing to ameliorate during the General Election period. Once again Churchill appointed a committee of Cabinet Ministers – this time chaired by Butler himself – to produce a programme of emergency measures and to report to the next meeting of the Cabinet in two days' time. He also proposed to send Attlee a copy of Bridges' note, and laid it down that Cabinet Ministers' salaries should be reduced from £5,000 a year to £4,000 for a three-year period of rearmament. He himself would take only £7,000 of the Prime Minister's salary of £10,000.

Eden then reported on the state of Foreign Affairs. The most urgent problem was that the Egyptians had renounced the 1936 treaty, which allowed Britain to keep troops at Suez; he proposed that the remainder of the 3rd Infantry Division should go to Cyprus. The Prime Minister commented that as the 6th Armoured Division had already been promised to General Eisenhower on the Continent, Britain herself would be denuded of protection and it might be necessary to reconstitute the Home Guard.[22]

After the Cabinet meeting Churchill had another meeting with Clement Davies, and pressed him to agree to his choice of Speaker. Davies, who had already refused office, agreed, and reaffirmed his party's support for any measures which were essential for the country's safety, even if they were not popular.

Next day at 2.30 p.m. the House of Commons reassembled, its first task being to elect a Speaker. When Churchill entered the House:

To the great amusement of Opposition members he advanced on the wrong side of the chair as if to take his place on the Opposition front bench. There was a roar of laughter as he turned back and, passing behind the Chair, he went to his proper place to the accompaniment of loud cheer from his supporters who stood in their places waving their order papers.[23]

But the morale of Labour members was also good. Very few seats had changed hands in the General Election, and Richard Crossman noted in his diary:

My first impression...is that everyone is so enormously relieved at having got back that they are in the highest spirits.[24]

In the discussion of the choice of Speaker Morrison and Milner were duly proposed, and then Churchill revealed the details of the discussions he had had with Attlee and his colleagues and explained that he could not go back on the promise he had made to Morrison. Crossman said of his speech: 'He couldn't remember the constituencies of any of the Members he had to refer to, but he is so deaf that he can't be prompted.'[25] But Milner cannot have polled the full Labour vote, for W.S. Morrison was elected by 318 votes to 251. This was the first occasion that the election of a Speaker had gone to a division since 1895.[26]

Next day, 1 November, the Cabinet held its second meeting. Butler put forward a memorandum indicating the financial difficulties that now beset the Government, and suggesting some remedies. He said: 'We are running an external deficit at a rate of £700 million a year, compared with an annual surplus of some £350 million in the corresponding period a year ago.' He therefore proposed to make heavy cuts in the programme of imports for 1952, including a suspension of stockpiling measures, a reduction in the tourist allowance from £100 to £50 and, for the first time since 1939, an increase in interest rates. Discussion of the economies continued at further meetings of the Cabinet on 2 and 5 November, when Butler decided after consulting the Governor of the Bank of England that the increase in bank rate should be only from 2 per cent to 2.5 per cent. 'He was satisfied that even the small increase which he proposed would have a valuable psychological effect on the market.' It was also decided to drop all mention of the university franchise from the King's Speech, as the legislation was not urgent – it was never to be resurrected – and to authorise the Minister of Supply to give 'formal directions' to the Iron and Steel Board to prevent any reorganisation of the industry taking place before legislation denationalising the industry was carried in the New Year.[27]

As the King was still recuperating only slowly from an operation to remove a lung, his Speech opening the new Session of Parliament was read for him by the new Lord Chancellor. In the debate that followed Churchill made a plea for peaceful discussion:

> For two whole years our island has been distracted by party strife and electioneering...What the nation needs is several years of quiet, steady administration, if only to allow Socialist legislation to reach its full fruition. What the House needs is a period of tolerant and constructive debating on the merits of the questions before us.

He outlined the economic difficulties that beset him on taking charge, emphasising in particular the coal shortage. He said that he was proposing a secret session on defence, but that Parliament would be adjourned from early December until early February 'subject of course to the usual arrangements for recall in case of emergency'. The Government would re-establish the Home Guard, in view of the shortage of military manpower in the United Kingdom. While only iron and steel could be denationalised in the coming session, other nationalised industries would be given more 'flexibility' and there would be an 'extension of road haulage activities'. The Monopolies Commission would be given more power.[28]

Next day Butler announced the economic measures which the Cabinet had decided on. The United Kingdom deficit in 1952, if no action was taken, would be of the order of £500–600 million. This was due to a worsening of the terms of trade, and to the loss of the Anglo-Iranian refinery at Abadan. He therefore recommended cuts in imports designed to save £350 million in 1952, of which £160 million was to be in the form of food. The strategic stockpiling programme was to be slowed down, the tourist allowance cut from £100 to £50, and new investment in building – although not housing – was to be cut. An Excess Profits Tax, promised in the election manifesto, was to be levied from 1 January, and the bank rate was raised to 2.5per cent. He welcomed an assurance from the General

Council of the Trades Union Congress that they were willing to continue consultation with the Government, and pledged reciprocity 'on all matters of common concern'.[29]

In reply, Hugh Gaitskell, who was Butler's predecessor as Chancellor, was concerned to establish that he had not concealed the degree of deterioration in the balance of payments taking place in the early autumn, and he cited a speech that he had made at the Mansion House early in October. He agreed that all the measures announced by the new Chancellor, except for the increase in bank rate, were what he would also have done. It was left to G.R. Strauss, former Minister of Supply, to introduce a partisan note when the debate was resumed on 12 November by moving an amendment to the Address attacking the proposals relating to iron and steel and road haulage. He said that Labour would restore ownership in both industries without additional compensation to investors. But, with the Liberals voting in support of the Government, the amendment was defeated by 320 votes to 281. Next day Herbert Morrison, Attlee's deputy, moved an amendment deploring the length of the vacation being provided for the Commons; but Crookshank, the Leader of the House, pointed out that it would only be one week longer than that provided after the 1945 election. This amendment was also comfortably defeated, by 318 to 281.[30]

Meanwhile Eden, accompanied be Selwyn Lloyd, had gone to Paris for a meeting there of the United Nations General Assembly. Eden, making his first speech to the United Nations since the foundation conference at San Francisco in 1945, deplored the 'bitter vehemence of the polemics exchanged'. He gave his support to a disarmament plan proposed by the three Western Powers – the United States, France and Britain – which had been worked out before the British change of government. The plan made one concession to the Soviet standpoint, and that was to include both atomic and conventional weapons. But Vyshinsky, the Soviet spokesman, had already denounced it in what Eden described as 'a cataract of abuse'. Eden said: 'Should we not, then, do much better to proclaim a truce to name-calling and angry words? Could we not, instead, apply our minds dispassionately to serious problems? I am sure that we should. Should we try from now onwards? That will be my task.'[31]

Eden then left Selwyn Lloyd to lead the British delegation, and returned to England and the Foreign Office. On the 15th he made a statement in the Commons about the Sudan, resulting, as he put it, from Egypt's 'unilateral action in purporting to abrogate the 1936 Treaty of Alliance and the two Condominium Agreements of 1899'. He said that a constitution for self-government would be in operation in 1952, and that the Sudanese could then 'choose their own future status with the United Kingdom and with Egypt.'[32] On the 19th there was a general debate on Foreign Affairs, in the course of which he made a *tour d'horizon* of all the problems of foreign policy. He looked forward to meeting Konrad Adenauer, first of all in Paris, and then later in London in early December, when he was to pay a brief visit. He hoped for an armistice in Korea, but, he said, 'it must include supervision and prisoners of war as well as a demarcation line.' As for the Persian oil dispute, he enunciated three principles by which the Government stood: practicability, which meant efficient operation, refining and marketing; fair shares between Persia and those undertaking the development; and fair compensation for the act of nationalisation.

He also dealt with the vexed problem of Anglo-Egyptian relations. He offered the Egyptians a revision of the Anglo-Egyptian Treaty of 1936, which they had denounced, pointing out that 'to give an ally any facilities on one's own soil is not necessarily derogatory to one's own sovereignty. If that is so, this country is doing precisely that thing now.' Meanwhile the Government had no option but to 'maintain their position in the Canal Zone, basing their rights to do so on the Treaty of 1936.' He called for an end to 'terrorist' activity in the area. He concluded his hour-long speech with a brief expression of his aspirations in foreign policy:

> What we can try to do is to build up our reputation for patience and sane counsel; to use the diplomatic experience of centuries, which is our heritage; to guide the nations, and to guard the peace.[33]

There was, in fact, less disagreement about foreign policy between the two Front Benches in Parliament than within the

Cabinet. David Maxwell Fyfe, who had been appointed a delegate to the European Assembly at Strasbourg, and who was sympathetic to the federalist cause, persuaded the Cabinet on
22 November – Eden being absent abroad – to allow him not
merely to 'welcome' the Schuman Plan for a Coal and Steel
Community, but also to say that Britain would 'set up a permanent delegate at the seat of the Authority to enter into relations
and to transact business with it.'[34] He later maintained that he
had also been authorised to welcome the European Army idea,
but his speech did not sound enthusiastic and Reynaud, the
former Prime Minister of France who was also present, warned
him that if Britain did not participate, as Churchill had indicated she would eighteen months beforehand by agreeing to a
European Minister of Defence, the French would also refuse to
participate. Only a few hours later, to Maxwell Fyfe's embarrassment, Eden told a press conference in Rome, where he had
gone for a meeting of the North Atlantic Council, that Britain
would in no circumstances participate in a European Army.[35]
Macmillan, who agreed with Maxwell Fyfe, for the time being
held his fire, though he enquired of Churchill whether he
should resign from the European Movement.[36] On 3 December
the Conservative members of the British delegation at
Strasbourg sent Churchill a letter criticising the 'shattering
blow' which Eden had delivered at Rome,[37] and on 6 December
Churchill himself dealt with the subject of the European Army
in a speech in the Commons, when Defence was under discussion, though not, as he had wished, in Secret Session. He said:

> As far as Britain is concerned, we do not propose to merge
> in the European Army but we are already joined to it. Our
> troops are on the spot, and we shall do our utmost to make
> a worthy and effective contribution to the deterrents against
> aggression and to the causes of freedom and democracy
> which we seek to serve.

Later on in his speech, he admitted that Aneurin Bevan had
been justified in maintaining that the rearmament programme would lag:

> I was giving him an honourable mention in despatches for
> having, it appears by accident, perhaps not from the best of
> motives, happened to be right.[38]

After he had sat down he again rose to utter a few words of praise for the former Minister of Defence, Emanuel Shinwell, for the effectiveness of his work in the development of rearmament:

> I am so glad to be able to say tonight, in these very few moments, that the spirit which has animated the Right Honourable Gentleman in the main discharge of his great duties was one which has, in peace as well as in war, added to the strength and security of our country.[39]

The relative cordiality between the two Front Benches, with the Labour leaders recognising the degree of continuity between their own policies and those of the incoming administration, accounted for the Government's success in the lobbies before the recess. As Patrick Buchan-Hepburn wrote to the Prime Minister about his task as Chief Whip:

> It is a great responsibility, with our not too great majority, but Harry Crookshank is a tower of strength, and the whips are very keen...I have been thinking about our large majorities and what they mean...

He attributed them to 'personal rivalries in the Socialist Party' and to the weakening influence of William Whiteley, the Labour Chief Whip, a Durham miner who was already almost seventy: 'As he fades out – as I think he means to do – control and discipline will suffer.'[40]

On 31 December Churchill set out for the United States on board the *Queen Mary*. He was accompanied by Eden, Ismay and Cherwell, as well as by two of the Defence chiefs, Field Marshal Slim and Admiral Sir Rhoderick McGrigor. The Cabinet Secretary, Norman Brook, and Churchill's doctor, Lord Moran, were also in the party, which altogether numbered 30. Although the American media were looking forward to the visit, the British Embassy in Washington warned that there was 'a measure of trepidation about the arrival of a great and powerful personality and a good deal of wariness regarding his proposals.'[41] On arrival in New York Churchill held a press conference and then flew in the President's plane to Washington, where he was received by Truman and most of the Cabinet. He lunched with the President at Blair House –

the White House being under repair – and dined on board the Presidential yacht, the *Williamsburg*.

The first contacts were social rather than seriously political and economic: Churchill persuaded Cherwell to estimate how much of the *Williamsburg's* stateroom would be filled by all the drink he had consumed during his life, at a quart a day for 60 years, and expressed comical dismay when Cherwell, using his slide rule, figured out that it would only fill the room knee high. But after dinner Churchill went on to give his views of the international situation, telling his hosts that the European Defence Community, being a mixture of nationalities, would be deficient in spirit.[42] On the other hand he praised the American rearmament which was a consequence of the Korean War, and said that the dangers of war were less than in 1948, at the time of the Berlin air lift. He also slipped in a suggestion (not warmly received) that the United States might send a brigade of troops to the Canal Zone of Egypt, 'as a symbol'.[42]

The next day, 6 January, was a Sunday, but Churchill visited the Pentagon for talks with Robert Lovett, the Secretary of Defence and his advisers. That evening Acheson and Lovett, together with the American Chairman of the Joint Chiefs of Staff, General Omar Bradley, dined with Churchill and Eden at the British Embassy. Churchill urged the Americans to provide 'support and unity of policy' in the Middle East. Referring to Iran, the Prime Minister said:

> ...the British had been kicked out of Abadan in a most humiliating way. If he had been in office, it would not have occurred. There might have been a splutter of musketry, but they would not have been kicked out of Iran.

Acheson commented drily that 'all the concessions which the oil company had made in bringing their dealings with Persia up to what was standard elsewhere had come too late.'[43]

Four Plenary Sessions of talks were held on Monday and Tuesday, 7 and 8 January. Very little was agreed between the two sides, but the talks were conducted in a friendly atmosphere. Churchill tried to persuade the Americans to agree to a modification of the agreement made by the Attlee Government whereby an American admiral would take charge of the North Atlantic naval forces. He did not succeed; after all, they were to provide most of the forces involved. Churchill himself rejected the idea of any agreement about the standardisation of rifles while the Korean War continued, but he persuaded Truman to put in writing the verbal understanding that already existed between the two governments about the use of American bombers from British bases. So far as the Middle East was concerned, the communiqué simply announced 'a broad harmony of view'; this also applied to the Far East, although the two governments acknowledged 'divergencies' in attitude to China. Important deals were also struck on the level of industrial materials: it was agreed that the United States should supply Britain with a million tons of steel in 1952; and that Britain should supply America with 20,000 tons of tin and 35 million pounds of aluminium.[44]

On the 9th Churchill heard Truman deliver his State of the Union address to Congress and then went by train to stay with his old friend Bernard Baruch in New York. On the 10th Eden, having stayed in Washington for further talks with the American Secretary of State, Dean Acheson, also went to New York to receive an honorary degree at Columbia University. Speaking of European federation, which was always of interest to Americans, he bluntly declared in his address: 'This is something which we know in our bones we cannot do.' He added, however, '[We] have the largest armoured force on the continent of Europe of any of the Atlantic Powers.'[45]

Most of the British party then proceeded to Ottawa by train, there to be received by Field Marshal Lord Alexander, Churchill's wartime Middle Eastern and Italian Front Commander-in Chief and now Governor-General of Canada. Churchill had to make a speech to the Canadian people, broadcast at an official banquet, but he also took the opportunity of summoning to meet him in the Canadian capital General Sir Gerald Templer, who was being recommended by Lyttelton, the Colonial Secretary, for the post of High Commissioner in Malaya. The appointment was urgent, as the previous High Commissioner, Sir Henry Gurney, had been assassinated on 6 October and Lyttelton, who had flown out to see for himself how effectively the war against the guerrillas was being waged, had come back with the clear impression that a powerful personality was needed to weld together both the armed forces and the police.[46] Churchill consulted

Alexander about him – for Templer had served under Alexander's command – and appointed him on the spot.

On 15 January Churchill returned to Washington, for a brief stay at the Embassy preparatory to making a speech to Congress two days later. At the last moment before leaving the Embassy, he was at a loss to describe how the United Nations forces would react if the Communists were to break a truce in Korea: 'prompt, resolute and effective' were the words suggested by his Foreign Office adviser, Sir Roger Makins. These words went into the final text, and although appreciated by Congress, they were to produce adverse reactions later at Westminster. Congress received rather coolly, however, his suggestion that American 'token forces' should be sent to the Suez Canal Zone.[47]

Nevertheless the speech, which was televised, was an impressive *tour de force*. As an American journalist described it:

> Mr Churchill spoke from a sheaf of notes; he extemporized and interpolated as he proceeded. The impact of the speech was enormously enhanced by this procedure, which is standard practice in the British Parliament, and almost unknown in Congress...Congressmen watched the man who had been trained by half a century in this practice with admiration mingled with affection and downright wonder.[48]

As Sir Oliver Franks, the British Ambassador in Washington, reported to the Foreign Secretary:

> The speech before the joint session of Congress, reaching many millions of Americans in most parts of the United States by television, created a deep and wide-spread effect and built up a fund of trust and goodwill which should stand us in good stead for some time to come.[49]

Before he left Washington, Churchill was able to obtain a concession about the Atlantic naval command: the Americans agreed that the area under British control should extend out to the hundred-fathom line, thus covering the entire area within which moored mines might be laid.[50]

Churchill then returned to New York for a few more days, and finally returned to Britain on the *Queen Mary,* arriving at Southampton on the 28th. Meanwhile, a major act of persuasion on his part was reported in the press: Field Marshal Lord

Alexander, who was not really interested in party politics, had agreed to give up his appointment as Governor-General of Canada and join Churchill's Cabinet as Minister of Defence. He was succeeded as Governor-General by Vincent Massey, the first native Canadian to hold the post. Alexander displayed his affection for Canada by not leaving the country until mid-February; he formally joined Churchill's Cabinet on 1 March, bringing the total number of peers therein to seven.[51]

Meanwhile on 6 February, early in the morning, King George VI had died in his sleep. He was thought to be recovering from a serious operation which, as we have seen, had involved the removal of a lung. The news did not reach Whitehall until later that morning, but it at once led to a suspension of normal activity and party politics. Churchill had been on the point of responding to criticism of his speech in Congress, as implying a change of policy on the Far East when he spoke of 'prompt, resolute and effective' retaliation if the Korean truce, when achieved, were broken by the Communists. Now Parliament was adjourned, and on the evening of the 7th Churchill broadcast a tribute, saying:

> During these last few months the King walked with death, as if death were a companion, an acquaintance, whom he recognised and did not fear. In the end death came as a friend.

More buoyantly he concluded:

> I, whose youth was passed in the august, unchallenged and tranquil glories of the Victorian Era, may well feel a thrill in invoking, once more, the prayer and the anthem, God Save the Queen.[52]

The sittings of both Houses of Parliament were suspended, except for a brief meeting on 11 February when Churchill moved resolutions of sympathy with the Royal Family. There was then a lying-in-state for three days followed by a funeral at Windsor on 15 February. The new Queen, who had been on her way with the Duke of Edinburgh to the Far East for a tour of Australia and New Zealand, had to cut short her trip and return to London by air; she and the Duke were received at Heathrow Airport by the Prime Minister, other Ministers and the Leader of the Opposition. Attlee was not less moved than Churchill by the loss of a monarch whom they had both known as a friend. A wreath from the Government that appeared on the coffin bore the inscription in Churchill's hand 'For Valour'.[53]

3 Robot and After

As soon as Parliament reassembled on 29 January, Butler made a statement announcing further measures to try to bring the balance of payments into equilibrium. Churchill had approved the measures at the first Cabinet on his return from America.[1] In his statement, Butler indicated that some of the measures to be taken arose from his meeting with Commonwealth Finance Ministers, who had come to London earlier in the month. In the second half of 1952, Butler, it was agreed, was to aim for a deficit of not more than £100 million with the rest of the world (excluding the sterling area); the Commonwealth countries and the colonies would provide the surplus of £100 million; and Britain would make up the difference by the supply of manufactured goods inside the Commonwealth. Some reduction of the defence stockpile of foodstuffs would be necessary, and the allowance of foreign currency to British tourists abroad would be cut to £25 a year. The food cuts would mostly be in the form of canned goods and certain fresh fruit, and there would be reduced imports of 'clothing, carpets, shoes and toys'. There would also be cuts in government expenditure: the Civil Service would be reduced by 10,000; education would be cut by 5 per cent; and there would be a ceiling of £400 million on the National Health Service, which meant the introduction of prescription charges, dental charges and charges for surgical aids. Little steel would be available for shops, offices or the still unreconstructed areas of cities damaged by the 'blitz'. The motor industry would be allowed to release only 60,000 each of private cars and commercial vehicles to the home market in 1952, as against 100,000 each in 1951. Butler also announced:

> The Minister of Labour is today making an order under Defence Regulations requiring employers seeking to engage workers to do so by notifying the local office of the Ministry of Labour, and to engage only workers submitted by a local office. There is no intention of attempting to compel workers to take jobs they are unwilling to take. No directions to workers are to be issued at all.

31

Finally, Butler declared that Budget Day would be advanced to 4 March.

Speaking next day, Gaitskell, who had preceded Butler as Chancellor, sought to explain the reasons for the crisis which had developed while he was still at the Treasury. These boiled down to the recent serious decline in American purchases of raw materials from sterling area countries, and Britain's consequent adverse terms of trade. He also mentioned the loss of Persian oil due to the closure of the Abadan refinery. As for Butler's proposals, while he endorsed them on the whole, he suggested it was a mistake to cut down the stocks built up for defence purposes – a point that had already been made in Cabinet by the Chiefs of Staff.[3] Gaitskell also complained that the Chancellor had:

> said nothing – or virtually nothing – on the vital question of production. He said nothing on what I would say is the equally important issue of wages, profits and dividends and the whole problem of restraining price inflation. He said nothing, practically speaking, of the relationship of defence to the present situation.[4]

The Chancellor, of course, had left many important issues to be dealt with in his Budget, and he had already received a paper from one of his senior Treasury advisers, R.W.B. ('Otto') Clarke, advocating, contrary to all previous advice, an early return to the convertibility of the pound. This would involve a floating rate for sterling, and 'the freezing (and funding) [of] all non-sterling area balances, except working balances'. The convertibility itself, however, would apply only to non-residents, and exchange control would continue on capital transactions. There would have to be 'tight non-discriminatory import licensing in the United Kingdom and the Rest of the Sterling Area on imports from the non-sterling world'. Clarke acknowledged:

> There are terrific risks in this, but if we have blocked balances effectively, and are adopting a *really* scarce money policy, and the Rest of the Sterling Area is taking it all seriously, it might be a starter.[5]

The Plan was given the codename 'Operation Robot' to indicate, as Sir Edwin Plowden, the Chief Planning Officer, put it, 'its role as an automatic regulator of the economy's performance'.[6]

It is clear that 'Robot' would have been very damaging to the Sterling Area because it had not been mentioned at the Commonwealth Finance Ministers Conference, and if it had been suddenly sprung on them only shortly afterwards, they would have been expected to reverse their policies at short notice. But Clarke had evidently despaired of Britain's being able to staunch the outflow of gold, and his fears were reinforced by Sir George Bolton, an Executive Director of the Bank of England.[7] The Chancellor mulled over 'Robot' for some time and then on 20 February wrote to the Prime Minister to give him an outline of it, and to say that he would have it ready for a meeting of Ministers the next day.[8] According to a letter by Bridges to Plowden, who was at Lisbon with Eden at the time, eight Ministers were at the meeting and all except Cherwell were in favour of it:

> The general feeling is that the scheme will be painful, that it will make great difficulty with the Commonwealth countries and play old Harry with E.P.U. [the European Payments Union] and will set up all sorts of strains in our external trading relations. It is agreed that its effects cannot be forecast. Nevertheless, it is felt that the scheme does give us a real chance of remaining in control of the situation and not just venturing into mid-stream.

Bridges added that no definite decision had yet been made except to postpone Budget Day by one week.[9] He did not say that the Ministers had only been shown the Clarke memorandum for the first time at the meeting, and that they had been asked to return their copies, which all of them except Cherwell did.[10]

Bridges' letter was taken out to Lisbon by Herbert Brittain of the Treasury, who with Eric Berthoud of the Foreign Office formed a delegation to explain the scheme to the Foreign Secretary. They also took a letter from Churchill to Eden referring to 'the new super-crisis which Rab [Butler] opened on us under the influence of the governor'. Churchill added:

> I must confess I was surprised that none of this dawned until recently upon the Governor or Rab, and it is awkward that it

was not ventilated when the Commonwealth Finance Ministers met. I gather it spells the doom of E.P.U. and you should bear in mind the dangers of the other powers complaining later that you knew of this but did not tell them. Yet you cannot tell them.[11]

Brittain also took a letter to Plowden from Robert Hall, who was Head of the Economic Section of the Cabinet Office. Hall described himself as 'very much disturbed and unhappy about the whole position'. He thought the scheme would lead to 'a considerable shrinking of world trade', and probably 'a considerable increase in unemployment'. He added:

> It is extremely hard for me to believe that the Foreign Office have yet grasped the implications for them of what is proposed, and I certainly do not think that Ministers will understand the proposals at all without a good deal of education.[12]

Eden was at first impressed by Churchill's talk of a 'super-crisis', and inclined to accept 'Robot'.[13] But Plowden, quoting Robert Hall to him, persuaded him to write back a cautious note:

> If this treatment is the only one that holds out hope of recovery, we must also understand the hurt it will inflict upon our people and do everything in our power to mitigate the suffering, and I fear unemployment, that must result.

He then referred to the evident necessity of reducing the rearmament programme, and said 'though we shall be much blamed by the U.S. amongst others, I feel more concern at the strain that will be placed on loyal Commonwealth countries, like Australia.' He added that he would be 'with you on Wednesday [27 February]. Could I have a discussion with you and Rab that afternoon?'[14]

Meanwhile Cherwell and Donald MacDougall, his economic adviser, organised the opposition to 'Robot', ironically from No. 11 Downing Street, where the Paymaster-General occupied rooms at the top of the building, Butler having decided to continue living in his house in Smith Square. Cherwell bombarded the Prime Minister with minutes recording opposition: on the 26th (Tuesday) he wrote:

We had a meeting of Ministers this morning to consider the economic plan. …Salter very strongly against and also Swinton, and the Chancellor told us that his economic advisers were violently opposed to it. Even he admitted that it might spell the ruin of the Tory Party.

He added that the plan 'emanated' from the Bank of England, although 'opinion there is divided'; in the Treasury a 'brilliant but volatile Under-Secretary [sc. Otto Clarke] seems to have persuaded Leslie Rowan [Second Secretary] to back it. Otherwise I do not think it has much professional support.'[15]

The issue was debated at three Cabinet meetings on Thursday and Friday, 28 and 29 February, but the record of the discussion was kept only in the Treasury.[16] On Thursday the line-up according to Robert Hall was: 'Cherwell, Salter…and Swinton against; Butler, Lyttelton and Thorneycroft for…' On Friday they met again and practically decided not to go on with the scheme, at any rate for the time being. 'Rab was exceedingly distressed…' Hall discovered afterwards that the Thursday Cabinet was 'left very even, as Eden has swung towards our side.'[17] The Foreign Secretary thus played a decisive role in financial policy for once.[18]

Butler wrote to Eden rather lamely on 1 March that he wanted to see him 'partly because I want to continue our long record of working together and not at cross purposes, and also because I do not think I can bring the Budget proposals into a final stage without your concurrence and support.'[19] The meeting presumably took place shortly afterwards, as the Budget was to be presented ten days later. Butler also took up with Salisbury a comparison the latter had made between 'Robot' and the Hoare-Laval Pact of 1935, which was also a sensational switch of policy shortly after a general election; Salisbury wrote an emollient reply, saying:

I am becoming more and more conscious…of the fact that it is likely to prove impossible to get through our present difficulties on a pure party basis; yet the plan…would be bound to widen still further the cleavage between the parties.

Salisbury added that he regretted 'any divergence of view between me and you, whose opinion I so greatly respect.'[20]

All these rebuffs were, of course, unknown to Parliament, the press and the public when on 11 March he delivered his Budget speech to the Commons. He said that he was seeking to 'eliminate the United Kingdom deficit with the non-sterling world' in the latter half of 1952, albeit 'taking into account such defence aid as we may receive from the United States.' This aid was expected to amount to $300 million, which had been allocated to Britain by Averell Harriman, President Truman's 'Special Envoy', who had served as Chairman of the Temporary Council Committee of NATO or 'Three Wise Men' as they were called, and who had assessed the economies of all the allies. Butler also expected an improvement in 'invisibles', that is income from shipping, insurance, etc., and he also hoped for an increase in the income from exports to the extent of £50 million. To help cut home investment and thereby raise exports still more, he raised bank rate still further to 4 per cent. The Excess Profits Levy, promised in the election manifesto, was to be 30 per cent, and was to start from the previous 1 January. Taxes on petrol and other road fuel were raised by 7d a gallon.

But the main change was in the food subsidies, which were cut from Cripps's ceiling of £410 million to £250 million. This meant immediate increases in the price of bread, meat and milk; other basic foodstuffs would have their price increases later. He reckoned that the cost per head would be about 1s 6d a week. To compensate, family allowances would be increased from 5s to 8s a week for each child in the family after the first child, and there would be increases in pensions also. The total of all the concessions would be £80 million, but the saving on food subsidies would be £160 million. Butler also raised the income tax threshold, thereby freeing two million people from paying the tax altogether.[21]

The speech took an hour and three-quarters to deliver, and when the Chancellor sat down he received an ovation from the Conservative benches.[22] The Budget was praised in Liberal as well as Conservative newspapers. The *Manchester Guardian* called it 'a dose of realism',[23] and the *News Chronicle's* economic editor, Oscar Hobson, also greeted it warmly.[24] The *Daily Mirror*, although critical, realistically commented:

It is the woman who will feel the full impact of dearer rations, in addition to other climbing prices. Tax reliefs will turn up in millions of wage packets and they must be passed on to the housewife.[25]

The Economist, while praising Butler for his 'lucidity', maintained that 'The opportunity... has not been fully grasped' because the public, after being 'warned of imminent disaster, has in the event been let down lightly.'[26]

The Opposition immediately turned its fire on Lord Woolton, who was in the Commons gallery during the speech, because he had said during the general election that the Conservatives would retain the food subsidies.[27] Woolton felt obliged to offer his resignation to the Prime Minister, who however replied firmly:

> Pray dismiss from your mind any idea of resigning from the Government because of malicious debating points made by those who have brought the British community into deadly economic and financial peril.[28]

The immediate effect of the Budget was to strengthen sterling quite markedly. MacDougal recorded:

> The pound had been at \$2.78, at which the Bank was obliged to support it, almost continuously since January...I watched the tape frequently, and by Friday (three days after the budget) the rate rose to nearly \$2.81 – then an unbelievably rapid change.[29]

All the same, in the aftermath of the Budget both he and Robert Hall found that relations with Treasury officials were 'very difficult', and 'the threat of "Robot" was continually present – a sword of Damocles hanging over our heads.'[30] On 20 March Rowan circulated a paper suggesting that the scheme be introduced on 1 April, or on 27 April.[31] Because Cherwell thought that Churchill was wobbling and talking of 'setting the pound free', he sent him a further critique of the idea:

> It is at first an attractive idea to go back to the good old days before 1914 when the pound was strong and we never had dollar crises...if a 6% Bank Rate, 1 million unemployed and a 2/- loaf is not enough, there will have to be an 8% Bank Rate, 2 million unemployed and a 3/- loaf. And so on until

the gap is closed. If the workers, finding their food dearer, are inclined to demand higher wages, this will have to be stopped by increasing unemployment until their bargaining power is destroyed. This is what comfortable phrases like 'letting the exchange rate take the strain' mean; nothing more and nothing less…To rely on high prices and unemployment to reduce imports would certainly put the Conservative Party out for a generation…[32]

Churchill sent this paper to Butler on 20 March, with the comment:

> This is a formidable statement and arises I am sure from a purely objective view. No decision is called for at the present time but all should be borne in mind.[33]

On 4 April Butler, in a Cabinet Paper, while describing the balance of payments as 'precarious', acknowledged that 'the improvement in our position gives us a little more time than we had previously expected to study the main alternatives.'[34]

If the Chancellor had wished merely to frighten his colleagues into taking the need to economise seriously, perhaps he could have pursued no wiser policy than to threaten them with 'Robot'. In mid-May he called for an early review of British overseas commitments, in which the Foreign Office and the Ministry of Defence would be involved:

> There is no escape from the conclusion that the load we are at present imposing on the metal-using industries for defence purposes gives us no hope of solving our balance of payments problem by the only way it can be solved, namely, by a rapid expansion in our export of metal goods.[35]

At the end of May the Cabinet asked both the Foreign Secretary and the Minister of Defence to report on the possibilities of making economies in their departments. Then in mid-June Robert Menzies, the Prime Minister of Australia, visited London and was invited to attend a meeting of the Cabinet. He was sounded on a suitable date for a Commonwealth Conference to discuss economic as well as other topics, and he recommended November. This was accepted by Churchill and his colleagues.[36]

Churchill, speaking at a Press Association luncheon on
11 June, took it upon himself to utter words of warning about
the economic situation:

> Around us we see the streets so full of traffic and the shops
> so splendidly presented, and the people cheerful, well-
> dressed, content with their system of government, proud as
> they have a right to be of their race and name. One wonders
> if they realise the treacherous trap-door on which they
> stand.... To speak like this is not to cry despair. It is the
> Alert; but it is more than the Alert; it is the Alarm.[37]

This rather contradicted Butler's own relatively optimistic
report to the Commons next day, when he said that Britain's
gold and dollar reserves had fallen by less than £10 million in
the two and a half months since the end of March, compared
with a fall of £227 million in the first three months of the
year.[38] Although this took into account about one-third of the
promised $300 million which had lately been received, it was
still very good news. It seemed as if his Budgetary medicine
was working.

Nevertheless, Cameron Cobbold, the Governor of the Bank
of England, was convinced that a sterling crisis was about to
take place 'about the end of August', and wrote Butler a
formal letter to warn him.[39] On 23 June Butler accordingly
summoned his principal advisers, and they at first agreed to
revert to the 'Robot' plan; but opposition soon revived,
though MacDougall complained that 'the same rush tactics as
in February' were being employed.[40] By 27 June Butler had received memoranda from Hall, Plowden and Salter opposing
the plan, and on 30 June, when the Prime Minister presided
over a meeting of Ministers to discuss it, it transpired that 'all
were against it except the Chancellor and Lyttelton.'[41] This
was probably the occasion of the note from Lyttelton which
Butler quotes in his memoirs: 'This goes ill. The water looks
cold to some of them. They prefer a genteel bankruptcy. *Force
Majeure* being their plea. Micawber Salter.'[42]

Early in July Macmillan, who had not been at this meeting
but wished to forestall any restriction of his housing plans, put
in a Cabinet Paper, a section of which was entitled 'The
Bankers' Ramp'. It declared: 'While all sensible people must

respect the authority, few can accept the dogma of the infalli-
bility of "the world of Banking and Finance".' He added:

> As an objective, convertibility is, of course, right...But the
> timing is vital... To act now, and to try to support such
> action, by widely advertised reductions in armaments and
> housing and social policies seems to me very dangerous. It is
> playing the old bankers' game. It is the same thing we were
> asked to do in 1931.[43]

On the housing issue, however, Macmillan forfeited the
support of Cherwell and MacDougall, but he still retained that
of Churchill. Cherwell wrote a note to the Prime Minister in
which he pointed out:

> Despite the housing queues and the undoubted hardship, it
> seems true that we are the best housed people in Western
> Europe. It seems equally certain that we are the worst fed. It
> is a political question whether we should annoy 50 million
> people a little by reducing their food rations, or 30,000 a lot
> by making them wait for their houses.

Churchill simply noted on this: 'We are pledged to 300,000.'[44]

On 16 July Churchill, in answering a question in the
Commons, spoke of 'the very serious measures which are
being taken in all fields.'[45] In view of the fact that 'Robot' had
been turned down, this was embarrassing for Butler, who was
shortly to face an economic debate, and the Prime Minister
apologised to him for the indiscretion.[46] When the debate
took place on 29 July, Butler could only point to the way in
which Britain was undertaking munitions orders for the
United States and for Belgium, a creditor for gold payments
under the EPU.[47] Gaitskell described his speech as 'an
amazing anti-climax'.[48]

Meanwhile Woolton wrote to Churchill reviving fears of an
early devaluation, and suggesting a reversion to 'Robot':

> The alternative policy which you must allow me to remind
> you I supported last February, is to let the burden of the
> deficit fall on the day to day rate of exchange. Maybe the
> rate will fall – in which case that fact alone will reduce
> the attractiveness of our imports...and will increase our
> chance of doing an export trade...by making our goods

cheaper...This is an old tried method which has worked for many decades.[49]

If Churchill had really understood the elements of economics he would have turned down this suggestion out of hand, but once again he asked Cherwell to comment, and Cherwell replied with the same arguments as he had used before. He added that devaluation of the pound 'would not significantly reduce imports which are already cut to the bone', and exports would not expand as 'metal goods are limited by lack of steel, and soft goods by the world textile slump.'[50]

In August a Working Party of officials met to consider what proposals they were to put before the Commonwealth Prime Ministers in November. Cherwell and MacDougall put forward the idea of an Atlantic Payments Union in place of that at present in existence which was limited to Western Europe. The Treasury officials twisted this round to make it an early approach to convertibility, provided that the United States backed the scheme with an exchange equalisation fund of five billion dollars. This was called the 'Collective Approach'.[51] Eden, who had chaired the Ministerial Committee, reported to the Cabinet:

> The general opinion in my committee was that the United Kingdom Government should put forward the 'collective approach' proposals, as modified, as the basis for discussion at the Commonwealth Economic Conference.[52]

Cherwell's comment to Churchill on the eve of the Conference was sceptical:

> The central theme of the plan is once more convertibility and a floating pound but this time the Commonwealth countries are to be asked to join in to approach the U.S. for help together with France, Benelux and perhaps Western Germany. I do not think this plan as disastrous as the so-called Robot plan which we rejected last February and again in June. For one thing it cannot be sprung upon the world unannounced; for another I do not believe it will come to anything.[53]

On 3 November the Cabinet agreed to put the plan forward to the Commonwealth Conference. [54] The Conference accepted the British lead, in spite of some concern among the Asian

Dominions about accepting 'fixed rates with sterling after sterling had become convertible.'[55]

Some time had to elapse before the plan could be put before the new American administration under Eisenhower, which took over only in late January 1953 and clearly needed time to assess its responsibilities. In the meantime a paper was prepared for submission to the State Department indicating the role that the British Cabinet now hoped the Americans would play.[56] The paper said:

> Nothing would be more conducive to the adoption of freer trade and currency policies by other countries than a real step forward by the United States to help other countries to live by 'Trade not Aid.' The particular policies which could be changed to provide greater opportunities to earn and save dollars have been extensively explored in recent years – tariff policy and customs procedure, the use of quota restrictions to protect agriculture, 'Buy American' legislation, shipping discrimination and subsidies, immigration, 'tied' lending (eg by the Import-Export Bank) &c...It is hoped that the United States will find itself able, by Government loans, private investment and through the International Bank, to participate in Commonwealth development...[57]

At the beginning of February Butler was able to report to the Commons that the sterling area had a surplus of £150 million in 1952 as a whole, compared with a loss of £700 million in 1951.[58] This success was due partly to the restrictions that had been imposed, but also to the fact that the terms of trade moved in Britain's favour – that is to say, raw materials were relatively cheaper, reversing the previous trend.[59] At the end of the month he and Eden left England together on the *Queen Elizabeth*, bound for New York and Washington.[60] When they arrived at New York they found that news of Stalin's stroke 'displaced all else.'[61]

The result of their mission, so far as the 'Collective Approach' was concerned, was very much as Cherwell had predicted. After only two days Butler sent a message to the Prime Minister indicating this:

> We have been put through an exhaustive cross-examination on the state of our internal economy and the prospective

strength of ourselves and the sterling area. While expressing genuine admiration of the extent of our recovery and achievement, the United States team, in which Lew Douglas has played a prominent part, doubted whether our economy was yet strong enough to sustain the risks of a convertibility operation, and indicated that the time was not yet, in their view, opportune for putting the collective approach into effect.

Lew Douglas had been American Ambassador in London at the time of the Labour Government's struggles with convertibility, so he knew the problems that Britain and the sterling area faced. Butler added:

> At this early stage of their administration they are not inclined to undertake to face Congress with any drastic measures designed either to win financial support for our scheme, to lower tariffs or otherwise to implement good creditor policies. But they are equally clear that they should encourage the momentum of our policies and do nothing to create an impression of 'impasse' or disagreement... It must be said that although no new proposal has emerged which is likely to ease our burdens, nevertheless the spirit of the talks and the personal contacts established have been very worth while.[62]

Even without the 'Collective Approach', however, Butler was able to plan a generous Budget for 1953. This was, as Plowden wrote, because 'the economy was running well below capacity.'[63] Unemployment, although still very low, had risen by about 100,000, and it seemed that some incentive was required. To the plaudits of the Conservative backbenchers, Butler's 1953 Budget reduced purchase tax by a quarter and income tax by 6d in the pound. The Excess Profits Levy was to terminate at the end of 1953, and initial allowances for capital investment were to be reintroduced. He also announced an increase in the sugar ration, and its forthcoming abolition. He concluded his speech by saying:

> We step out from the confines of restriction, to the almost forgotten but beckoning prospects of freer endeavour and greater reward for effort.[64]

Although Gaitskell next day pointed out that 'the real justification for Budgetary concessions is not the flourishing state of the economy but the stagnation into which production has fallen',[65] his harsh reminder did nothing to damage Butler's rising reputation on the Government benches.

As the *Daily Mail* said on the following day:

> Many a sugar-coated pill has emerged from the familiar red dispatch box on Budget Day. But Mr Butler has done something unique. He has literally given us the sugar with no pill.

In spite of the rejection of 'Robot' and the relative failure of the 'Collective Approach', he was now clearly established as Number Three in the Cabinet – a position already symbolised by his presiding over the Cabinet in the absence of the Prime Minister in September, and reinforced by the replacement of Salter as Minister of Economic Affairs at the end of October and the resurrection of the post of Economic Secretary for one of Butler's old protégés, Reginald Maudling. The serious illness of Lord Woolton, who collapsed with peritonitis at the Conservative Party Conference at Scarborough in October and was out of action for six months, removed a colleague who claimed superior knowledge of economics; and Cherwell devoted more of his time to the development of the atomic programme after the explosion of the British atomic bomb at Monte Bello Islands, Australia, at the beginning of October. The long illness of Eden and, as we shall see, of the Prime Minister himself, made Butler's position all the more secure – but all the more exacting.

It was no doubt the favourable impact of Butler's 1953 Budget that enabled the Conservatives to pick up an Opposition seat at Sunderland South in May – an exceptional success for a Government in power. *The Times* attributed it to the fact that the Tory party had 'changed almost beyond recognition since 1939'.[66] This was a mistake.

4 Korea and Colonial Problems

Churchill's Government inherited from Attlee's the commitment to support the United Nations Command in Korea, but this was not like one of the joint commands of the Second World War. The British contribution was relatively small in relation to the Command as a whole, which had been entrusted in the first instance to the United States, originally in the person of General Douglas MacArthur. When so-called Chinese volunteers intervened in the struggle in November 1950, MacArthur's troops had suffered a severe reverse, for they were scattered across North Korea attempting to clear the whole country of the enemy. President Truman and the American Chiefs of Staff accepted that honour would be satisfied if the United Nations forces re-established a position near the 38th Parallel, which had been the original border between North and South Korea. As we have seen, however, MacArthur wanted to go further, openly demanding authority to strike directly at China, and expressing pessimism about the prospects in Korea unless this were done. In April 1951 Truman relieved him of the command, and transferred it to his Army Commander, General Matthew Ridgway.

By mid-1951 Ridgway had restored the front line to a position roughly along the Parallel, and he also held off some fierce counter-attacks. In July, after the Soviet Ambassador to the United Nations had indicated that an armistice might be attained, negotiations began. At this time there was a single Commonwealth Division in Korea, consisting of two British brigades and one Canadian, and two Australian infantry battalions. The Division also included a New Zealand artillery battery.[1] But Ridgway's main forces consisted of some seven American Divisions and as many as nine of the South Korean Army. Britain also provided some warships, including an aircraft-carrier and marine commandos, but the RAF had no fighter aircraft which could compete with the Russian Mig-15, though the American Sabre jets could. Under these circumstances the British Government could hardly ask for

45

more than a right to be consulted on major issues, and certainly could not claim a place at the negotiating table.

Churchill was unhappy to find the armistice negotiations still going on when he took office. He minuted to Eden in mid-November:

> No one knows what is going on in Korea or which side is benefiting from the humbug and grimaces at Panmunjom [where the armistice talks were taking place]. We must try to penetrate the American mind and purpose. We may find this out when we are in Washington. Nobody knows it now. The other side clearly do not want an agreement. It is important to think how prolonging the deadlock can benefit them. Obviously it diverts United Nations resources. But what else do they hope for? Meanwhile a war is being carried on and British troops are engaged, with sharp losses.[2]

A month later, after receiving a fresh report from Tokyo about the stalemate in the truce talks, Churchill again addressed Eden on the matter:

> Obviously the Communists are manoeuvring with the United States in order to gain time. The question is For What? The six months parleyings have enabled the Chinese Communists to add sixty thousand to their strength; to build up their artillery, and above all to let the Russians teach them how to fly the Russian planes. The United Nations' position is actively and relatively far worse than it was six months ago. We may be grateful that we have only a small say in these matters. I am glad we do not bear the responsibility of having to guess the Communist motives. There can however be no doubt that so far time had been almost entirely on their side.[3]

In April General Eisenhower's decision to run for the Presidency resulted in further changes in the Korean army command. Ridgway, who had proved his abilities both as Army Commander and as Far East Commander-in-Chief, now became Supreme Commander in Europe, and his place in the Far East was taken by General Mark Clark, who had commanded an army under Alexander in Italy during the Second World War. General Van Fleet was the new Army Commander in Korea. In the late spring of 1952 Mark Clark invited

Alexander to visit the Korean front, and so early in June Alexander flew to Japan, taking with him Selwyn Lloyd to represent the Foreign Office. By this time the front was more or less static, and on his return to Tokyo from Korea Selwyn Lloyd wrote to Eden to say:

> We were greatly reassured about:-
> (i)   the strength of the U.N. defensive positions
> (ii)   the U.S. conduct of the whole prisoner of war affair
> (iii) the U.S. conduct of the Armistice negotiations.

He added that he was 'more worried than Alex about the South Korean political position', owing to the arbitrary behaviour of Syngman Rhee, the President, who was unwilling to accept a conclusion of the war without unification of the entire country; but Lloyd also commented that:

> The Commonwealth Division really is a remarkable Commonwealth effort, and our chaps were a model of efficiency and good morale.[4]

It was unfortunate that while Alexander and Lloyd were still in Washington on their return journey the United States Air Force extended its bombing campaign to a complex of power stations on the Yalu River – right on the border of Manchuria. The two British Ministers had been given no hint that this operation was pending, and it caused the Government some embarrassment in the Commons, Attlee asking a sharp question about it on 25 June.[5] One outcome of the visit was a proposal by Mark Clark that a senior British or Commonwealth officer should be appointed as one of his Deputy Chiefs of Staff. Churchill accepted this proposal, and it was announced in the House of Commons – though Selwyn Lloyd warned that the officer concerned would not supersede the normal channel of communication through the Joint Chiefs of Staff in Washington.[6]

Almost at once, however, Churchill had second thoughts. Next day the British Ambassador in Tokyo sent a despatch reporting a meeting with General Mark Clark, at which the General had said that 'With the appointment of a British Deputy, who would know about operations before they happened, he hoped that in future Her Majesty's Government would be in a position to say that they had been consulted and that they approved the operations.'[7]

Churchill described this as 'a disturbing telegram...[We] have a more direct responsibility without real power.'[8] After finding some weeks later that the Chiefs of Staff were opposed to the appointment he wrote to Eden: 'I should prefer to say that we do not propose to take advantage of General Mark Clark's friendly offer upon full consideration of all the circumstances.'[9] Eden replied at once. 'I do not see how we can now change our plans. It should be made quite clear that the Deputy Chief of Staff would be responsible solely to General Mark Clark':

> ...If we were to change our minds now it would be very confusing for the House of Commons and for public opinion in this country and the Commonwealth. Apart from the charge of order, counter-order, disorder, it might be suggested that there was some new discord in Anglo-American relations.[10]

At the Cabinet meeting on 22 July it was decided to go ahead with the appointment, but the statement of the officer's duties was carefully revised.[11]

There was not in fact very much for the officer concerned – Major-General S.N. Shoosmith – to do in the way of liaison anyway. The troops had orders to limit their activity to defensive measures only, and from July 1952 onwards the one issue that divided the two sides in the armistice negotiations was an issue on which the British and American Governments were completely agreed, namely that the prisoners of war should only be repatriated voluntarily. The obstacle here was that there were 20,000 Chinese prisoners in United Nations custody, of whom 14,000 refused to return. The Chinese made an issue of this, no doubt partly because their excuse for intervening in Korea had been that their troops were 'volunteers', and also because the 1949 Geneva Convention on prisoners' rights was unfortunately vague. The Cabinet had approved the American stand on this issue as early as April,[12] and in July Churchill wrote to Sir William Strang, the Permanent Secretary at the Foreign Office:

> In my view there can be no question of forcing any Chinese prisoners of war to go back to Communist China against their will. These are the ones, above all others, who carry

with them the moral significance, as the ones who had opted for us would certainly be put to death or otherwise maltreated.[13]

There were also 35,000 Korean prisoners, out of a total of 118,000 who refused repatriation, but they naturally presented less of a problem.

The armistice talks remained deadlocked on this question throughout the summer and autumn, and in October the Americans decided to recess the talks for the winter. Attention turned to the General Assembly of the United Nations, where an Indian resolution, after careful amendment by the British delegation to ensure that it accepted voluntary repatriation, was adopted on 3 December by the large majority of 54 votes to five.[15] Although Selwyn Lloyd and Gladwyn Jebb, the Foreign Office official who was Britain's permanent representative on the Security Council, had been in New York throughout, Eden also visited in November and spoke on behalf of the Indian resolution on 11 November. Not only did it emphasise voluntary repatriation in its amended form, but it commended itself to Eden as likely to rally Asian opinion and, as he put it to the Cabinet, 'avoid snubbing the Indian initiative and thus in effect kicking India back to the top of the fence just when she showed signs of descending on our side of it.' Eden added: 'It was particularly encouraging that General Eisenhower [now President-elect] agreed with us on this point.'[15] But Dean Acheson, the 'lame duck' Secretary of State, was hotly against it, and on 19 November he saw both Eden and Selwyn Lloyd for a meeting which lasted two hours and which Eden described as 'one of the most disagreeable that he has ever encountered.'

Dean [Acheson] assailed Selwyn in a manner that was only half jocular, accusing him of not having dealt honourably with the United States in this matter, of being a Welshman and so on, for nearly an hour. He said that if Britain could not make up her mind that she was with the United States on this matter, it would be the end of Anglo-American co-operation, there would be no N.A.T.O., *et cetera*. Hickerson [State Department] had the impertinence at one point to say, 'Anthony, you have got to choose between the United States and India. Which will you have?' They both spoke in contemptuous terms not only of Krishna Menon and the Indians but also of Mike Pearson and Canada. Dean described Mike as an 'empty glass of water.'

Eden had his Principal Private Secretary, Evelyn Shuckburgh, report this both to Strang at the Foreign Office and to Sir Oliver Franks at the British Embassy in Washington.[16] Franks commented sagely that he was sure that 'Dean Acheson's state of mind was largely occasioned by the intolerable situation of being and having to act as Secretary of State when he has no real power or position.'[17] But Eden thought the fracas sufficiently important to report it to the Cabinet in mid-December.

Although General Eisenhower had promised during his election campaign that he would pay a visit to Korea if elected, and in fact did so in December 1952 while still President-elect, no notable development took place after his inauguration except a decision which he announced in his 'State of the Union' message to Congress on 2 February to allow the Chinese Nationalists on the island of Formosa [now Taiwan] to attack the mainland if they wished. Eden promptly dissociated the United Kingdom from this decision, in a statement to the House of Commons.[18]

It was perhaps the death of Stalin in early March that permitted the final acceptance of the United Nations' terms. An exchange of sick and wounded prisoners took place on 20 April, but it was not until Dulles had visited Nehru in Delhi in May and asked him to transmit to Peking a threat to broaden the war that the final UN condition for the exchange of the prisoners was agreed.[19] Even so, a hitch occurred on the United Nations' side which held up the signature of the armistice for a month. On 18 June Syngman Rhee, who objected to any peace that left Korea divided, released 25,000 Korean anti-Communist prisoners without waiting for the repatriation procedure. Nevertheless, the armistice was agreed on 19 June – South Korea dissenting – and was formally signed on behalf of the two sides on 27 July.

The importance of ensuring that India was sympathetic to the Western viewpoint about the prisoners was demonstrated when both sides accepted an Indian contingent as the agent for determining the desire of each of the remaining prisoners for voluntary repatriation. But suspicion between the two sides remained acute, and the 16 nations which had contributed fighting forces to the United Nations Command issued a joint declaration to say that if there were any breach of the armistice 'we should again be united and prompt to resist. The consequences of such a breach...would be so grave that, in all probability, it would not be possible to confine hostilities within the frontiers of Korea.'[20]

The armistice included a stipulation that a political conference should be held within 90 days in order, if possible, to secure the reunification of the country. But arrangements for its convening remained deadlocked, and it was not until a Foreign Ministers' Conference on Germany and Austria in February 1954 that it was agreed to take up the issue at Geneva in April of that year. Unfortunately, the Geneva Conference also resulted in deadlock, and the two Koreas remain divided to the present day.

The United States had suffered over 140,000 casualties, of whom 33,629 died. Britain suffered 686 killed, out of a Commonwealth total of 1,263. There were also 1,102 British missing or prisoners of war, of whom almost all returned.[21]

While it was the United States that bore the primary responsibility for conducting the Korean War, insurgency that had arisen or was to arise in the British colonies was entirely a matter for the British Government. The extent of these territories is now difficult to recall. As Oliver Lyttelton reported in 1953, they amounted to 35 in number 'by a method which takes Governors or High Commissioners as its unit', and the total area was 'a little more than 2 million square miles (compare in round terms the United Kingdom's 95,000 and the United States' 3,750,000).' The total population was about 74 million.[22]

In Malaya, when the Churchill Government took office, a serious insurgency was taking place. The Governor, Sir Henry Gurney, had been assassinated and his successor had not been appointed. Oliver Lyttelton, the Colonial Secretary, took charge at once and announced at the Cabinet's first meeting that he intended to visit Malaya at the end of November, at a time when a Conference of Governors was assembling at Singapore. Before setting out he told the Cabinet that:

it was his intention to establish stronger direction and more
unified control of the campaign for establishing law and
order. His present bias was in favour of concentrating in the
hands of a single individual the powers of the Governor-
General and Commander-in-Chief.

But, he said, he would take no action until he had visited the
area.[23] He also submitted to the Cabinet an appreciation of the
situation by Lieutenant-General Sir Harold Briggs, the retiring
Director of Operations. Briggs emphasised the need to win over
the Chinese population of Malaya. As a Colonial Office report
put it: 'It is difficult to police a country which is nearly half
Chinese with a force which is 95% Malay, and which cannot
speak the language of the people it purports to control.'
   The linguistic problem beset not only the police, but still
more the seven British infantry battalions – as large a force as
had been sent to Korea – and the three 'Colonial' (i.e. East
African and Fijian) battalions also serving there. There were
also ten RAF squadrons and two squadrons of the Royal
Australian Air Force. Although Malaya was valuable to the sterling area for its substantial exports of rubber and tin, the
estimated expenditure on the emergency in a full year was
£57 million.[24]
   On his return from the Far East, which also involved a trip
to Hong Kong, Lyttelton set about finding a suitable senior
officer, to act both as High Commissioner for Malaya and to
'direct all military and police operations in the Federation.'
His first choice was General Sir Brian Robertson, who was
reaching the end of a term as Commander-in-Chief, Middle
East Land Forces; Robertson was summoned home, but he
successfully pleaded that he had been too long abroad and
hoped for a home posting. Then Lyttelton turned to the Chief
of the Imperial General Staff himself, General Sir William
Slim, but Slim refused on the ground of age – he was over
sixty. Then Lyttelton thought of General Sir Gerald Templer,
and arranged for him to fly out to Ottawa to meet the Prime
Minister; as we have seen, Churchill approved the appointment on the spot, and he took up his post in February 1952.[25]
   Under Templer's command things soon began to improve.
The 'terrorists' in Malaya, by Lyttelton's estimate, were never
more than about 4,000 to 6,000. But they could get supplies by

battening on the Chinese squatters until the latter were brought into 'new villages' rendered 'reasonably secure inside well-lighted and well-wired fences'. This was the Briggs Plan, initiated by Briggs in his brief tour of duty before Templer took over.[27] Lyttelton reported in the spring of 1953:

> The improvement in the security situation has been striking. Terrorism has been greatly reduced but terrorist casualties have increased: the Security Services have themselves suffered progressively fewer casualties…The foundation for recent progress in the campaign against terrorism was laid in the resettlement programme inaugurated by the late Sir Henry Gurney and the late Lieutenant-General Sir Harold Briggs. By the end of 1952 over 470,000 squatters, the majority of them Chinese, had been moved to protected New Villages.[28]

Although the 'shooting war' was not yet over, its end was within sight, and Lyttelton could promise that it would be possible to withdraw some of the forces sent to cope with the emergency 'within a year or two'.[29]

But no sooner was one crisis moving to a conclusion than another appeared, this time in East Africa. Over-population in Kenya had led to a growth of land-hunger, especially in the 'White Highlands' which had been reserved for white settlers. It was in this area that a native movement among the Kikuyu tribe called 'Mau Mau' began to develop. Members of Mau Mau took oaths of secrecy, and early in 1952 initiated attacks mostly on fellow-Africans, but sometimes on the white settlers themselves. In April 1952 Lyttelton appointed a new Governor, Sir Evelyn Baring, but owing to ill-health he did not take up his post until September. In October he was obliged to declare a state of emergency, and a British battalion and reinforcements of the King's African Rifles were moved to the colony. The cruiser HMS *Kenya* put in at Mombasa, and Lyttelton himself arrived to take stock of the situation.

But Kenya was not like Malaya. There could be no question of replacing the Governor, who had only just been appointed. Nor were the Mau Mau Communists, in spite of their implacable hostility. The disorders culminated in the 'Lari massacre' of about a hundred Africans, only 25 miles from Nairobi, the capital, on 26 March 1953.[30] This resulted in the despatch of further military reinforcements – two British infantry battalions and a brigade headquarters, and a flight of Harvard aircraft.[31] Jomo Kenyatta, the leader of the Kenya African Union, was among a considerable group of Africans, mostly of the Kikuyu tribe, who were detained. Kenyatta was tried before a former judge of the Kenya High Court and sentenced to seven years' imprisonment – itself a useful qualification for his later career as President of the ex-colony.

There was more continuity of Colonial policy than would appear from the House of Commons debates, for Lyttelton had an abrupt manner and made few verbal concessions to his political opponents. Unlike Eden, he was not the master of the 'soft answer' that, according to Proverbs, 'turneth away wrath.' As he wrote in his memoirs, 'I began to be an unpopular Minister, and a popular target for attacks.'[32] But he and the Cabinet as a whole were just as committed to constitutional progress as their predecessors. Templer's instructions were not merely to restore 'law and order' in Malaya but to pave the way for 'political advancement'.[33] In Africa too Lyttelton encouraged the same process and allowed the Gold Coast leader, Dr Kwame Nkrumah, to be designated as 'Prime Minister'.[34] In the much larger country of Nigeria, he recognised that internal differences were so great that the constitutional solution would have to be on federal lines. He described the conference that he convened under his own chairmanship in London at the end of July 1953 as 'the most successful of the many negotiations in which I was engaged during my term of office.'[35]

The British parties clashed most frequently over policy towards Southern Africa, though here again the Conservative and Labour leadership had much in common, at least to begin with. It was the Labour Government which in 1950 had banished Seretse Khama, the hereditary claimant to the Chieftainship of the Bamangwato in Bechuanaland (later Botswana), because he had married a white woman while in England. This was because Sir Evelyn Baring, then British High Commissioner to South Africa (and Governor of the three High Commission Territories including Bechuanaland) felt that the South African Government, which had lately adopted the policy of apartheid, would otherwise absorb the three territories and leave the Commonwealth.[36] The decision was confirmed and made permanent by Ismay during his period as Commonwealth Secretary in 1951–52, although Churchill, when in opposition, had described the Labour Government's action as 'very disreputable'. Churchill had changed his mind after a message from his old friend General Smuts to the effect that allowing Seretse to take the Chieftainship might 'damage the relations of South Africa to the Commonwealth.'[37]

Fear of the extension of apartheid from South Africa to Rhodesia was also the background to the creation of the Central African Federation, consisting of the Rhodesias and Nyasaland (now Zimbabwe, Zambia and Malawi). Relations with Southern Rhodesia were conducted by the Secretary of State for Commonwealth Relations, as the country was already semi-independent. The Labour Secretaries of State for Commonwealth Relations and for the Colonies, Patrick Gordon Walker and James Griffiths, both favoured action on these lines, provided that African opinion could be persuaded to accept it – though unfortunately the real reason could not be openly declared. Lyttelton and his successive colleagues at the Commonwealth Office – Ismay, Salisbury and Swinton – took the same view.[38]

A conference was held at Lancaster House in London in April 1952, and a second conference followed in January 1953. But African opinion was either lukewarm or hostile, and the views of the British Labour Party veered in the same direction. Attlee personally visited the territories in September 1952, and in December led a delegation to the Colonial Office to stress Labour's reservations prior to the second conference.[39] But Salisbury, Swinton and Lyttelton jointly warned the Cabinet:

> We have no doubt that if we postpone or abandon the scheme...Southern Rhodesia, soured and isolated, will be drawn more and more into the orbit of the Union.[40]

They asked, and the Cabinet agreed, to go ahead with the second conference as they had planned.[41] When the Federation Bill came to the Commons for second reading in May 1953, it met strong opposition from Labour, which regarded the safeguards for African interests as inadequate. Nevertheless, the bill was passed and the Central African Federation came into existence in August of the same year.[42]

The heaviest commitment of British troops and equipment, apart from that in Germany, was not in the Colonies but in Egypt, in the Canal Zone. Of a total of 11 and one-third divisions composing the entire British Army, the equivalent of two infantry divisions and a parachute brigade group were in Egypt in 1952.[43] The total number of mouths being fed by Britain had reached 81,000, far more than the 10,000 specified in the Anglo-Egyptian Treaty of 1936.

As we have seen the treaty had been abrogated by Egypt during the British election campaign. The Egyptians also claimed to cancel the Condominium Agreements relating to the Sudan, under which Britain and Egypt shared authority over the territory, and King Farouk of Egypt was proclaimed King of the Sudan. The Labour Government had refused to recognise these acts, and had strengthened the forces in Egypt by the equivalent of four brigade groups; the Churchill Government confirmed this move, although it left the home country completely bare of either infantry or armoured formations. The town of Ismailia, where many British troops were billeted, was subject to rioting in mid-October, and the Egyptian labour force of some 50,000 was almost entirely withdrawn. In mid-November the Egyptian police themselves provoked incidents in Ismailia, and so British personnel were evacuated from the town. At the beginning of December Eden asked the Cabinet to authorise the British Commander-in-Chief, Sir Brian Robertson, to detain Egyptian 'terrorists' indefinitely, but not to try or punish them; this was agreed.[44] Eden also saw the Egyptian Foreign Minister in Paris at the General Assembly of the United Nations, told him of the action taken, and urged him to press his Government to join four-power talks on defence arrangements to replace the 1936 Treaty. The other powers in the proposed Middle East Defence Organisation were to be, in Eden's view, the United States, France and Turkey.[45] The Cabinet decided to release £5 million from the Egyptian sterling balances at the end of the year, in accordance with an agreement made by the Labour Government in the previous March.[46]

On 25 January, with the approval of Churchill and Eden, General Robertson ordered the disarming of the Egyptian police at Ismailia. They resisted and fought back vigorously, surrendering only when 46 of their number had been killed, together with three British soldiers.[47] This was immediately followed by rioting in Cairo, directed at British and foreign property, which resulted in 20 deaths and the destruction of notable landmarks including Shepheard's Hotel. Eden contemplated authorising 'Operation Rodeo' – a plan to rescue British and other nationals in Cairo – but before he could order this the Egyptian Army restored order unaided.[48] Then on 14 February Eden obtained the authority of the Cabinet to negotiate a new treaty with Egypt, allowing the permanent retention of 'a small combatant force in the Canal Zone'. This was in spite of some grumbling from the Prime Minister, who was averse to any concessions. On 1 March King Farouk replaced his existing Government with a new one led by Hilali Pasha. Eden regarded this as 'a considerable improvement', and felt that: 'They seem to be as good a Government as we can hope for in Egypt.'[50] He persuaded the Cabinet to agree to negotiate on 'the principle of evacuation' and the provision of equipment for the Egyptian armed forces. But the Cabinet insisted on two preconditions – that Egypt should agree to join 'a collective defence organisation for the Middle East' with other powers, and also 'recognise the right of the Sudanese to self-determination'.[51]

These conditions were a stumbling-block, as the Egyptian Government could not retreat on the recognition of the King to suzerainty over the Sudan. Negotiations were stalled, although the American Secretary of State, Dean Acheson, anxious to keep Egypt aligned with the West, tried hard to encourage both parties to make concessions.[52] Eden himself was inclined towards the American view, and after some more months had been lost he presented his Cabinet colleagues with a general statement of his views about 'British Overseas Obligations':

If on a longer view it must be assumed that the maintenance of the present scale of overseas commitments will permanently overstrain our economy, clearly we ought to recognise that the United Kingdom is over-committed and that we must reduce the commitment. The only practical way to removing the permanent strain would be for the United Kingdom to shed or share the load of one or two major obligations, e.g. the defence of the Middle East, for which at present we bear the responsibility alone, or the defence of South-East Asia, where we share the responsibility with the French. Our present policy is in fact directed towards the construction of international defence organisations for the Middle East and South-East Asia in which the United States and other Commonwealth countries would participate.

Eden concluded with the Macchiavellian observation:

Our aim should be to persuade the United States to assume the real burdens in each organisation while retaining for ourselves as much political control – and hence prestige and world influence – as we can.[53]

In July 1952 a military coup took place in Egypt, led by General Mohammed Neguib. He forced the abdication of the King and formed a government mostly composed of junior military officers. Sir Ralph Stevenson, the British Ambassador in Cairo, reported favourably on Neguib: he described him as 'an honest man who is doing his best in an extremely difficult situation'; but Churchill, who always read the English newspapers, noted that Neguib 'uses the expression that the Sudan and Egypt should work together "against the common enemy." This seems to me a fairly clear indication of his views.'[54] He continued to spar with Eden on this subject in August, just before Eden's marriage to his niece Clarissa Churchill:

Surely it would be very unwise to use the bait of re-arming the Egyptian forces or improving their equipment in the hope that they will take a reasonable view about making our forces withdraw from Egypt in spite of our Treaty rights? I believe it is an Eton custom to make parents of pupils pay for the birch!

Eden, who was an Etonian, replied with an allusion to Churchill's links with Harrow:

We will not let them have this equipment yet anyway. Even if we did so, I doubt if they would make the mistake of trying to push our forces into the Egyptian equivalent of Ducker![55]

While Eden and Clarissa were on their brief honeymoon in Portugal – Clarissa having gone out to her Registry Office wedding at Caxton Hall from No. 10 Downing Street – Churchill explained his views more fully to Selwyn Lloyd, the Minister of State:

> ...Since we took office we have followed the resolute policy of the late Government and have not hesitated to fire at Ismailia and elsewhere the decisive volley. ...I am not opposed to a policy of giving Neguib a good chance provided he shows himself to be a friend. I hope he will do something for the fellahin, but we must not be afraid of him or be driven by the threats of cowards and curs from discharging our duty of maintaining the freedom of the Suez Canal for all nations until we can hand it over to some more powerful combination.[56]

In spite of Churchill's intransigence, Eden asked the Cabinet at the end of October for fresh instructions to be given to the Ambassador to negotiate with Neguib. He wrote that 'The emergence of the new regime in Egypt may offer a better chance of coming to terms than we have had in the past.' He wanted, 'as part of a general settlement', to allow the Egyptians to take over the Suez base, and he was also willing to help to rearm the Egyptian forces with Centurion tanks and jet aircraft.[57] But Churchill still sought to persuade the United States to take part in the protection of the Suez Canal 'as an international waterway', and thought it was premature to think of moving the British troops to Cyprus. The Cabinet, without deciding on the larger issues of Middle East defence policy, authorised the Minister of Defence to discuss with the Chancellor of the Exchequer the cost of building accommodation for troops in Cyprus.[58]

Eden had undertaken in the autumn of 1951 to ensure self-government for the Sudan within 12 months. In the autumn of the following year, therefore, El-Mahdi, the son of the leader whose followers had killed General Gordon at Khartoum in 1884, visited London to obtain assurances that elections would not be postponed.[59] The Foreign Office made sure that he was warmly received, and he was greeted by Churchill himself at No. 10 Downing Street.[60] On 22 October Eden announced Britain's consent to Sudanese self-government; this meant that the only obstacle now would be the Egyptian Government.[61] On 26 October General Neguib, in what Eden in his memoirs described as 'an act of statesmanship', dropped the Egyptian claim to the unity of the Nile countries.[62] King Farouk's abdication had already eased the path. After lengthy negotiations marked by some mistrust on both sides – the British being particularly anxious to protect the position of the inhabitants of the Southern Sudan *vis-à-vis* the Muslim Northerners – agreement was reached and announced by Eden to the House of Commons on 12 February 1953. But Eden had to cope with a 'highly critical' group of the Government's own supporters in the House of Commons before the announcement was made – an unpleasant augury of difficulties to come.[63] After elections for a Sudanese Parliament, there was to be a transitional period of three years culminating in full self-determination. During these three years, the Sudanese Government would be 'Sudanised' – that is, native officials would be substituted for British.[64] In spite of much Egyptian lobbying, the elections resulted in the election of Sudanese who were determined to be independent. So the upshot was at least a partial success for Britain.

As for negotiations about the Canal Zone, the British view was that these should be conducted if possible by Britain and the United States together. In view of the impending change of administration in Washington, the discussion of how the approach should be made was entrusted to a State Department official, Henry Byroade, who visited London early in January 1953. Byroade wished to win Egyptian goodwill by an early delivery of arms, but the British demurred at this, thinking the arms might be used for guerrilla operations against their troops in the Canal Zone.[65] Churchill meanwhile had gone off for a month to Jamaica, and when he returned he:

> was in a rage against AE (Eden), speaking of 'appeasement' and saying that he never knew before that Munich was situated on the Nile. He described AE as having been a failure as Foreign Secretary and being 'tired, sick and bound up in detail'. Jock [Colville] said that the Prime Minister would never give way over Egypt. He positively desired the talks on the Sudan to fail.[66]

But he suggested to Eisenhower as soon as the latter took office that the two countries should negotiate together with Neguib through their ambassadors, each aided by a senior military representative. Churchill was proposing to ask Field Marshal Slim to undertake the task for Britain, and when Eden visited Eisenhower in the White House early in March he repeated the invitation. Eisenhower went so far as to nominate General John E. Hull of the US Army, but he added the proviso that he 'did not in any way commit the United States to participation in the early phases of the negotiations.'[68] And when the Egyptians indicated that they did not approve of joint negotiations by the two powers, the Americans withdrew, and Eisenhower wrote to Eden to say 'I feel we have been clumsy', and he elaborated his views more generally:

> I am certain that nothing infuriates an individual in one of these meetings so much as an insinuation or implication that they may be representing a country, whose convictions, because of some national reason, are not really important. I know, for example, that the French frequently feel that the United States and Britain are guilty of power politics on this point, and they resent it fiercely.

He asked Eden to maintain 'an attitude of absolute equality with all other nations, in every kind of multilateral conference in which we jointly participate.'[69]

Churchill then took up the correspondence, saying:

> I hope...that though you may not be able to help us positively it will not look as if the United States is taking sides against us. ...At present we seem to be heading for a costly and indefinite stalemate both in the Middle East and the Far East...[70]

Shortly after this, Eden fell seriously ill with gall bladder trouble, and was out of action for about six months; Sir Ralph Stevenson, the British Ambassador in Cairo, was also in hospital, and this gave Churchill the opportunity to despatch Robin Hankey (whom he relied upon to take a hard line) to Cairo to conduct the negotiations. Slim had to take up an appointment (already announced) as Governor-General of Australia, and so General Sir Brian Robertson, previously the British Commander-in-Chief in the Middle East, was appointed to take his place. Hankey's instructions from Churchill were, in effect, to play a waiting game: he was to be a 'patient sulky pig'.[71] For some months more, therefore, the impasse continued, and the Conservative Government avoided any charge of 'scuttle', but, to Butler's distress, lost any opportunity of defence economy.

5 The European Defence Community

The Korean War had sharpened the concern of the Western Allies about the danger of an attack on Western Europe, and the need to protect West Germany. For if, as was widely believed, Stalin had encouraged the North Koreans to attack the South, he might equally well launch the East Germans – who had a substantial force at their disposal – against West Germany, which, apart from small police forces in the separate Länder, was without an army. The Allied occupation forces were far too weak to hold back a determined assault from the East, especially if it were supported by the Red Army and if the other satellites also joined in the attack.

Churchill himself while in opposition realised the danger. As we have seen, he attended the Strasbourg meeting of the Consultative Assembly of the Council of Europe in August 1950, and sponsored a resolution which was then carried, calling for 'the immediate creation of a European army under a unified command and in which we shall bear a worthy and honourable part.'[1] Churchill envisaged the army as comprising contingents from Britain, from the United States and from the Western European countries, including West Germany. But the French were reluctant to agree to the rearmament of Germany. In October 1950 they put forward what was called the 'Pleven Plan' for the formation of a European army. This had been hastily devised by Jean Monnet, the author of the Schuman Plan for a Coal and Steel Community: to avoid the danger of recreating the German General Staff, it proposed that the army should be integrated 'at the level of the smallest possible unit' – presumably at battalion level. The army was to be under the control of a European Minister of Defence.

In December 1950, at a NATO Council meeting, it was agreed that American forces in Europe would be strengthened, and that all the Western Powers would rearm and place their troops under the command of an American general. General Eisenhower, who had commanded the troops in the campaign in Western Europe from D-Day onwards, was unanimously invited to take charge once more. It was accepted that German forces should be recruited, up to the level of the brigade group. But it was not only the French who had their doubts about the rearmament of Germany. In February 1951 Attlee set out the Labour Government's conditions for this to take place:

> Obviously, the rearmament of the countries of the Atlantic Treaty must precede that of Germany. Second, I think the building up of forces in the democratic states should precede the creation of German forces. Third, the arrangements must be such that German units are integrated in the defence forces in a way which would preclude the emergence of a German military menace. Fourth, there must be agreement with the Germans themselves.[2]

In the course of the following year – 1951 – the three major Western Allies undertook to negotiate with Dr Adenauer, the West German Chancellor, an agreement to restore political independence to the occupied tri-zone. While these negotiations took place in Germany, a simultaneous conference was meeting in Paris to develop the Pleven Plan into a European army – the European Defence Community (EDC) as it was called. Britain was represented only by an 'observer', as the British Labour Government had no intention of allowing its forces to be subject to a European Minister of Defence. Meanwhile the Russians, who feared German rearmament, proposed a conference of the four occupying powers on 'the German problem'. For reasons of public relations, this invitation was accepted, and Foreign Ministers' deputies met at the Palais Rose in Paris to agree the agenda of a conference, but after 74 meetings they were unable even to get that far, and so the attempt collapsed.[3]

When the Conservatives took office in October 1951, many European leaders thought that the British attitude towards Europe, and in particular the EDC, would be more positive. On this issue, differences existed between Eden and some of his Cabinet colleagues. Maxwell Fyfe, as leader of the Conservative delegation at the Strasbourg Assembly in November and December, took a different and more friendly line to the EDC than Eden. Although Maxwell Fyfe maintained in his memoirs that his statement at Strasbourg and Eden's were 'totally contradictory', this does not seem to have been the case.[4] Maxwell Fyfe's speech was followed by one from Paul Reynaud, in which the former French Premier warned that Britain's absence from the EDC would cause the whole scheme to collapse.[5]

It was on the following day that Churchill himself circulated a Cabinet paper explaining his own views:

> I am not opposed to a European Federation including (eventually) the countries behind the Iron Curtain, provided that this comes about naturally and gradually. But I never thought that Britain or the British Commonwealth should, either individually or collectively, become an intregral part of a European Federation, and have never given the slightest support to the idea.

Turning to the concept of the European army, he wrote:

> I should doubt very much the military spirit of a 'sludgy amalgam' of volunteers, or conscripts to defend the EDC. or similar organisations. The national spirit must animate all troops up to and including the divisional level.

He then criticised the French contribution as 'pitiful', and argued:

> They have no ground of complaint against us who have already dedicated four divisions to General Eisenhower's command. We must not lose all consciousness of our insular position. I noticed some time ago the faulty structure of the present French arrangements, and in particular how the few combatant divisional formations they have will be deprived of all training efficiency by the vast mass of recruits annually flowing in upon them.[6]

The French weakness that Churchill noticed was occasioned by the heavy commitment of their officers and NCOs to the war in Indo-China, and to the decision of the French Assembly not to send any conscripts to serve in the Far East.[7]

On 3 December the British Conservative delegation to the European Assembly at Strasbourg sent a joint telegram protesting at their new Government's lukewarm attitude to the EDC. No reply was received.[8] As for the 'Europeans' in the Cabinet – besides Maxwell Fyfe there was Macmillan – they were stymied by the opposition to their views of both the Prime Minister and the Foreign Secretary. Eden secured support for the policy which he and Churchill favoured from Eisenhower himself, who wrote to him early in December to say:

> I personally believe it would merely complicate matters if Great Britain should, at present, attempt to participate directly in the formation of a European defence force or in joining a European political union. I have pointed out the great benefit of Great Britain's continuing to carry out her world-wide responsibilities.[9]

All that Eisenhower expected of the British Government was an attitude of encouragement towards the EDC from outside, and when Churchill and Eden visited Paris in mid-December before their trip to the United States, they duly promised in their joint communique to 'associate' Britain with the EDC when it came into existence.[10]

Macmillan in a letter to Eden shortly afterwards accepted defeat on the 'European' issue:

> If we had been 'in' on the Schuman Plan or European Army Plan 2 years ago, we might have moulded it to our liking. But it would have been impertinence, as well as folly, to butt in at the last stage of the negotiations. It would have been a wrecking policy.[11]

Macmillan had earlier consulted Churchill on whether he – and the Prime Minister himself – should resign from the European Movement, which the latter had founded in 1948. One of Churchill's secretaries assured them both that Eden had decided this was unnecessary.[12] But the bitterness aroused by the revelation of the British attitude caused the resignation of the President of the European Assembly, the Belgian Paul-Henri Spaak.[13]

In February Eden was the host in London to a meeting of the three Western Foreign Ministers. For France, Robert Schuman wanted an Anglo-American guarantee against the unilateral secession of one of its members from the EDC – he was evidently thinking of West Germany. But the American Secretary of State, Dean Acheson, could not provide this without Congressional approval, and so the communiqué on the talks merely repeated British and American 'support' for EDC from outside, and their willingness to maintain armed forces in Europe 'in association with the European Defence forces'. Adenauer, who was invited to join the talks at their conclusion – he was in London in any case for the funeral of King George VI – while insisting on equality of status for West Germany, agreed to accept a form of words which banned the production of atomic, biological or chemical weapons 'in strategically exposed areas' – which in reality meant West Germany.[14]

The meeting of the North Atlantic Council at Lisbon shortly afterwards therefore found much of its business already pre-pared by the major powers. The Council accepted a formula for mutual security undertakings between NATO and the EDC. West Germany was to pay a financial contribution assessed by the NATO Temporary Council Committee – the 'three wise men' who had undertaken the same task for the other powers. The German contribution was to be used as assistance for Allied troops on German soil and for the beginning of West Germany's own rearmament, now expected to begin in the financial year 1952/3. The Lisbon Conference also agreed to establish a permanent base for NATO with a Secretary-General. This was in accordance with the views of Acheson and Eden as expressed in Washington, but although Eden had pressed for London as the headquarters, the French insisted on Paris.

On the other hand, it was urged that Britain should provide the first Secretary-General. Eden was strongly tempted to offer himself for this post, confiding to his diary that 'I would really enjoy the work, and would give so much to be on my own.'[15] This was an interesting comment on his state of mind at the time, and his relations with Churchill. The latter, however, refused to release his Foreign Secretary, and the post was then offered to Oliver Franks, who was retiring from the Embassy in Washington. Franks, however, refused the offer, and finally Churchill persuaded his loyal wartime colleague Ismay to serve. It was with considerable reluctance that Ismay gave up his post as Secretary of State for Commonwealth Relations, which he was beginning to enjoy.[16] But he had become 'expendable' to Churchill now that Alexander was about to become Defence Secretary. His post as Commonwealth Secretary was now taken by Salisbury, who held the largely nominal post of Lord Privy Seal. Salisbury in turn gave up the Seal to Crookshank, who was Leader of the Commons as well as Minister of Health.

Crookshank was relieved of the Ministry of Health – on which
he had made little impact – by Iain Macleod, a backbencher still
in his thirties who had impressed Churchill by his capacity in
debate on health matters against Aneurin Bevan.[17]

While the negotiations for the restoration of German sovereignty were proceeding in Bonn, the details of the EDC Treaty
were being thrashed out at a conference in Paris. Although
Britain was fully involved in the former, in the latter it had
only observer status. But it having been agreed that Britain
would make arrangements to associate her troops in some way
with the European army, one of Alexander's first commitments was, at Eden's suggestion, to arrange a date to visit Paris
and discuss this matter.[18] When the meeting took place,
Marshal Juin of France, who was Commander-in-Chief of the
NATO forces in the Central Front, argued that 'logistic'
difficulties would arise 'when it came to incorporating EDC
units in a British Army Corps'. But Alexander, calling upon his
own experience during the war, said:

> It should be remembered that these problems had been
> successfully overcome in the Italian campaign...Combined
> exercises might help to find satisfactory solutions.[19]

His old wartime colleague, Montgomery, however, who was
now Eisenhower's Deputy Supreme Commander, took the
view that the only solution of the inter-Allied problem was for
Britain to undertake to join the EDC. He wrote to Churchill in
December 1952:

> An announcement now that the British will participate in
> the EDC and the European Army would, in my opinion,
> secure its passage through the German and French
> Parliaments. Without such an announcement, I believe the
> ship will crash on the rocks.[20]

Churchill acknowledged this missive rather brusquely, but said
he had shown it to Eden;[21] the latter had already begun to
contemplate the prospect of the failure of EDC. As he told the
Cabinet:

> If the French Assembly ratifies the Treaty subject to condi-
> tions which would involve its complete re-negotiation or

indefinite delay, or if it rejects the Treaty, Her Majesty's Government, after prior consultation with the United States Government, should put forward a plan for a German contribution to Western defence through the North Atlantic Treaty Organisation; the essence of this plan would be accession by Germany to the North Atlantic Treaty, the extension of the duration of the North Atlantic Treaty, and the development of the NATO structure so as to provide a measure of control over German rearmament.[22]

Meanwhile the Soviet Foreign Office had not been idle. In mid-March 1952 it had sent a note to the three major Western powers proposing a four-power meeting to discuss a peace treaty for Germany as a whole. Commenting on this to the Cabinet Eden said that the proposal was 'clearly designed to placate public opinion in Germany and at the same time to arouse misgivings in France...The test of their [i.e. the Russians'] sincerity would be their willingness to agree to the holding of free elections, under independent supervision, throughout Germany.'[23] The three Western powers duly drew up a joint note along these lines.[24]

When the Soviet Government resumed the diplomatic offensive with a further note on 9 April, it at least provoked the German Social Democrat Opposition leader, Kurt Schumacher, to suggest exploring the possibility of an agreement between the four wartime Allies which would end the division of Germany.[25] Eden was, as he recorded in his diary, 'Troubled by the turn EDC negotiations are taking and relation of our reply to Soviet note to them.' He was 'not happy with American line nor with ours which seemed too negative'. He had to think of public opinion not only in Germany but in France and for that matter in Britain, where there lingered a good deal of hostility to German rearmament. With the aid of Frank Roberts, his Deputy Under-Secretary of State, he altered the text until it seemed 'exactly right'.[26] As he had told the Cabinet in April, the Western reply should 'leave the door open for further discussion' while the agreements with West Germany on guarantees to the EDC and the contractual arrangements were hastened.[27] The three Western powers, replying with identical notes on 13 May, remained emphatic that they could not agree to negotiations with Germany as a whole

until after free elections, and that free elections were dependent upon the findings of an 'impartial enquiry'.[28]

By late May the EDC Treaty and the Contractual Agreements
were both ready for signature, but on 24 May a further Soviet
note arrived which seemed to the Allies to take the proposal no
further.[29] The three Foreign Ministers attended the signature of
the treaties and their associated documents in Bonn and Paris
on 26 and 27 May, and Eden said to Acheson: 'We have won the
battle of the notes.'[30] But as ratification of the agreements had
still to come, the struggle was by no means over.

The British and French Foreign Ministers were anxious, for
the sake of domestic opinion, to keep up the exchange with
the Soviet Union, but Acheson, with the EDC Treaty and the
Contractual Agreements already signed, was now in favour of
going no further than restating what had already been said.
He worried about American Senatorial ratification of the
agreements:

> Proposal for mtg now wld jeopardise ratification here and in
> Ger...[P]roposal for immed mtg with Sovs wld lead Senate
> to take position that situation might be changed and thus
> no need for their giving this matter priority.[31]

In addition, John J. McCloy, the American High Commissioner
in Germany, reported Adenauer as being 'extremely upset and
nervous' at the prospect of 'a separate deal between the Allies
and Russia over Ger.'[32] In the end the joint note sent on
10 July did no more than repeat the Allied offer of an impartial committee of enquiry into whether free elections could be
held, and then a meeting of the four powers to discuss the
arrangements for holding the elections.[33] A further note emanated from Moscow on 23 August, revealing little change of
position, and after another Allied reply giving no ground, the
exchange came to a close.[34]

Although the American Senate approved the ratification of
the rearmament of Germany readily enough, the same did not
apply to Britain, where the Labour Party, despite having been
committed to it before the election, found occasion to make
an issue of the proposal now that it was in opposition. More
importantly, the ratification of the EDC Treaty by the six
continental powers hung fire. Although it had been a French

initiative, it became apparent in the autumn of 1952 that the French Assembly would take a lot of persuading to ratify the treaty, involving as it did the merging of the French army into a larger entity. Both the Gaullists and the Communists opposed the idea, and Robert Scott, who was an Assistant Under-Secretary of State at the Foreign Office, commented: 'Since Turkey recovered twenty years ago France has taken her place as the sick man of Europe' – a comment that drew Eden's approval.[35] The trouble was that so much of the French regular army was committed to the Indo-China war, and there were still issues of importance between France and Germany, for instance the future of the Saar.[36]

In Britain, the issue was solely that of German rearmament. Eden brought the treaties before the Commons at the end of July 1952, and there was a two-day debate. He spoke both at its introduction and at its conclusion, pointing out that the agreements were the logical outcome of the Labour Government's policy. But for the first time in the new Parliament the Labour Party chose to divide the House on a major issue of foreign policy. Shinwell, the former Minister of Defence, moved an amendment describing the Government's proposals as 'inopportune, particularly at a time when attempts are still being made by the Western Powers to discuss the German problem with the Union of Soviet Socialist Republics', adding also a reaffirmation of 'the conditions first laid down in this House by the present Leader of the Opposition on 12th February 1951'.[37] The so-called 'Attlee conditions' were, as we have seen, outlined when Attlee was still Prime Minister. But the party was swung into opposing Eden's policy by its own left wing – an unusual combination of the anti-German Hugh Dalton and the Bevanites.[38]

The Times Parliamentary Correspondent described Eden's two speeches as 'brilliant and persuasive' and said that:

> his reasoned argument against delay in ratification appeared to add to the embarrassment of the disunited opposition.[39]

Certainly there must have been some Labour abstentions, as the Government's motion was carried by 293 votes to 253.[4]

Early in 1953 fresh delays were holding up ratification. Adenauer needed a two-thirds majority in the Bundestag, which he did not command unless the Constitutional Court ruled in his favour, so he decided to bide his time. Meanwhile the new French Government of René Mayer had only managed to take office on the understanding that it would add 'protocols' to the EDC and seek assurances of still closer association from the United Kingdom.[41] It was not a very good sign that the Mayer Government depended on the support of the Gaullists, as General de Gaulle, then in self-imposed exile, described the EDC as a 'Frankenstein'.[42] Churchill commented on a note from Eden: 'Two if not three years have been lost through French obstruction.'[43]

So ratification by the potential members of the EDC had proceeded no further by the spring of 1953. Eden and Butler were actually on the way to America when the death of Stalin took place. The news obscured all else, but Eisenhower, who had just taken office, found time to see Eden. He recorded in his diary:

> He was very friendly but still rather vague in his ideas and found Winston's messages tiresome. 'Here comes trouble' he said he had told someone when the first one arrived. He promised me as much time as I wanted while I was here, and I think he meant it.[44]

Back in Britain in mid-March, Eden was pleased with the outcome of an official visit to the country paid by Marshal Tito of Yugoslavia, which paved the way for the eventual settlement of the dispute over Trieste – British and American troops were still in occupation there, eight years after the end of the war. Meanwhile Churchill took up the idea of paying a visit to Molotov, and on Good Friday (3 April) sent round a draft telegram, which, according to Eden:

> …showed that he hadn't really understood our reasons for not caring for early meeting or alarming Ike with report that we were doing so now.[45]

Next day Eden, who had been in poor health for some time, was obliged to go into hospital for an operation for 'chronic inflammation of the gall bladder'. He had been just about to go on a tour of Mediterranean countries – Turkey, Greece and Italy. He was to see them only on his convalescence four months later.[46]

6 Privatisation

The Churchill Government was pledged to 'simplify the administrative machine', to repeal the Iron and Steel Act and to give private hauliers the chance to return to business.[1] As we have seen, one of the first decisions of the new Cabinet was to prevent the Iron and Steel Corporation, as set up by the Attlee Government, from reorganising the companies which had only been nationalised that year.[2] At first the Cabinet had considered the possibility of denationalising iron and steel before Christmas, and had appointed a Committee under Crookshank to look into this.[3] Crookshank quickly discovered that this was impracticable, but said that a directive could be given to the Board of the Corporation to 'refrain from any action which might prejudice the position further'.[4] The form of the directive to this effect, to be issued by the Minister of Supply, was approved by the Cabinet on 12 November, and thereupon announced in the House of Commons.[5]

It was hoped that the bills for the denationalisation both of road haulage and of iron and steel would be ready for introduction when Parliament reassembled at the end of January.[6] But the death of the King early in February delayed parliamentary business for about two weeks, and there were also delays involved in the drafting of the legislation. Meanwhile Conservative backbenchers were becoming exercised about the renewal of the BBC's Charter, for some of them vigorously opposed the perpetuation of the monopoly. Salisbury and Woolton were deputed to calm the 1922 Committee on this matter.[7] But when they put the case for retaining the monopoly, they encountered 'a very strong body of opinion in favour of ending' it. They agreed to continue to negotiate with 'a small delegation appointed by Government supporters who were specially interested in the question'.[8]

At this juncture the Prime Minister declared himself 'disturbed' by a recent announcement on increases in railway and bus fares in the London area. Strong feelings were also expressed in Parliament, although the Transport Tribunal had been considering the application from the Transport Commission for almost a year. At a meeting of the Cabinet on

73

7 March 1952 Churchill secured approval for a public statement that the fare increases were not the responsibility of the
Government.[9] He was evidently worried about the prospects
for the party in the impending county council elections. At a
later Cabinet the Chief Whip was asked to arrange a meeting
in London for the Home Secretary and other Ministers.[10] It
was to no avail: in the county council elections Labour increased its majority in London by 22 seats, and took control of
four other counties – Essex, the West Riding, Lancashire and
Northumberland.[11] *The Times* commented:

> It is possible there is evidence here of a permanent shift in
> political power – the result of the granting of universal
> suffrage...Certainly there is some new factor at work in
> elections.[12]

Some of the Conservative backbenchers remained discontented and suspicious about the Government's failure to act
on its election pledges of denationalisation. As *The Economist*
put it in early March:

> There has been no bonfire of controls and the two dena-
> tionalisation measures, for steel and road haulage, have
> taken an unconscionable time in the machinery.[13]

Cuthbert Alport, Conservative MP for Colchester, put down
a motion urging early action to deal with the nationalised
industries: it attracted 46 signatures in a short time and led
to Churchill's decision to reaffirm in the Commons the
Government's intention to denationalise road haulage and to
reorganise the iron and steel industry 'under free enterprise
and with an adequate measure of supervision'.[14] The difficulty
for the Government was the fact that, owing to their small lead
over Labour, controversial bills could not be entrusted to
standing committees, on which their majority was only one.

In mid-April, taking further fright over the impact of fare
increases, the Cabinet decided to direct the Transport
Commission to hold up its increase in charges until Ministers
had considered the report of the Central Transport Consultative
Committee.[15] When this became known, *The Times* declared:

> [T]he Government have conspicuously allowed themselves
> to become rattled; after disclaiming any responsibility they

have now gone to the opposite extreme and have debarred the Commission indefinitely, by Ministerial direction, from increasing fares at all... The propriety of subsidising the railways with one hand and reducing food subsidies with the other is one of the many aspects that would be open to critical question.[16]

The Economist put its criticism more bluntly:

Why...should it have lost touch with reason when faced with a much delayed increase in railway fares, decided after careful inquiry and necessary to meet proved increases in costs...? This act of interference prevents the Transport Commission from discharging its statutory duty of paying its way.[17]

The Opposition forced a debate on the transport charges on 28 April, and enjoyed a field day at the Government's expense. The unhappy Minister of Transport, John Maclay, fell ill before the debate, and the Home Secretary took his place as chief Government spokesman, but on this sort of issue he was no match for Herbert Morrison, who was, as Crossman put it, 'back in his element attacking the Tories on transport' after an unhappy experience as Bevin's successor at the Foreign Office.[18] Maclay resigned shortly afterwards, to be succeeded by Alan Lennox-Boyd, but the post remained outside the Cabinet, Lord Leathers being the Co-ordinating Minister for Transport, Fuel and Power.[19] At the same time the Labour Party made substantial gains in the borough elections of early May, and regained control of several major cities.[20] *The Economist* said: 'Mr Churchill and his colleagues must be regarded, at least for the present, as a minority government.'[21] Late in May Butler confessed to Harold Nicolson, to whom he had offered a lift in his car, that:

Winston is so brave in war and so cowardly in peace; the Tory Government ought to convey the impression of people who are absolutely sure of themselves; as it is, they convey the impression of a wobble.[22]

It may partly have been owing to the Government's lack of success in dealing with transport that the Cabinet came to the conclusion that a Transport Bill should be presented to Parliament before that on iron and steel.[23] A White Paper on

Transport Policy was accordingly laid before Parliament in early May, proposing that the railways should be decentralised, but not denationalised, and the Transport Commission's road haulage assets – except for those which it already possessed at the time of nationalisation – should be sold to private interests. There was also a provision for a levy on the road hauliers of £4 million per annum to compensate the railways for their capital loss and for their expected loss of traffic.[24] *The Times* said of the White Paper that it 'appears to speak rather as though the great problems of the limits of competition between road and rail, with which Ministers, parties and transport managements all wrestled for so many years, do not exist.'[25] *The Economist*, even more challengingly, said:

> The Government is not deliberately stepping out in the right direction after careful analysis of the economics of transport... It is following its political nose on the problem of ownership, but on the much more vital problem of costs and charges, it seems to be groping in the dark and groping the wrong way.[26]

When the White Paper was debated later in May, the new Minister, Alan Lennox-Boyd, bravely opened the debate. But grave doubts about it were expressed, not only by the Opposition, but also by at least one prominent Conservative backbencher, Sir Ralph Glyn, a former railway director, who said:

> I still have many friends in the transport industry, and it is a strange fact that I have not met one person who approves of the White Paper... I think that the proposal with regard to the levy is going to be quite disastrous for the relationship between the road and rail service.[27]

Churchill was forced to say that the White Paper was 'a guide rather than a rule',[28] but Leathers was at first unwilling to reconsider the measure.

When the new session of Parliament approached in the autumn, Churchill wrote to Leathers proposing the abandonment of at least half of the levy on road haulage.[29] Churchill was backed on this by Swinton as well as by Boyd-Carpenter, but the issue had to be voted on by the Cabinet in October, the Prime Minister saying:

The Government ought not to mind bowing to opinion in the House of Commons on a matter of this kind: on the contrary, it was valuable to demonstrate that Parliament had an active part in shaping legislation.[30]

By mid-October Churchill wanted to go still further and drop the levy altogether, pointing out to Leathers:

After all, the main and precise difficulty we have to face is the disposal of the 41,000 vehicles. This would surely be helped by the purchasers not being burdened by the levy.[31]

At its meeting on 29 October the Cabinet accepted the Prime Minister's view, in spite of objections from Butler – no doubt on financial grounds – and from Maxwell Fyfe, who felt committed to the levy by having argued vigorously for it in the Commons.[32]

As Churchill had indicated, the total number of vehicles to be sold was only 41,000 which was only 4 per cent of all the commercial vehicles on the roads. The great bulk of vehicles were owned by businesses carrying their own goods, and before the new legislation they were limited to a 40-mile radius. The Transport Commission was permitted to keep an extra 3,500 beyond what was already allotted to them, and, allowing for depreciation of others, only 32,500 were available for sale, together with 'garages, depots and other premises'. Sales only began in January 1954, and by the end of June of that year the number sold was about 6,000, the Disposals Board having difficulty in selling the premises along with the lorries. As Lennox-Boyd put it in a report to the Cabinet:

The Board is inclined to think that there is insufficient capital at the disposal of the small investor to buy more than some 10,000 vehicles at the price which it would be reasonable for the Board and the Commission to accept, while the large investor is deterred by the speculative nature of the industry and by the threat of renationalisation... On present indications, therefore, some 15,000 vehicles will be left unsold.[33]

By the end of January 1955 the number of disposals had risen to 12,698,[34] and in August, on the recommendation of the Chairman of the Road Haulage Disposals Board, the Government decided to allow the Commission to retain an additional 5,000 vehicles.[35]

If the release of road haulage involved only 'one-twentieth' of the industry, as Churchill himself explained to the Commons in the debate on the White Paper[36] – and in the event, as we have seen, much less than that – the approach to the iron and steel industry was more comprehensive. But the industry was still to be supervised by a national board on the lines advocated by the Trades Union Congress in 1950 in its statement *The Public Control of Industry*. This favoured something like the immediate postwar Iron and Steel Board which was 'composed of representatives of employers and workpeople with independent members'.[37]

The preparation of the bill took a great deal of time in 1952, as its parliamentary draftsman, H.S. Kent, has recorded, and this accounted for its belated presentation to the Cabinet. It was not only the long deliberations of the Minister of Supply, Duncan Sandys, which was responsible; they also spent fruitless hours in trying to devise a formula which would prevent subsequent Parliaments from renationalising the companies, but in the end this proved impossible. There were, according to Kent, 'innumerable conferences in the minister's room'.[38] A White Paper was submitted to the Cabinet on 3 July. Sandys said that:

> The acknowledgement that the return of the companies to private ownership would take 'some years' to complete would forestall suggestions that securities of the nationalised company would be summarily sold at whatever loss, or if the process of disposal proved to be slow, that the denationalisation was a failure.[39]

But even so, the Cabinet was not united in accepting the proposals. In view of Labour's threat of renationalisation, Salisbury, for one, thought:

> The wiser course would be for the Government to seek every means of finding some basis of agreement, within the steel industry and between the Parties, which would take the industry out of politics.[40]

Salisbury was so emphatic that he threatened to resign on this issue, but next day the Cabinet agreed that:

> The Minister of Supply should revise the draft White Paper so as to lay greater emphasis on the proposals for the future supervision of the industry and less on the proposals for returning it to private ownership.[41]

This was to appease Salisbury, as appears from Crookshank's diary, in which he noted for that day: 'I still hope we can get a compromise & prevent Bobbety's [Salisbury's] resignation.'[42] Salisbury wrote to Swinton, probably the next morning:

> I opposed Steel last night; but the broad view of those at the meeting was in favour of going on with it...I remain opposed, & rather depressed. I find myself more & more out of sympathy with Winston, who seems to me purely out to reverse what has been done, instead of trying to create a new and healthier atmosphere of co-operation in meeting our difficulties.[43]

Eden had missed these meetings, owing to an attack of jaundice – no doubt a precursor of his later, more serious, gallbladder trouble. In answer to a telephone call, as he noted in his diary:

> I suggested someone should be put to work to draft the kind of statement that might be made if we didn't issue a White Paper. Then this, together with White Paper, might be discussed on Tuesday when I returned...Bobbety readily fell in with this, though he was clearly exasperated with W[inston]. Rang Winston, who accepted this arrangement, though with only a somewhat cold expression of thanks.[44]

The crisis ended with an agreement on a form of words to be delivered by Butler on 29 July, in a speech about the economy generally, but calling for 'constructive criticism' of the White Paper on the Steel Industry, which had just been published. It did not receive any response from the Opposition except a rather disdainful observation from Gaitskell about Butler's 'queer-looking olive branch'.[45] But the White Paper received a far warmer welcome from the press than the transport White Paper, *The Economist* commenting:

In contrast to [the Transport] Bill, the White Paper on the iron and steel industry propounds a reasoned, even an astute, Parliamentary exercise, to be followed by a financial operation that is at any rate plausible. ...It is, moreover, tactfully constructed to appeal to the trade unions, whose co-operation would be required.[46]

When the bill came up for its second reading in late November, Sandys emphasised the need for 'public supervision' in the fields of 'prices, development and raw materials'.[47] The debate was much less tempestuous than that over transport, and with Liberal support the Government secured satisfactory majorities for its proposals. The bill finally received the Royal Assent in May 1953.[48] The new Iron and Steel Board then came into existence, and Lincoln Evans, the General Secretary of the main trade union in the industry, the Iron and Steel Trades Confederation, who had already accepted a knighthood in the New Year Honours, became the full-time vice-chairman of the Board. Two other members of the TUC General Council joined the Board as part-time members. Evans had already been attacked by the Bevanite journal, *Tribune,* for accepting the knighthood, but had been sturdily defended by his colleagues; now the attack was renewed, with all three nevertheless supported by the General Council and by the Congress in the following September.[49]

Dr Kathleen Burk, in her valuable study *The First Privatisation,* has dealt fully with the City's preparations for the restoration of the iron and steel companies to private ownership. Discussions were held long before the bill was enacted, in fact as early as 1950.[50] But the process of disposal was, as Sandys foresaw, a very gradual one. In March 1954 Woolton wrote to the Prime Minister expressing the concern of party members at the slow progress that was being made: 'We have passed the Acts, but the question they are asking is to what extent the denationalisation of road transport and of iron and steel is, in fact, taking place.' Churchill passed this note to the Cabinet Secretary with a request for a report from the Departments to the Cabinet.[51]

The Iron and Steel Holding and Realisation Agency was being managed by the Treasury, and it was therefore Butler who sent a reply. He reported that '15 per cent of the nationalised steel industry...in terms of employment, or 17 per cent in terms of ingot production' had so far been sold. Churchill minuted 'This is satisfactory so far.'[52] But the information did not reach all members of the Cabinet, for Crookshank wrote to the Prime Minister about six weeks later with a similar query:

> I wonder if you would consider calling for reports from the Ministers concerned, so that the Cabinet could consider whether there is anything which can properly be done to speed up sales.[53]

Churchill ordered 'As proposed', but no record appears in the Cabinet minutes. It is likely that Butler was reluctant to give details of further proposed flotations other than orally, and Crookshank confined himself to asking, and securing, agreement for a Select Committee on Nationalised Industries in the following session of Parliament.[54]

Dr Burk points out that the sale of the companies into private hands went somewhat unevenly, and early in 1954 'the share prices of both United Steel and Lancashire Steel fell to substantial discounts.'[55] But the market improved later in the year, and in January 1955 there was what the chairman of one of the underwriters called an 'overwhelming response.'[56] Even so, although by 1957 86 per cent of the productive capacity had been denationalised,[57] Richard Thomas & Baldwin remained in public ownership until the advent of another Labour Government, which again restored the entire industry to the public sector by an Act of 1967.

Thus the Government's pledges about denationalisation had, first of all, been carried through their parliamentary stages in the 1952–3 session, and then, so far as was possible, been put into practice in the two remaining years of the Churchill Government. But what was striking about the whole exercise was the limited extent of the whole operation, comprising less than one-twentieth of the road haulage industry, and leaving the iron and steel industry subject to a supervisory board of a character which satisfied the trade unions. The Cabinet was not even united in proceeding so far as they eventually did, and they were always inhibited by the fear that another Labour Government would thwart their intentions. It was the parliamentary party and the party in the country which, in the last resort, insisted on their pledges being fulfilled.

The division between the Cabinet and the back benches was even more marked over the future of the monopoly of the BBC. There was no election pledge, but the Corporation's Charter was due to expire at the end of June 1952, and many MPs were opposed to monopoly in any form, although other Conservatives – especially those in the Lords – were warm in support of the BBC. In April 1952 Woolton sought to reconcile those pressing for the Charter's unfettered renewal, and those opposing the monopoly. He suggested a compromise whereby the Corporation would maintain its monopoly of sound broadcasting, but that 'in due course' a sponsored television service would be established to compete with BBC television:

> The sponsored television service would be subject to some form of public control and would not be started until the Corporation had been able to develop an adequate national television service and to improve its sound broadcasting service...

This was agreed, and approval was given for a White Paper to be drafted on these lines. He also proposed that the appointment of Governors of the BBC should be 'removed from the political arena', and suggested, oddly, that this could be done by vesting the duty in a committee consisting of the Prime Minister, the Leader of the Opposition, the Archbishop of Canterbury, the Lord Chief Justice and the President of the [Scottish] Court of Session.[58]

Later that month, however, a hitch occurred. Woolton, in discussion with John Profumo, the leading backbench advocate of sponsored television, found that he and his colleagues would not accept the compromise. He therefore withdrew his proposals. At this point Churchill commented: 'It would be best to postpone for two years – and Cabinet must decide.'[59] In spite of Churchill's desire for postponement, something had to be done urgently about the Charter, and Derek Walker-Smith, the Chairman of the 1922 Committee, wrote to the Prime Minister to warn him that:

> The view of the large majority of the Committee is opposed in principle to a continuance of the monopoly at present

enjoyed by the B.B.C. This applies both to sound and television, but with particular force to the latter.[60]

So the White Paper was redrafted and resubmitted to the
Cabinet, which approved it on 13 May.[61] One alteration was
that the Speaker was substituted for the Archbishop on the appointing committee. The White Paper proposed a ten-year
Charter for the BBC, but said 'in the expanding field of television provision should be made to permit some element of
competition.'[62] When the White Paper was published on 15
May, *The Times* recognised that it was a compromise:

> Those members of Parliament and others who are in favour
> of commercial broadcasting will find cold comfort in the
> Government's memorandum...and whole-hogging believers
> in total and uncommercialised monopoly will be made a
> little nervous by it...Had any part of its [the BBC's] time,
> either on sound or on television, been invaded by sponsors,
> a Trojan horse would have been insinuated into a free and
> healthy broadcasting institution.[63]

The first parliamentary debate on the White Paper took
place in the House of Lords a week later, on the initiative of
Lord Reith, who had been the BBC's first Director-General,
and who now cast himself in the role of its defender. He had a
large number of supporters of all parties in the two-day
debate. Viscount Samuel, the Liberal leader, had visited
America and found a television set in his hotel room, which
for two dollars would supply programmes for 24 hours: 'One
day I paid my two dollars and listened at intervals during the
day with the most depressing results.'[64] Criticism of American
television was, in fact, a feature of all the debates. Lord
Halifax, who had served as Ambassador to the United States
during and after the war, said sadly:

> I am profoundly sorry that it should be the Party with whom
> I am associated who have made themselves responsible for
> it...It may well be that the effect here will never be likely to
> be so bad as it has been in America. I do not feel too
> confident about that, but I hope it is true.[65]

Among the other Government supporters opposing the White
Paper were Lord Brand and Lord Waverley, and thus the

official spokesman of the Government, Lord De La Warr, who as Postmaster-General was responsible for broadcasting, was heavily outgunned until the very end of the debate when Lord Simonds, the Lord Chancellor, stepped down from the Woolsack and gave him some support: 'The time has come for the monopoly, like all other monopolies, to come to an end.'[66] No vote was taken.

When the issue was debated in the Commons, the case for the Government's White Paper was put by Maxwell Fyfe; Herbert Morrison led for the Opposition. This put the issue more clearly on a party basis, and although one Government supporter, Beverley Baxter, ventured to speak out against the White Paper, he admitted that he would vote for it because there was a three-line Whip.[67] A few days later Churchill told the Commons that, because the Opposition rejected the idea of the proposed committee for appointing governors, the Government was also abandoning it, and the task would revert to the Prime Minister.[68]

After this there was a long delay before the issue of commercial television could again be taken up. In the meantime Woolton, its principal supporter in the Cabinet, was struck down by peritonitis in October 1952 at the Conservative Party Conference at Scarborough; he was out of action for several months, and in November Churchill transferred him to the less exacting post of Chancellor of the Duchy of Lancaster.[69] A general reshuffle of offices took place at the same time: Salisbury became Lord President in Woolton's place, and Swinton succeeded him as Commonwealth Secretary, thus formally joining the Cabinet for the first time since before the war. Eden, who was in New York at the time, told his Private Secretary, Evelyn Shuckburgh, that this was 'little more than a juggle with the old-stagers'; Shuckburgh diplomatically suggested to him that this 'was just as well. The more Winston ignored the younger men in the party the more they would develop pressure for a change at the top.'[70]

By January 1953, the number of television licences was reported to have exceeded the two million mark, and four-fifths of the population of the Kingdom were within reach of the service.[71] But in March the Postmaster-General told the Cabinet that he could not extend the range of BBC coverage to include the cities of Portsmouth, Plymouth and Aberdeen in time for the Coronation on 2 June.[72] The BBC coverage of the Coronation was, nevertheless, a triumph for the medium. The cameras were allowed inside the Abbey and filmed even the Communion Service, and the cause of the monopoly received a boost from the American relay (by NBC) when the film was interrupted by what Asa Briggs, the BBC's historian, calls a 'notorious interview' with J. Fred Muggs, the 'charismatic chimpanzee'.[73] Even the *Daily Express* exploited this incident.

Two days after the Coronation *The Times* published a letter signed by Lady Violet Bonham-Carter, Lord Brand, Lord Halifax, Tom O'Brien (Chairman of the TUC General Council) and Lord Waverley proposing the formation of a body to be called the National Television Council, to encourage the Government to 'remain true to the principles which have given us the finest broadcasting system in the world' and to 'resist the introduction of commercial television'.[74] The Organisation was soon joined by other members of 'the Establishment' – the two Anglican archbishops and no less than fourteen university vice-chancellors.[75]

The success of the Coronation broadcast and the peers' letter to *The Times* faced the Government with a parliamentary dilemma. The Chief Whip reported to the Cabinet that of the Government's supporters in the Commons:

> 180 (including Ministers) were in favour of commercial television; 43 were against it; and...15 were doubtful. The attitude of 67 was unknown, though none of these was thought to be strongly opposed to it. Among the 43 opposed to it, there were at least 12 who could not be relied upon to vote in favour of it even if a three-line Whip were issued. While there had been no pronounced shift of opinion in recent weeks, there had undoubtedly been a greater feeling of uncertainty, resulting in part from constituents' letters hostile to sponsored television...[I]t was his personal opinion that the Government would avoid defeat. Nevertheless when account was taken of the fact that the Liberals would not vote with the Government, the possibility of the Government's defeat could not be excluded.

Although Maxwell Fyfe at once declared himself in favour of sponsored television, the Prime Minister had his doubts:

It would be most unfortunate if the Government were to risk defeat in Parliament in an effort to carry through proposals which were unpalatable to respected elements both amongst Government supporters and in the country generally. This seemed to him to be the sort of issue which could more reasonably have been regarded as a matter of conscience than of Party politics.

He advocated a free vote, and Salisbury said that the Lords would be unlikely to approve sponsored television. Crookshank agreed. But Butler came up with a compromise: the Government should announce their policy in more detail, and should explain the safeguards that they would provide. It was then agreed that there should also be a delay in putting it to the vote so that 'public opinion, which had been stirred by the televising of the Coronation, might have time to settle down and an opportunity had been obtained to explain more fully the safeguards which could be applied to prevent abuse...'[76]

This was in spite of Eden's views, which had been conveyed to the Cabinet Secretary before he left to have a third operation in the United States. The Cabinet Secretary reported him as agreeing with the views of the National Television Council, and thinking that 'sponsored' television would be even worse in Britain than in America, because 'export markets are the prime concern of manufacturers', and so 'sponsored television...would probably be run mainly by newspaper proprietors.'[77]

The National Television Council did not take long to provoke a rival body into existence. In July a Popular Television Association was founded, with the Earl of Derby as its President. Both the NTC and the PTA were professedly non-party bodies, but the PTA had links with Conservative Central Office, as was demonstrated when the Conservative Party Conference of October 1953 passed a resolution supporting the idea of competitive television.[78] But this was after Lord De La Warr had announced late in August that the Government would not propose direct sponsoring but would 'envisage a system whereby the station and not the advertiser is responsible for the programmes.'[79] A second White Paper, embodying this change, was published in November: a new public authority was to supervise the new commercial system and regulate the programme companies.[80]

As before, the Lords were the first to debate the White Paper, on a motion put down by Lord Halifax. But he was ill when the motion came up for debate, and his place was taken by Lord Hailsham, a peer who had just inherited his title after being in the Commons for several years. He brought his Commons style of speaking with him to the Lords' debate, which did not help his cause. He said that 'the White Paper is a retrogression because it falls between two stools.' But De La Warr argued that it was 'a compromise between two strongly held views' and he emphasised that 'the continuance of the B.B.C. as it is, the controlling body armed with the ownership of the transmitting stations, and no sponsoring – are our three safeguards.' This time the Lords voted on Halifax's motion, and on a two-line Whip it was handsomely defeated.[81] The Commons debate on the White Paper again came later, and Maxwell Fyfe was able to cite a Gallup poll in favour of commercial television. The House divided on party lines, and the White Paper was approved by the Government's usual majority.[82]

The Television Bill was published early in March 1954, and its second reading in the Commons took place later that month. It was only a one-day debate, and was notable only for a threat by Herbert Morrison that if the Independent Television Authority had not started operations when Labour won the next election, they would 'scrap it entirely'.[83] In fact, the bill received the Royal Assent on 30 July 1954. The Independent Television Authority, under the chairmanship of Kenneth Clark (at that time Chairman of the Arts Council), met for the first time on 4 August, but the first broadcast was not made until September 1955 – five months after Churchill had retired and four months after another Conservative election victory.[84]

The record of legislation altering the existing monopolies showed how hostile to change the Churchill Cabinet proved to be. While most of the Attlee Government's measures of nationalisation remained in place, the two specific changes to which the Government was pledged, the freeing of the road haulage industry and the denationalisation of iron and steel,

were duly accomplished. But the number of road haulage vehicles returned to private hands was a tiny proportion of the
total, the railways remained in national ownership, and the
iron and steel industry was subject to a supervisory board as
recommended by the Trades Union Congress. As for so-called
'independent television', it was accepted only with reluctance
by the Prime Minister, in spite of his prewar difficulties with
the BBC, and was subject to a compromise which brought into
existence yet another public body, the Independent Television
Authority. If this was 'setting the people free', then the phrase
had a very limited meaning in the legislation of the early
1950s.

But as well as legislation there was derationing of food, and
there, as we shall see, the phrase 'setting the people free' had
some validity.

7 The Struggle Against Illness

After the death of Stalin in early March 1953, Western political leaders were naturally anxious to discover whether the new regime, headed by Malenkov, but only as the foremost member now of a collective leadership, would differ markedly from the previous one. It was not in Western eyes a good sign that Molotov remained as Foreign Minister. Nevertheless Eden was prepared to put the issue to a test. Before the end of March Sir William Strang, the Permanent Under-Secretary, sent a message to Sir Alvery Gascoigne, the British Ambassador in Moscow, to say that Eden was considering the possibility of an early meeting with Molotov 'in view of indications of new trends in Soviet policy in post-Stalin period':

> Discussions might start on Anglo-Soviet topics and then perhaps broaden out. We have been thinking of possible agenda on Anglo-Soviet basis and must confess that it looks a bit thin. I should be grateful for any suggestions you can give us for agenda both (a) Anglo-Soviet and (b) other, and also for any reflections or advice on proposal in general.[1]

Two days later Eden summoned Gascoigne home for consultation, asking him to come at once because he (Eden) was due to leave on 6 April for a visit to Turkey and Greece. He instructed him, before leaving, to thank Molotov for his assistance in the repatriation of the British civilian internees who had been trapped by the first swift North Korean invasion, including the British Minister and his staff.[2]

It may well be that the initiative had come from Churchill and not from Eden, for Eden's diary records that on 3 April he had been arguing with the Prime Minister against an 'early meeting' with the Russians, thereby 'alarming Ike [Eisenhower]'.[3] But it was that weekend (Easter, as it happened) that Eden's doctor, Sir Horace Evans, ordered him to cancel his engagements and have an immediate operation to relieve inflammation of the gall bladder.[4] Certainly some changes were occurring inside the Soviet Union: on 3 April

Beria, who was a member of the 'collective leadership', stated that the 'Doctors' Plot', announced in Stalin's last months, was a hoax. Several doctors, many of them Jewish, who had been arrested and imprisoned on a charge of plotting to remove Soviet leaders, were now released from prison.[5] *The Times* commented:

> Surely there is no precedent in Soviet history for this public admission of fraudulent and evil methods in the State police and judicial system. The admission implies a promise of reform.[6]

Churchill, losing no time, had already cabled to Eisenhower:

> Anthony and I have been thinking a good deal, as we know you have also, about the apparent change for the better in the Soviet mood. I am sure we shall be in agreement with you that we must remain vigilantly on our guard and maintain all that process of defensive rearmament from which any real progress must have resulted. We think, as I am sure you do also, that we ought to lose no chance of finding out how far the Malenkov regime are prepared to go in easing things up all round. There certainly seem to be great possibilities in Korea and we are very glad of the steps you have taken to resume truce negotiation.

Churchill then added:

> We are sending our Ambassador back to Moscow with instructions to try to settle with Molotov a number of minor points which concern Britain and Russia alone and have caused us trouble in the last few years. They included such matters as the recent Soviet notice to terminate the temporary Anglo-Soviet Fisheries Agreement of 1930, the cases of certain individual British subjects in Russia, exchange rates and restrictions on movements. Talks on these may give some further indication of the depth of the Soviet purpose. We shall of course gladly keep your people informed of how we progress.[7]

On 7 April Churchill visited Eden at the Foreign Secretary's flat at No. 1 Carlton Gardens, and arranged to take over the Foreign Office for the six weeks it was expected that Eden would be out of action. This decision was announced at once, and it was also stated that Selwyn Lloyd, the Minister of State, would regularly attend Cabinet meetings while Eden was ill.[8] Indications of moderation in the Kremlin were supported when the Soviet delegation at the United Nations withdrew its opposition to the appointment of Dag Hammarskjöld of Sweden as the new Secretary-General, and he was duly elected. Gascoigne, on flying back to Moscow, asked to see Molotov and was able to discuss his 'minor points' with him for three-quarters of an hour.[9]

Meanwhile Eisenhower had replied to Churchill's cable, saying that 'I feel sure that you will find our thinking on the subject largely paralleling your own' and adding that he was thinking of making a 'formal speech' indicating the 'steps or measures which we believe necessary to bring about satisfactory relationships throughout the world.' He sent Churchill a draft of the proposed speech, and said that he would also 'check with France, and with Adenauer, who arrives here tomorrow.'[10]

Churchill, looking at Eisenhower's proposed speech, thought that the tone was wrong, and so he urged him to wait a little longer:

I believe at the moment time is on our side. The apparent change in Soviet mood is so new and also so indefinite and the causes for it so obscure that there could not be much risk in letting things develop. We do not know what these men mean. ...Nevertheless great hope has risen in the world that there is a change of heart in the vast, mighty mass of Russia and this may carry them far and perhaps into revolution. It has been well said that the most dangerous moment for evil Governments is when they begin to reform. Nothing impressed me so much as the Doctors story. This must cut very deep into Communist discipline and structure. I would not like it to be thought that a sudden American declaration has prevented this natural growth of events.

Because Eisenhower was proposing in his speech to call for a political settlement for the whole of Korea under United Nations auspices, and also roll-back of Soviet power from the satellite countries of Europe, Churchill thought this was asking too much all of a sudden. He added:

It seems to me very unlikely that the terms that you require for the political settlement of Korea as set out in your statement would be accepted as they stood by the other side. I fear the formal promulgation...at this moment might prevent the hope of an armistice...Anthony and I...cannot see what you would lose by waiting until the full character and purpose of the Soviet change is more clearly defined and also is apparent to the whole free world...[11]

Eisenhower replied that he was already committed to make a speech on 16 April, but that he would 'soften the parts concerning Korea and change certain other expressions so that there can be no misinterpretation of our position.'[12] The speech was delivered to the American Society of Newspaper Editors, and was also broadcast. It showed signs of alteration from the original draft:

Even a few...clear and specific acts, such as the Soviet Union's signature upon an Austrian treaty, or its release of thousands of prisoners still held from World War II, would be impressive signs of sincere intent...The first great step along this road must be the conclusion of an honourable armistice in Korea.

The President also proposed a disarmament treaty, and the diversion of the money saved from armaments to 'a fund for world aid and reconstruction'.[13]

In the House of Commons, both Churchill and, for the Opposition, Herbert Morrison commented favourably on the speech after its delivery, and Churchill sent Eisenhower the relevant section of Hansard, adding 'No dissent was expressed in any part of the House.' But he went on to say:

There will, however, be a strong movement here for a meeting between Heads of States and Governments. How do you stand about this? In my opinion the best would be that the three victorious Powers, who separated at Potsdam in 1945, should come together again...I am sure the world will expect something like this if the Soviets do not turn your proposals down abruptly. If nothing can be arranged, I shall have to consider seriously a personal contact. You told me in New York you would have no objection to this...[14]

The reference to New York was to their meeting when
Eisenhower was President-elect early in the year.

It was now Eisenhower's turn to show alarm. The idea of
personal negotiation with Communist leaders, before there
was even a Korean armistice, shocked both him and Dulles.
He replied as follows:

> As to the next step, I feel that we should not rush things too
> much and should await the Soviet reply or reaction longer
> than a few days. There is some feeling here also for a
> meeting between heads of states and governments, but I do
> not think this should be allowed to press us into precipitate
> initiatives. ...We have so far seen no concrete Soviet actions
> which would indicate their willingness to perform in con-
> nection with larger issues...My thinking concerning a per-
> sonal contact at this moment runs somewhat along the same
> line. The situation has changed considerably since we talked
> in New York and I believe we should watch developments
> for a while longer before determining our final course.
> However, if you should find it necessary for some special
> and local reason to seek a personal contact, we would hope
> for as much advance notice as you could possibly give us.[15]

Eisenhower seems to have recognised that Churchill had
the bit between his teeth, and indeed Churchill followed up
the loop-hole thus offered by submitting to the President a
draft message that he was proposing to send to Molotov. After
saying that Eden's illness would prevent any contact at Foreign
Minister level, he enquired:

> I wonder whether you would like me to come to Moscow so
> that we could renew our war-time relations and so that I
> could meet Monsieur Malenkov and others of your leading
> men. Naturally I do not imagine that we could settle any of
> the great issues which overhang the immediate future of the
> world but I have the feeling that it might be helpful if our in-
> tercourse proceeded with the help of friendly acquaintance
> and good-will instead of impersonal diplomacy and propa-
> ganda. I do not see how this could make things worse...

Churchill added for the President's benefit 'The sort of date I
have in mind would be three or four days in the last week of
May.'[16]

The President replied at once with a note of strong discouragement:

> Foster and I have considered it deeply and since you sought my views I must say that we would advise against it. You will pardon me, I know, if I express a bit of astonishment that you think it appropriate to recommend Moscow to Molotov as a suitable meeting place...I do not feel that the armistice negotiations are going well and this to me has been the first test of the seriousness of Communist intentions. Far from there having been any Communist actions which we could accept as indications of such seriousness of purpose the *Pravda* editorial repeats all the previous Soviet positions and we are now faced with new aggression in Laos.

The President, who was now seriously worried about South-East Asia, went on to argue that a visit by Churchill to Russia would 'infuriate the French, especially when the situation is hanging in the balance.' Also, such a trip would arouse great expectations:

> Whatever you said publicly about the purposes of your solitary pilgrimage, I suspect that many in the Far East as well as the West would doubt that you would go all the way to Moscow merely for good will. I feel this would be true in this country, and the effects on Congress which is this week taking up consideration of our Mutual Defense Program and extension of our reciprocal trade act, would be unpredictable.

He concluded:

> Naturally the final decision is yours, but I feel that the above factors are so important that I should in all candour and friendship lay them before you.[17]

Churchill's reply to this powerful missive was to point out at once that:

> None of the four men who I am told are working together very much as equals, Malenkov, Molotov, Beria and Bulganin has any contacts outside Russia except Molotov. I am very anxious to know them and talk to them as I think I can frankly and on the dead level.

But he concluded:

> I will consult with my colleagues upon the position and your weighty adverse advice. At any rate I will not go until after your Budget has been settled by Congress which would mean delaying till after the Coronation and about the end of June. Perhaps by then you may feel able to propose some combined action.[18]

Having failed to obtain Eisenhower's approval for his 'solitary pilgrimage', Churchill decided to declare his views, not to the Cabinet but to the House of Commons and thereby to the world. On 11 May he made a major speech in a debate on foreign affairs. Of relations with the Soviet Union, he first said: 'We have been encouraged by a series of amicable gestures on the part of the Soviet Government,' but promptly added:

> These have so far taken the form of leaving off doing things which we have not been doing to them. It is, therefore, difficult to find specific cases with which to match their action.

He then electrified his audience by saying:

> I believe that a conference at the highest level should take place between the leading Powers without long delay. The conference should not be overhung by a ponderous or rigid agenda, or led into mazes and jungles of technical details, zealously contested by hoards of experts and officials drawn up in vast cumbrous array. The conference should be confined to the smallest number of Powers and persons possible. It should meet with a measure of informality and a still greater measure of privacy and seclusion. ...At worst the participants in the meeting would have established more intimate contacts. At the best we might have a generation of peace.[19]

According to *The Times*, 'A spontaneous cheer endorsed this statement.'[20] But the Foreign Office did not approve, fearing the impact in America and on the other allies – although Selwyn Lloyd was in Colville's words 'personally enthusiastic'.[21]

After the speech had been made, the adverse reaction that the Foreign Office had anticipated did not take long to manifest itself. In particular, the French Government of Mayer, with Bidault as the Foreign Secretary, was sufficiently worried at the danger of finding itself excluded from a 'summit' meeting to suggest a colloquy of the three Western powers. When this was put to Eisenhower, he at once saw it as a useful way of holding Churchill back. He telephoned to Churchill during the nights of 20/21 May, and suggested that they should all meet on 15 June, in Maine, 'because of the lovely weather there this time of year'. Churchill, however, although happy to take part, at once asked to be the host at Bermuda, and Eisenhower accepted this. The President favoured the utmost informality: 'I am personally restive if not irritable under the restrictions of formal agenda', he told the Prime Minister.[22] Churchill said he would arrive in Bermuda on the 16th after attending the Coronation Naval Review. 'My present idea is that we should all stay at the Mid-Ocean Golf Club...I do not play golf any more so I shall bring my paint box.'[23]

Meanwhile the French Government had collapsed, and an interregnum of five weeks ensued before another Government could be formed. Churchill and Eisenhower agreed to fix the later date of 7 July, and Churchill planned to arrive on the battleship HMS *Vanguard* on the 6th.[24] They hoped that by fixing a firm date they would encourage the formation of a new French Government, which did come about on 26 June with Joseph Laniel as Prime Minister and Bidault once more at the Foreign Office.[25] It was not, however, the French Government but Churchill himself who precipitated the indefinite postponement of the Bermuda meeting.

Although Eden's bile-duct operation was supposed to cause him an absence of only six weeks, it turned out that his two operations had left the bile duct actually severed. Fortunately an American specialist in this field of surgery, Dr Richard Cattell, was visiting London in May, and he promised to undertake the necessary third operation if Eden was willing to go to Boston to Cattell's New England Baptist Hospital. This Eden agreed to do, and after spending two weeks by invitation at Chequers recovering his strength, he and Clarissa left Heathrow by air on 15 June. They were seen off by Winston and Clementine; Vincent Massey, the Canadian Governor-General, provided the aircraft for the flight, and Eden's son Nicholas, who was serving as an ADC to the Governor-General, met him at the airport in Boston.[26]

Churchill was under intense pressure in this period. Not only was he in control of the Foreign Office as well as No. 10, he also had to play his part in the Coronation ceremonial. The Queen had invited him to become a Knight of the Garter, and he underwent the exhausting investiture on 24 April. When the Coronation itself approached (on 2 June) he had many official engagements, including – as well as the ceremony itself – a dinner for the Commonwealth Prime Ministers on 27 May, the chairmanship of five successive sessions of the Commonwealth Conference which began on 3 June and a Foreign Office banquet for the Queen at Lancaster House on 5 June. On 23 June he hosted a dinner at No. 10 Downing Street for the Italian Prime Minister, Alcide de Gasperi. According to Butler, he 'made a special effort in his speech':

> He said that only in the time of the Roman occupation and when our heirs met American heiresses was there hot water and central heating in these islands. He concluded by evoking the need for a free liberty-loving Italy.[27]

But after the formalities he slumped down in a chair, and his son-in-law and Parliamentary Private Secretary, Christopher Soames, noticed that he could not walk. Soames told de Gasperi that the Prime Minister was 'very much over-tired', and the Italian party took the hint and made their departure. As Mary Soames later wrote:

> A few had noticed the slur in Winston's speech and his un-steadiness, but attributed it to his having had a little too much to drink; nobody guessed the real reason – that he had sustained a stroke.[28]

As usual, Lord Moran, his personal physician, was tele-phoned for, but as he was out for the evening he was asked to call next day at 9 a.m. Moran diagnosed 'a spasm of a small artery' as had occurred at Monte Carlo in August 1949.[29] Nevertheless he failed to prevent Churchill from dressing and conducting a Cabinet meeting, at which most of those present did not notice anything untoward except an unusually quiet Prime Minister.[30] Moran returned later that morning with

Sir Russell Brain, a specialist in neurology, and they warned
Churchill against going to the Commons to answer questions
in the afternoon. Next day – the 25th – he went to Chartwell,
and both doctors found that the thrombosis was spreading.
They drew up a medical bulletin, referring to 'a disturbance of
the cerebral circulation'. But Salisbury and Butler, who were
on the scene at lunchtime, decided that this would be too
alarming, and changed the bulletin to:

> The Prime Minister has had no respite from his very
> arduous duties and is in need of a complete rest. We have
> therefore advised him to abandon his journey to Bermuda
> and to lighten his duties for at least a month.[31]

Churchill had told Colville, his private secretary, 'not to let
it be known that he was temporarily incapacitated'. So Colville
contacted Churchill's three closest friends in the press,
Camrose, Beaverbrook and Bracken. As Colville later
recorded:

> All three immediately came to Chartwell and paced the
> lawn in earnest conversation. They achieved the all but in-
> credible, and in peace-time possibly unique, success of
> gagging Fleet Street, something they would have done for
> nobody but Churchill.[32]

Colville, who had a ready entry to royal circles after serving
the Queen as a private secretary before her accession, took the
precaution of warning Sir Alan Lascelles, the Queen's current
Private Secretary, about the possibility that Churchill might
have to resign. There would be obvious difficulties in choosing
a successor, as Eden, the 'heir-apparent', was still gravely ill in
America. Nevertheless Colville wrote to Clarissa Eden to say 'I
think (with pretty good reason) that the Queen will ask
Bobbety [Salisbury] to form a Caretaker Government for six
months.'[33] The convention was already well established that a
peer could not normally serve as Prime Minister, but it was
thought that if this was to be purely temporary, it would be
acceptable.

The bulletin, as revised, was published in the press on
Saturday 27 June, and it was also announced that for the time
being R.A. Butler would preside at Cabinets and Salisbury
would assist Churchill in supervising foreign affairs. But

Churchill's paralysis was still spreading, and that day affected his left leg in particular, so that 'the foot drags and the toes catch the carpet.'[34] On Sunday Jane Portal, one of Churchill's secretaries but also R.A. Butler's niece, wrote to her uncle:

He is definitely weaker physically and fell down today. In fact he cannot really walk at all and his swallowing is bad. However he is very cheerful and his courage is remarkable – he seems completely detached in a funny sort of way.[35]

The public were to be given no such insight, however, and Christopher Soames told reporters reassuringly on that day:

I have seen Sir Winston this morning. He is about, and has been doing a little work. He was seen by Lord Moran this morning. His condition is not such that it is likely to deteriorate or to improve from day to day. He is simply suffering from general fatigue, which is probably more mental than physical.[36]

Meanwhile Eden had been operated on – successfully – in Boston, on the day after Churchill's stroke. As soon as he heard of Churchill's illness he was naturally anxious for more information. Butler wrote to him on the same day as Colville, to confirm the seriousness of Churchill's illness but also to reassure him about his own position:

At Cabinet…Winston was firm and courageous if very slow… Bobbety and I did not realise till Thursday night or Friday. We went down on the Friday to lunch at Chartwell both of us having realised that Bermuda must be postponed. We spoke in this sense together and easily prevailed on the idea that Bobbety might run Bermuda vice Winston. …We found great courage but much underlying sorrow and pain…You may be sure we shall guarantee *him* peace and *you* your place when you return. We need not rush you out of your well earned convalescence. We'll get the House up somehow, then the summer pause comes to our aid.[37]

On the Sunday (29 June) Moran noticed that Churchill was relaxing, and beginning to read Trollope's *Phineas Finn*.[38] But Churchill also wrote a letter to the Queen, to say that he hoped to carry on until the autumn, when Eden would be recovered. He responded to a request from the Opposition to appoint Salisbury as Acting Foreign Secretary, and not just 'assisting'. This was all the more important as on 30 June a meeting of the Foreign Ministers of Britain, the United States and France was announced to convene on 10 July – but at Washington, and not Bermuda.[39]

On 1 July Churchill acknowledged a letter of sympathy from Eisenhower, and in return took him into his confidence:

> I am so sorry to be the cause of upsetting so many plans. I had a sudden stroke which as it developed completely paralysed my left side and affected my speech. I therefore had no choice as I could not have walked with you along the Guard of Honour of the Welsh Regiment complete with their beautiful white goat, whose salute I am sure you would have acknowledged. Four years ago, in 1949, I had another similar attack and was for a good many days unable to sign my name. As I was out of office I kept this secret and managed to work through two General Elections and a lot of other business since. I am therefore not without hope of pursuing my theme a little longer but it will be a few weeks before any opinion can be formed. I am glad to say I have already made progress. I have not told anybody these details which are for your eye only.

Churchill then recommended Salisbury to the President, as Britain's representative at the Washington meeting, and added:

> I had never thought of a Four-Power meeting taking place till after EDC was either ratified or discarded by the French and I thought November would be the sort of time. Adenauer and Bonn seem to be moving towards a united Germany and now they speak of a Four-Power Conference with approval.[40]

At a Cabinet on 6 July Salisbury presented the terms of his general approach to the Washington meeting. He had received a note from the Prime Minister urging him to press for the early ratification of EDC by the French and an early four-power meeting (including the Russians) on Germany.[41] A week later Selwyn Lloyd told the Cabinet that Salisbury's colleagues in Washington accepted the idea of a four-power meeting of Foreign Ministers on the German problem, but felt

that its primary business must be to 'discuss the means of creating the conditions in which free elections could be held.'
Butler reported that Churchill had seen the telegrams and
agreed that Salisbury would have to accept, although 'he in-
ferred from them that the French and Americans intended
the Four-Power Meeting to end in a breakdown.' Churchill
wanted Salisbury to insist that 'Heads of Government might
attend in the later stages', and the scope of the agenda might
then be widened.[42]

A few days later Churchill resumed his personal correspondence with Eisenhower:

> Please consider at your leisure whether it might not be
> better for the 4-Power meeting to begin, as Salisbury urged,
> with a preliminary survey by Heads of Government of all
> our troubles in an informal spirit. I am sure that gives a
> much better chance than if we only came in after a vast new
> network of detail had been created. Moreover, Bidault made
> it pretty clear he wanted this meeting to break down in
> order to make a better case for EDC before the French
> Chamber, whereas it would have been a great advantage to
> go plus EDC. with friendly hands in strong array.

Churchill added that physically he was progressing. 'I can
now walk about. The doctors think I may be well enough to
appear in public in September.'[43]

Eisenhower replied quickly, welcoming Churchill's physical
improvement, but rejecting his idea of an informal summit
meeting:

> I like to meet informally with those whom I can trust as
> friends. ...But it is a different matter to meet informally
> with those who may use a meeting only to embarrass and
> entrap. I would prefer the Foreign Ministers to make the
> first exploration on a limited and specific basis.[44]

Meanwhile, the Western Foreign Ministers had sent their
separate but identical invitations to the Soviet Government for
a four-power meeting in late September, to discuss an Austrian
treaty and 'the organisation of free elections throughout
Germany'.[45] Eisenhower also wrote an open letter to
Adenauer to amplify the conference communique, to sympa-
thise with him about the violent Communist suppression of

rioting in East Berlin on 27 June, and to say that a 'prosperous' Western Germany had exerted 'an attractive power which has already been demonstrated by the steady stream of refugees in recent months.'[46]

On 24 July Churchill moved from Chartwell to Chequers, and on the 27th he was visited there by Anthony and Clarissa Eden, who had just flown home from America. Anthony had lost a stone and a half in weight, and Colville noticed how 'thin and frail' he still was.[47] But he and Clarissa were looking forward to a Mediterranean holiday on board HMS *Surprise*, a frigate then being used as an Admiralty yacht – the ship had been promised to them by Jim Thomas, the First Lord of the Admiralty.[48] The Korean armistice was signed on the day of their meeting, and both Churchill and Eden must have warmly welcomed the news. But, as Salisbury pointed out in the Lords in reporting on his Washington trip, the sudden dismissal of Beria, one of the four presumed co-equal Russian leaders, 'introduced a new element of uncertainty into the situation.' He added, nevertheless: 'But are we to ignore these few faint fluttering gestures towards a greater liberalism? I cannot help feeling that that would be foolish.'[49]

The Soviet note in reply arrived on 5 August. It was certainly discouraging, as it proposed a five-power meeting including China, and since the United States had not recognised the new Chinese Government, it was, as Salisbury told the Cabinet, 'evidently designed to exploit such differences as existed between the three Western powers.[50] On 9 August Malenkov was reported as saying that the Soviet Union now possessed the ability to deploy the hydrogen bomb,[51] and shortly afterwards British and American monitors recorded a test explosion.

In August Churchill, although still not fully fit, began to chair Cabinets again, and at the end of the month he effected a minor reconstruction of the Government. He summed it up in a letter to Eden, who was in the Mediterranean:

The merging of the Ministries of Pensions and National Insurance involves the departure from office of Heathcoat-Amory, for whom it is on all hands thought desirable that a post should be found. Fred Leathers has also asked to be relieved before the end of September. You know what difficulty I had to persuade him to serve at all. I have therefore felt this was the moment to make a series of changes, to which I have given a great deal of thought...The 'Overlord' system for which I was responsible, which is not as necessary in peace as it was in war, disappears. Secondly Education, Agriculture, and Food come into the Cabinet, the first two gratifying powerful interests, the third eventually to disappear. Thirdly there is a compression of three Offices, with substantial net economies and reduction of staff.

Churchill also indicated that the Chief Whip was recommending 'new blood' among the Junior Ministers, so further changes would have to follow.[52] The first set of changes, announced at the beginning of September, also involved Woolton's appointment as Minister of Materials in addition to the sinecure post of Chancellor of the Duchy of Lancaster, and Heathcoat Amory's promotion to be Minister of State at the Board of Trade, to encourage exports and overseas trade. But *The Times* complained that the changes were 'something of an anti-climax after many forecasts of more sweeping changes...Apart from Mr Heathcoat Amory...no new men of promise have been moved or promoted.'[53]

In the Bundestag elections in West Germany Adenauer secured an absolute majority for the first time – a welcome development for the other Western powers and, of course, a rebuff for the Soviet Union. Meanwhile, the Queen had invited Churchill and his wife Clementine to accompany her to the St Leger at Doncaster and thereafter to stay for a short time at Balmoral. On 13 September he attended church there – as he had done with King Edward VII in 1908.[54] He returned to London by air and presided over a Cabinet on the 16th, and then, accompanied by his daughter Mary and her husband Christopher Soames, he flew off again, this time to Beaverbrook's villa at Cap d'Ail. From there Jane Portal, who went to provide secretarial assistance, reported to her uncle that Churchill was:

...utterly exhausted after Balmoral, but was reviving and beginning to prepare his Conservative Party conference speech, which is a good thing and it comes quite easily, but apart from anything else how he will stand on his pins for an hour is a frightening thought.[55]

Meanwhile Eden, having disembarked from *Surprise* at Athens, had been cruising in the Aegean in a smaller yacht which he had been able to borrow through the British ambassador there. He co-ordinated his return to England with Churchill's, for 30 September. Next day they met for an hour at No. 10 Downing Street, and according to Eden's diary he 'made it clear to W. that I was ready to serve in any capacity, but he made it evident he wanted me to stay on at F.O.'[56] It was then announced that Eden would take up his duties at the Foreign Office again on Monday 5 October. A few days later Eden attended the Conservative Party Conference at Margate, where he received a warm reception, even though he had to warn his audience that 'the last Soviet reply to the three-Power note...shows no agreement for a meeting at any level.'[57]

The Conference was also a test of Churchill's capacity to deliver a major speech, which the Leader traditionally made at the end of the Conference. Early in his speech he said:

> ...we have no intention of plunging the nation into electioneering strife this year, and indeed so far as my immediate knowledge is concerned that applies to next year too.[58]

At the end of his 50-minute address he spoke of his own position:

> If I stay on for the time being bearing the burden at my age it is not because of love for power or office. I have had an ample share of both. If I stay it is because I have a feeling that I may through things that have happened have an influence on what I care about above all else, the building of a sure and lasting peace.[59]

The Times commented:

> An anxious and oft-repeated question was answered. After all the surmises and rumours that spread around during his illness the old fighter and sage was back. The flashes of wit, the love of resounding phrase, the zest for the party tussle (breaking out even in the very moments when he repudiated it), the manner of shaping policy by what seemed to be

private soliloquy, and, above all, the gift for capturing and transmitting the thoughts of the British people on the great questions of peace and war – all these were there.[60]

Churchill's doctor, Lord Moran, called on him that evening at No. 10 Downing Street and found about his patient 'an air of complete relaxation'.[61] He was now thinking, he told Colville, of retaining power 'until the Queen returned from Australia in May'.[62]

8 Bermuda and Berlin

By the autumn of 1953 members of Churchill's Cabinet were beginning to think of the next general election, and how to fill in the intervening parliamentary time. It was probably at a Cabinet meeting in September that Butler scribbled a note on No. 10 Downing Street paper to Patrick Buchan-Hepburn, the Chief Whip:

1) We can't have an Election for a bit owing to the illness and personal problems. 2) We have built the 300,000 houses and we can't really stand against the criticism that Conservatives have done nothing to 'conserve' old houses. 3) We have the priceless chance of using Harold. 4) Our legislative programme otherwise was v. thin. 5) I would not preclude the possibility – after this is through and depending on the intl situation Budget situation etc of an election October year.

All that is absolutely precluded is an election this autumn or next spring...RAB

To this the canny James Stuart, who saw the note, added:

But a G E in October 1954 is too early if we do Housing next Session.[1]

In mid-September Butler wrote to Eden, who was still in the Eastern Mediterranean, and raised with him another domestic problem as well as housing:

If, as I hope, we take on the Repair of houses we shall have a useful Session. Our agriculture policy is proving very complicated indeed. Moving into a free economy is by no means popular with the Producer. Moreover the public is beginning to see that most of the remaining subsidy payment goes to the Farmer. I am helping Tom [Dugdale] and the others where I can.[2]

The priority to be given to Housing was raised by the Minister most directly concerned, Harold Macmillan, at the Cabinet on 16 September:

As the policy necessitates an increase in rent for something like 5 or 6 million houses, it is unlikely to be popular. It is important therefore that, if legislation is introduced, there should be ample time to judge its generally good effects. I hope that the White Papers may be published just before the Prorogation of Parliament and discussed during the debate on the Address. The second reading of the Bills might take place before Christmas and the Royal Assent received about May 1954. This time-table would mean that some of the effects of the measure would begin to be seen by the autumn of 1954.

The Prime Minister agreed and put the argument even more bluntly:

I have no doubt that the policy would invite a good deal of criticism, and the Government's aim should be to push it through as rapidly as possible so that its beneficial effects could be seen at an early date.

The scheme was then agreed in principle, but referred back to Crookshank's committee for minor redrafting.[3]

In the debate on the Address Churchill spoke in the House of Commons for the first time since his stroke in June. It was a conciliatory and reflective speech:

It is not really possible to assume that one of these fourteen million masses of voters possesses all the virtues and the wisdom and the other lot are dupes or fools, or even knaves and crooks. Ordinary people mix about with each other in friendly, neighbourly relations, and they know that it is nonsense for party politicians to draw such harsh contrasts between them. Even in this House it is difficult for the specialist in faction to prevent Members from getting very friendly with each other and worrying about their common difficulties and the grave strain and expense of modern Parliamentary life. We have at least that in common.[4]

On domestic policy, he referred to Macmillan's Housing Bill, which was now set out in two White Papers, one for England and Wales and one for Scotland, and he mentioned the policy of guaranteed farm prices which Dugdale would introduce to take the place of rationing, as expounded in yet another

White Paper. His comments on foreign policy apparently reflected a desire not to alienate Eden, who had disapproved of his speech on 11 May and opposed what Eisenhower had called the 'solitary pilgrimage' to Moscow.[5]

The *Times* correspondent described Churchill's speech as a 'rhetorical triumph... Every facet of the Churchillian gift for parliamentary oratory shone with undiminished lustre...', and Henry Channon, the American-born backbencher, recorded in his diary:

> Brilliant, full of cunning and charm, of wit and thrusts, he poured out his Macaulay-like phrases to a stilled and awed House. It was an Olympian spectacle. ...In eighteen years in this honourable House I have never heard anything like it.

Channon also described the aftermath of this demonstration of Churchill's powers:

> [T]hen he sought refuge in the Smoking Room and, flushed with pride, pleasure, and triumph sat there for two hours sipping brandy and acknowledging compliments. He beamed like a school-boy.[6]

The debate on the Address continued all week. Next day Macmillan expounded his housing proposals. Having said that he had 'every hope' that 300,000 new houses would be built in 1953, he went on to deal with the problem of the seven and a half million houses built before 1914. The repairs to these houses now cost three times as much as in 1939, but rents were controlled, some since 1914, some since 1920. The landlords were entitled to have their rents increased, but 'the repairs increase must be earned and it will be earned by the repairs.' Speaking of slum houses which could not immediately be pulled down, the Minister said that the local authorities should 'accept responsibility for the care and maintenance and, within the limits of what is possible, for the improvement of the houses which must be temporarily reprieved.' There was a third category of 'dilapidated houses', which 'are in a bad state but, nevertheless, are capable of being put right.' Finally, there were large houses for the middle class, now too large but suitable for conversion into flats.[7]

On the following day, 5 November, Eden gave a brief account of the state of foreign affairs as he found them on his return to office. He said that five of the seven issues that Sir Alvery Gascoigne had raised with Molotov had been resolved, but that Soviet propaganda 'continues as before', and 'the continued oppression in Eastern Europe' gave no cause for optimism.[8]

Eden's pessimism about change in the Soviet Union was confirmed by the Kremlin's reply to the Western powers' invitation to a conference at Lugano, which was entirely negative, prompting *The Times* to comment next day:

> Today, eight months precisely since Stalin died, the Western Powers have to study a Soviet Note that might have been written by Stalin himself.[9]

The Commons debate extended over the weekend, and it was only on Monday, 9 November that Sir Thomas Dugdale, the Minister of Agriculture, was able to explain the 'new structure of marketing arrangements and price guarantees'. He said that food rationing would end in 1954, and that it was 'the policy of the Government to consider sympathetically proposals for the establishment of producer marketing boards'.[10]

The three Western Foreign Ministers had met in London in mid-October to discuss current issues, in particular the reply to the Soviet Union about talks on the German problem.[11] It was the discouraging response from Moscow, already referred to, that led Churchill to propose to Eisenhower a revival of the meeting of Heads of Government at Bermuda:

> The Soviet answer puts us back to where we were when Bermuda broke down through my misfortune. So why not let us try Bermuda again? I suggest four or five days in the first fortnight in December... All arrangements were very carefully worked out last time, and it only takes a word of command to put them all on again.[12]

Eisenhower replied next day agreeing to a meeting at Bermuda on 4 to 7 December.[13] Churchill was delighted, and said that he thought 'we might both "brace the French up" on EDC.'[14] It was agreed that all three Heads of Government would bring their Foreign Secretaries, and Churchill also invited Cherwell, to discuss 'atomics' with his American counterpart, Admiral Strauss. Ismay was to attend to report on progress at NATO.

At his first bilateral meeting with Churchill at the Mid-Ocean Club on Bermuda the President said that if there were a deliberate breach of the armistice in Korea by the Communists, 'we would expect to strike back at military targets with atomic weapons.' Churchill said that 'he quite accepted this' but went on to propose a meeting with the Soviet Union as soon as possible, 'preferably early in January'.[15] Later on, at a meeting also attended by the French leaders, Eisenhower put forward a proposal for an international atomic energy agency, which he was going to suggest in a speech at the United Nations in New York on 8 December: each of the three atomic powers would contribute 'uranium and fissionable materials', which would then be used for peaceful purposes. This met with general approval. At the first plenary meeting they discussed whether there was a 'new look' in the Soviet Union since the death of Stalin. Churchill said 'let us make sure that we do not too lightly dismiss this possibility', but Eisenhower rejected the idea brutally, likening the 'new look' to that of 'a whore with a new dress'. John Colville, who was present as Churchill's Private Secretary, later wrote: 'I doubt if such language has ever been heard at an international conference.'[16] Next morning, however, the Foreign Ministers agreed to propose to the Russians a four-power meeting in Berlin early in January.

On 5 December Churchill and Eisenhower discussed atomic matters with their two principal advisers, Lord Cherwell and Admiral Strauss. Churchill called for the resumption of 'full-scale co-operation', as during the war; the President expressed sympathy, but pointed out the he was bound by the McMahon Act of 1946 not to release atomic information. Churchill said that Britain, having successfully concluded weapons tests in Australia, had delivered a first weapon to the Royal Air Force. But Cherwell said, to general surprise, that Britain did not intend to make hydrogen bombs, as 'they felt able to get one megaton or possibly two from boosted fission weapons and …in their view few targets needed a larger yield.'

The President then said that he believed that 'atomic weapons were now coming to be regarded as a proper part of conventional armament', but this prompted Churchill to withdraw his approval of their use in Korea in the event of a breach of the armistice at least until he had consulted Eden.

He then produced a photostat of the original signed copy of the Quebec Agreement of 1943 between himself and President Roosevelt and read it to Eisenhower. It pledged the two governments not to use the weapon without mutual agreement. Strauss had never seen it before, but knew, of course, that it could not stand against the McMahon Act.

On the afternoon of the 5th Laniel, the French Prime Minister, went down with pneumonia, and missed the remainder of the conference. This left Bidault, his Foreign Secretary, to sustain an emotional appeal from Churchill supported by Eisenhower to ratify the EDC. Then that evening, when Churchill and Eisenhower dined in the company of Eden and Dulles only, Churchill and Eden felt that if the atomic bomb was used 'there was danger of our taking action which would be morally repellant to most of the world.' Churchill and Eden, who saw the draft of Eisenhower's proposed United Nations speech, managed to persuade him not to refer disparagingly to colonialism as 'bondage', and, more importantly, not to threaten to use the atomic bomb in Korea.

On the 6th (a Sunday) the Foreign Ministers met with their advisers in the morning to draw up a reply to the Soviet note, urging a meeting in Berlin in early January.[17] The draft was transmitted to Germany for approval by Adenauer. Ismay then reported to them on the progress of the NATO forces, and emphasised their growing cohesion, but he admitted that there was a 'levelling-off' in military budgets. Nevertheless, he thought that the 'present strategic concept of forward strategy (i.e., defence as far east as possible)' should be retained. The Foreign Ministers agreed, and Eden summed up their conclusions to the effect that 'there had been general approval for the "long haul" concept whereby all that could be expected in the next few years was the present level of forces plus the German contribution.'

Eden and Dulles discussed the Middle East informally on 6 and 7 December. Eden said that a section of the Conservative Party was staging a 'revolt' against further concessions to the Egyptians. (Selwyn Lloyd had cabled him that a group of about 35 backbenchers, annoyed by Egyptian 'breaches of faith in their execution of the Sudan Agreement', were tabling a motion opposing any more negotiations with them.[18)] Eden and Churchill were, therefore, both in intransigent mood about the

Suez Base. Eden thought a compromise would be possible on 'the wording of the availability formula, so long as it kept 'the U.N. principle' – that is, the base could be reopened to British troops in the event of an attack recognised as aggression by the United Nations. However, he 'did not think they could give way at all on the subject of uniforms' – that is, the British technicians maintaining the base should wear uniform on duty. Eden asked Dulles to delay the provision of military assistance to the Egyptians at least until the New Year, and suggested instead that the aid might go to Iran, where a joint Anglo-American coup masterminded by Kermit Roosevelt and the CIA had removed Mossadegh from power and restored the Shah.[19] Britain resumed diplomatic relations with the new regime in Iran during the Bermuda Conference.[20]

On their last day together Churchill, Eisenhower and the three Foreign Ministers discussed the Far East. Eden was anxious to enable Malaya and other British dependencies to renew their trade with China. 'He understood that this situation was charged with dynamite in the United States, but on the political side they also had difficulties at home.' If the armistice in Korea were broken, the British Government neither favoured the use of atomic weapons, nor any attempt to blockade the coast of China, for blockade would not be effective 'unless Soviet ports were included.'

At the last plenary meeting Bidault gave an account of the difficulties of his country's war in Indo-China. He said the French were very grateful for American aid in the struggle. Churchill said he admired the French for persisting in Indo-China when 'Great Britain cast away her duties in India.' He suggested, though, that the French could ease their own difficulties by prolonging their military service. 'He felt that a longer service term would save lives and would give the nation a higher return.'

The communiqué was the final business of the conference. Although all the regions discussed received a mention, the main emphasis was on the need for EDC ratification in order to 'secure the defensive capacity of the Atlantic Community', but, as the British leaders had wished, it also indicated that replies had been sent to Moscow by the three Governments 'which should lead to an early meeting of the four Foreign Ministers.'[21]

Eisenhower was the first to leave Bermuda on the 8th in order to make his speech at the United Nations in New York, but Churchill did not leave until late on the 10th, on which day his wife Clementine and daughter Mary were in Stockholm receiving the Nobel prize for Literature on his behalf.

On their return from Bermuda Churchill and Eden were faced with the backbench revolt of which Selwyn Lloyd had warned them. Before they set out for the conference, on 30 November, Eden had in fact known that this was coming, in the light of the Sudanese elections having gone badly for British interests in that pro-Egyptian forces had apparently triumphed. (As it turned out, he was mistaken.) He wrote to the Prime Minister:

> ...there will certainly be widespread indignation in our party. If a Foreign Secretary is to carry on in these exacting days he can only do so if he has the support of the overwhelming majority in his own ranks. This clearly does not apply to me in existing circumstances.[22]

If this letter was ever sent, it did not take Eden long to change his mind: no mention of the incident appears in his own diary, or in the published diary of Evelyn Shuckburgh, his private secretary. On his return from Bermuda he at once saw Captain Charles Waterhouse, who was the leader of the so-called Suez Group of rebels, and several of his colleagues.[23] On 15 December the Cabinet was told that arrangements had been made for ten of the leading dissidents to have dinner with General Sir Brian Robertson, the retiring base commander, who had also been entrusted with a role in the negotiations, and that Lord Alexander, the Minister of Defence, would address a meeting of about forty, 'including some belonging to the Foreign Affairs Group', on the 16th.[24] Churchill himself addressed a luncheon meeting of the 1922 Committee on the 16th and, in a 25-minute speech, appealed for their 'faith' in the Government's handling of the situation.[25] In spite of these efforts to ward off the revolt, Waterhouse and 35 other Conservative backbenchers tabled their motion calling on the Government to 'suspend' negotiations with the Egyptian Government,[26] and by the 17th the number of signatories had risen to 41.[27]

On that day Churchill reported to the Commons on the Bermuda meeting. Without mentioning Egypt, he stressed the importance of Anglo-American relations, described Eisenhower's speech at the United Nations proposing an international atomic energy pool as 'one of the most important events in world history since the end of the war', and repeated a warning delivered by Dulles in Paris on the 14th about an 'agonising reappraisal' of strategy if the French Chamber failed to ratify the EDC.[28] Attlee, following in the debate, described Churchill as 'a Father Christmas without any presents', but Eden, who did deal with the Middle East, forecast an early exchange of envoys with the new regime in Iran, and promised the Suez dissidents that when 'heads of agreement' for a treaty with Egypt were arrived at, they would be referred to the Commons before signature.[29]

On 26 December the Soviet Union replied to the Notes from the three Western powers agreeing to a four-power Foreign Ministers' meeting at Berlin, but postponing its date until 25 January.[30] Although hopes had been raised by the Soviet acceptance, Eden went to Berlin with no great expectation: as he told the Cabinet on 18 January:

> The best that we can hope to secure ... is a further demonstration of the solidarity of the Western Powers, possibly an agreement that further technical work should be done on the German and Austrian questions with a view to further meetings of the Foreign Ministers and, in private meetings with M. Molotov, a clearer indication of the real trend of Russian policy.[31]

The Ministers were in session in Berlin for three weeks. Eden, reporting back to the Cabinet on 22 February, said that the Conference had been marked by 'the extreme rigidity of the Soviet attitude towards European problems'. In this sphere there had been no agreement, not even over Austria. On the other hand, 'there was no heightened tension in the relations between the Four Powers... M. Molotov had shown himself most anxious to reach agreement on a Five-Power Meeting at Geneva.' Also, the unity of the Western powers had been demonstrated:

> M. Molotov had signally failed to cause any break or dissension among the Foreign Ministers of the three Western

Powers. M. Bidault had retained his resolution despite Russian blandishments and bullying. Mr Dulles had taken a considerable political risk in supporting the Five-Power Meeting at Geneva.[32]

When Eden reported to the Commons on the Berlin Conference, he quoted some pathetic and telling letters that he had received from Germans in the Eastern Zone who had been forced to sign bogus petitions supporting the Soviet concept of 'democracy'.[33]

The Government's relations with the trade unions, and especially the TUC General Council, had been friendly in its first two years of control, and, in spite of the cut in the food subsidies, the level of strikes had been no worse than when the Labour Government was in power. But in December 1953 the country was faced by the threat of a national rail strike just before Christmas. All three unions in the industry had rejected the offer of a flat-rate increase of four shillings a week proposed on 4 December by the Railway Staffs National Tribunal. The offer was, as the Minister of Labour himself admitted in Cabinet, an 'exceptionally low figure' compared with previous settlements – but it no doubt reflected the view that the retail price index had risen in 1953 by only four percentage points, compared with nine in 1952 and ten in 1951.[34] This in turn was due to the terms of trade moving in Britain's favour with the end of the Korean War and the cessation of American stockpiling. Trade unions in Britain, however, had become used to demanding – and achieving – substantial increases for their members.

The Transport Commission then offered to reconsider the wage structure; the Transport Salaried Staffs Association and the Locomotive Engineers agreed to this, but the National Union of Railwaymen, many of whose members were in the less skilled grades, persisted with the strike call – and it was obvious that they alone could bring the whole network to a standstill.

At a Cabinet meeting six days before the strike was due to begin, the Prime Minister himself suggested that the Transport Commission could allow a more generous settlement if 'some part of the interest charges with which they were saddled on nationalisation' could be 'transferred to the National Debt: a dramatic gesture of this kind', he said, 'might avert the threatened strike.' But Butler promptly demurred: such a move 'would be seen as a direct Exchequer subsidy in support of wages' and 'would be a dangerous precedent for the future.'[35] Monckton, however, although just recovering from flu, next day brought the two sides together at the Ministry of Labour and persuaded the Commission to make enough concessions to enable the strike to be called off. The Commission and the union agreed to 'confer, in order to evolve ways of increasing the efficiency of the railway organisation, not only by such adjustments of wages and salaries as may result...but by all other appropriate means.' The *Economist* commented:

> In all essentials...the settlement has settled nothing, except the convenience of the public at Christmas. The moral that the other unions will draw from this week's negotiations is not that wage increases are now dependent upon a relaxation of restrictive practices and upon working economies... Once more inflation has been thought preferable to a stoppage...[Sir Walter Monckton's] triumph is really one more retreat from reality.[36]

Monckton himself was well aware that the settlement was a defeat. He told the Cabinet that it was:

> (1) a surrender to force; (2) a victory for the Communists; and (3) damaging to constitutional negotiating machinery and voluntary arbitration... It is probable that, in the negotiations which are at present going on or pending in a number of industries, the unions will not be prepared to settle for less than seven shillings a week – the minimum amount the N.U.R. [Railwaymen] indicated they were prepared to accept.[37]

As if to underline this, the Confederation of Shipbuilding and Engineering Unions imposed a ban on overtime and a limitation on piecework. To deal with their claims Monckton appointed two courts of inquiry with identical membership, before departing to Spain for a ten-day holiday.[38] On 9 January *The Times* in a leading article suggested that 'current wage disputes...mark a turning point in the course of labour relations since the war.' Until recently, the article maintained, there had been 'a readiness to compromise in the interests of industrial peace'. But now, the article continued, 'It is clear that the system of arbitration which has ruled for so long is discredited.' The writer concluded gloomily:

> Are we to go back to the old days of strikes and lock-outs, or is there some other way – short of simply paying ransom, to the gathering detriment of British industry and trade, for the sake of peace?[39]

The problem had been exercising the Ministry of Labour, and its Permanent Secretary, Sir Godfrey Ince, suggested in a speech on 20 January that all negotiating machinery should provide for a final settlement by arbitration.[40] Sir Walter Monckton met members of the General Council of the TUC on 19 March to discuss this, but after brief consideration by both employers and union leaders the idea was rejected in April.[41]

At the end of February the courts of inquiry for the engineering and shipbuilding industries recommended a 5 per cent increase for both industries, but this was rejected by the unions; a final agreement was made at the end of March for a 6 per cent increase.[42] Another major settlement in the winter was an increase for miners – as much as eight shillings and sixpence for the underground workers, which was accepted after a ballot of the men. The miners' leaders also undertook to maintain the voluntary Saturday shifts, which for a time the Labour Government had abandoned.[43]

But the demand for pay increases spread beyond industry. At the end of January the Minister of Defence, aided by his three subordinate colleagues, put in a claim for an increase on the grounds that service recruitment had become difficult.[44] They won their case, and on 2 March Nigel Birch, the Parliamentary Secretary of the Ministry of Defence, when introducing the Defence White Paper, announced selective increases in service pay, and also increases in pensions.[45]

Butler had spent January at a Commonwealth Finance Ministers Conference at Sydney, Australia, on which he reported to the Commons on 2 February. His speech indicated how far the Commonwealth was dependent on American policy for avoidance of a slump:

Apart from what we ourselves must do, we look for good creditor policies by the United States. Over the last year they have been paying out gold to the rest of the world. This has largely been due to heavy military expenditure. We want to see some more permanent pattern emerging.

He also spoke of the need for a more active role by 'international institutions':

We welcomed the prospect of I.M.F. credits becoming more readily available whether to help the world to ride out the effects of an adjustment in the American economy or to augment the reserves as a step towards freer trade and payments.[46]

When the Cabinet met on 3 March, the day after the Defence White Paper was presented, Butler stressed the difficulties he was having in keeping expenditure within bounds. He said that:

If I am to avoid increasing the level of taxation in 1955, early consideration would have to be given to policy changes designed to secure substantial reductions in public expenditure.

Eden thereupon commented that the Middle East was the only theatre in which he saw any early prospect of reducing commitments. The Prime Minister invited Butler to suggest means of making the necessary savings.[47] Accordingly, Butler suggested that there should be two committees of Ministers to propose savings in 1955, one of £100 million in the civil estimates, and one of £150 million in defence.[48]

It was not surprising, therefore, that Butler's Budget at the beginning of April had virtually no tax concessions to offer. He said that the balance of payments surplus for 1953 was some £320 million, but admitted that this was largely due to a 'further movement of the terms of trade in our favour' and that 'we cannot expect to enjoy both favourable terms of trade and easy export markets at the same time.' Unemployment, at 373,000 in January 1954, was 80,000 lower than a year earlier, but 'output per man in manufacturing industry in 1953 was, on average, little above the 1951 level.' Investment in private industry had been insufficient, and he therefore proposed to

1. Conservative Central Office press conference, October 1951. R. A. Butler, the Chairman of the Party's Political Committee, is flanked by Lord Woolton (right), Chairman of the Central Office and J. P. L. Thomas (left), Vice-Chairman

2. 'Hot Seat' cartoon by David Low, published in the *Daily Herald*, 30 October 1951. Churchill, Eden and Butler occupy the front bench but find it uncomfortable. Attlee, Morrison and Gaitskell retreat into the background

3.   Churchill and General Eisenhower in Paris, December 1951. The General was
Commander-in-Chief of the NATO forces

4. Eden's wedding, August 1952. From left to right, Clementine Churchill, Eden, Clarissa Churchill, Winston Churchill

6. Lord Salisbury, Lord President from 1952 and Acting Foreign Secretary in 1953 during Eden's illness

5. Oliver Lyttelton, Colonial Secretary, 1951–54

8. Harold Macmillan, Minister of Housing, opens a new house in the course of his successful bid to complete 300,000 houses in 1953

7. Lord Cherwell, Churchill's scientific adviser, joining an aircraft to fly to Australia and visit the Woomera Rocket Range

9.   Churchill in Coronation procession, 2 June 1953. He is wearing the insignia of the Garter

10. Cabinet Ministers at Blackpool, October 1954. Left to right: Miss Horsbrugh (Education), Thorneycroft (Trade), Macmillan (Housing), Monckton (Labour), Alexander (Defence), Butler (Exchequer), Maxwell Fyfe (Home Office)

11. Churchill's eightieth birthday; cartoon by Vicky captioned 'One man in his life plays many parts'. *Daily Mirror*, 30 November 1954

extend investment allowances. Only milk and bread would now be subsidised, but 'agricultural guarantees' would be substantial. An increase in old age pensions could be postponed pending the report of the Phillips Committee on 'the problems of an ageing population'. He concluded:

> I am proposing a carry-on Budget, a Budget conceived as re-affirming our basic policies, rather than as marking any major change of emphasis or direction.[49]

The *Times* parliamentary correspondent described the speech as 'unexciting', and suggested that the Chancellor deployed his facts and figures with 'consummate if rather soporific lucidity'.[50] The *Manchester Guardian* described the Budget as 'colourless', but explained this by suggesting that the Chancellor might be worried by 'the course of the American trade decline'.[51] Two days later Butler displayed 'a genial and comfortable style' in answering questions from William Clark, the *Observer* correspondent, for the first time televised from No. 11 Downing Street.[52] With his wife and younger children he then took a well-earned fortnight's holiday in Majorca.[53]

9 The H-Bomb and Eden's Diplomacy

To his colleagues and inner circle of secretaries, Churchill seemed to be increasingly feeble early in 1954. In February Malcolm Muggeridge published in *Punch*, which he edited, a cruel cartoon of Churchill and an article about a Byzantine emperor who could not decide whether to retire, or when.[1] According to Shuckburgh, Eden's private secretary, Jane Portal, told him that the Prime Minister was 'getting senile and failing more and more each day... Life is a misery to him; he half kills himself with work, cannot take in the papers he is given to read, and can hardly get himself up the stairs to bed.' But she added: 'Yet he thinks he has a mission on three subjects – Russia, Egypt, and the atomic bomb'.[2] On 11 March he told Eden that he might retire in May, when the Queen returned from her Commonwealth tour, or at the end of the session, 'depending on his health'.[3] And next day he told Butler that he felt 'like an aeroplane at the end of its flight, with the petrol running out, in search of a safe landing'.[4]

But he still kept a close eye on the newspapers, and early in the year he read with close attention an article in the *Manchester Guardian* which reported Congressman Sterling Cole, Chairman of the American Joint Committee on Atomic Energy, giving details of the explosive power of the first hydrogen bomb test at Eniwetok Atoll in November 1952.[5] The details did not arouse much attention in Britain until after a second hydrogen bomb test at Bikini Atoll on 1 March 1954 and then not for some days. But in late March it was reported that a Japanese fishing boat had been contaminated by radioactive ash, although it had been 71 miles away from Bikini Atoll and well outside the exclusion zone; the fishermen had developed blisters from which one of them later died.[6] Later that month Churchill wrote to Eisenhower, stressing first the need to increase trade with the Soviet Union, so as to lead to a 'wider enjoyment by the Russian masses of...consumer goods'. Then he turned to the threat of the hydrogen bomb, saying 'There is the peril which marches towards us and is nearer and more deadly

120

to us than to you.'[7] We have already seen that the Russian leadership had exploded a hydrogen bomb of their own in 1953. Eisenhower's reply was largely concerned with the limitation of strategic exports from the West to Russia, on which subject he had already despatched a senior official, Harold Stassen, to negotiate in Europe and to make some concessions.[8]

On 5 April the Commons debated, on the initiative of the Opposition, a motion calling for the 'immediate' summoning of a conference of the great powers to consider 'the reduction and control of armaments'.[9] Attlee, opening the debate, said:

> I move this Motion in no party spirit; I seek no party advantage; nor do I offer criticism of this or any other Government...in our view, we face today a new situation in the history of the world... We are all sorry that those innocent fishermen have suffered, but they will not have suffered in vain if they have brought home to people the great extent of the danger.

He concluded:

> The time has come to make the United Nations organisation a reality... We believe that now is the time... British initiative may well save world civilisation.[10]

Churchill spoke for an hour in reply. At the outset he acknowledged Attlee's 'public spirit' and said that the Government would accept the Motion provided they could put their own interpretation on the word 'immediate'. But, having been nettled by criticism of himself in the left-wing press, he launched into a long prepared speech in which he attacked the Labour Government for having abandoned the Quebec Agreement, signed by himself and President Roosevelt in 1943, which he had read to Eisenhower at Bermuda and now read to the Commons. It contained the declaration 'we will not use it against other parties without each other's consent.' Attlee was angered by this and rose to ask:

> What possible reason had I to expect that the United States Government, with a Bill affecting an agreement like that with us, would not have informed their own supporters and Senator McMahon? I did not know. They did not tell me. How could I know?

It was the McMahon Act of 1946 that had prevented technical collaboration on atomic matters with Britain. Churchill continued:

> I think it would have been an obvious precaution to have confronted them with that agreement. Anyhow, they were not confronted with it.[11]

Labour MPs were exasperated by the way in which what should have been a virtually unanimous discussion had become a partisan debate, and Churchill thereafter was subjected to constant interruption. As *The Times* reported, 'the proceedings...degenerated into a sterile, angry, and pitiful party wrangle. And the responsibility was the Prime Minister's.'[12] Crookshank in his diary described his performance as 'disastrous'.[13] And Richard Crossman, who had come in for some of Churchill's criticism, wrote in his diary: 'All that evening the lobbies and Smoking Room hummed with talk of Churchill's failure.'[14]

On 7 April Eisenhower displayed his concern about the danger of Communist expansion in South-East Asia by publicly invoking the 'domino' theory.[15] He was especially worried about Vietnam, where a French garrison at Dien Bien Phu near the Chinese border was besieged by Vietminh guerrillas, and he proposed to send Dulles to London to consider joint action.[16] Dulles duly arrived on Sunday, 11 April, and next day had talks with Eden at the Foreign Office and then dinner with Churchill at No. 10.[17] Reporting to the Commons on the 13th, Eden said that he had agreed with Dulles that his Government would participate in 'an examination of the possibilities of establishing a collective defence...of South-East Asia and the western Pacific'.[18] Eden had previously pointed out to the Cabinet that such a treaty would suit Britain, as it would supersede the treaty between the United States and the two Commonwealth countries, Australia and New Zealand, from which Britain was excluded. This, known as ANZUS, had been signed in 1951 when Labour was still in office. Eden had said in a Cabinet Paper on 7 April:

> It would dispose of the anomaly of our exclusion from ANZUS and contribute to the security of Hong Kong and

Malaya. At the same time, with the Geneva Conference in prospect, I have grave misgivings about the timing of the proposed arrangement.[19]

Eden's statement in the Commons, cautious as it was, received an equally cautious welcome from the Opposition, but Aneurin Beven suddenly declared that the statement 'would be deeply resented by the majority of people in Great Britain'. Next day he resigned from the Shadow Cabinet, to which he had been elected at the beginning of the session.[20] Labour divisions in the Commons emerged even more markedly when a debate took place to establish an Atomic Energy Authority along lines advocated by Cherwell: 63 MPs from the Opposition voted for an amendment to impose a restriction upon the new Authority to prevent it manufacturing hydrogen bombs.[21]

But Churchill and Eden were at one in rejecting Dulles' call for Anglo-American intervention in Vietnam. On Sunday, 25 April there were two emergency meetings of Ministers to discuss this proposal; Eden returned from Paris to attend them and state his views. He told the Ministers:

Military intervention in Indo-China cannot be authorised by the United States Administration without the approval of Congress; and Mr Dulles believes that Congress would be more likely to accord this approval if the intervention were undertaken on a joint Anglo-American basis.

He added:

The Chiefs of Staff agree that air operations cannot now have any appreciable effect on the battle for Dien Bien Phu... I consider that anything like open war with China might well involve the Soviet Union and lead to a third world war.[22]

Eden then made his way to Geneva, but when the Cabinet met a few days later the Prime Minister reverted to the topic to say:

I have no doubt that the Foreign Secretary has been right in recommending that the United Kingdom should decline to associate themselves with any immediate declaration of intention to check the expansion of Communism in South-East Asia or to join in any precipitate intervention in Indo-China. I think it possible that the United States authorities may eventually be brought to share our view on this matter.

Churchill also said that the French Prime Minister had urged him to reconsider, but he had rejected this call.[23] But Dulles was very disappointed by the British attitude. He reported to Washington on 29 April that:

> U.K. attitude is one of increasing weakness. Britain seems to feel that we are disposed to accept present risks of a Chinese war, and this, coupled with their fear that we would start using atomic weapons, has badly frightened them.[24]

Dulles, together with the other principal protagonists of the Geneva Conference, were now assembled in that city. The first topic of the conference was Korea, but when it proved impossible to persuade the Communist powers to agree to a reunion of the divided country under the auspices of the United Nations, with free and secret elections in both North and South, it was agreed to abandon the search for a solution and to turn to the other topic of the conference, namely Indo-China. This part of the conference began on 8 May, which was the day after the fortress of Dien Bien Phu had fallen to the Vietminh. Dulles refused to sit at the same table as the Chinese, and in any case left Geneva for America before the Indo-China phase began. His deputy, General Bedell Smith, remained, but the co-chairmen of the conference were Molotov and Eden.

The burden on Eden to find a solution was all the heavier. Before the Indo-China conference began, on 5 May, he gave a dinner for Molotov and, according to Shuckburgh, did most of the talking:

> The theme was the middle position of U.S.S.R. and U.K., with an implication that we deprecate the wildness of the Americans (and Chinese), the hopelessness of the French. Rather an admission, it sounded, of the divisions in the Western alliance... AE seems now to be accepting the 'New Look' idea which he has been so roundly abusing in the P.M. ever since 11 May.[25]

This approach to Molotov paid off, for he showed himself unexpectedly helpful. As Eden said in his memoirs (quoting a note of his own), Molotov 'clearly thinks he and I have a special task in this conference to try and facilitate agreement.'[26] On the other hand, relations with the United States grew difficult, and Eden received anxious letters from Roger Makins, the new British Ambassador in Washington.[27]

At any rate it proved possible to make agreements for military armistice teams to be set up for the three French dependencies, Vietnam, Laos and Cambodia, and while they were completing their task, most of the principal delegates left Geneva for their home countries. In France Laniel's Government fell, and he was succeeded by Pierre Mendès-France on 18 June. Mendès decided to act as his own Foreign Minister and to pledge himself to resign after a month if he could not secure a ceasefire in Indo-China. He went to Berne in Switzerland for a meeting with Chou En-lai, the Chinese Foreign Minister, and on 22 June Eden told the Cabinet that 'a negotiated settlement...was not beyond reach.'[28]

Churchill and Eden then paid a visit to Eisenhower and Dulles in Washington, at Eisenhower's invitation. Churchill had wanted more information on the hydrogen bomb, and had asked for a meeting in late April, hoping they could convene some time in May.[29] They eventually agreed to meet on 25 June, and in advance of the meeting Churchill told Eisenhower that he had changed his mind about the importance of the Suez base, owing to 'thermo-nuclear developments' and the establishment of a forward tier of allied states, the 'Tito-Greeko-Turko front' as he called it, with Iraq and Pakistan.[30]

Churchill was accompanied by Cherwell and Sir Edwin Plowden, the head of the newly created Atomic Energy Authority, as well as by Anthony Eden and Churchill's doctor, Lord Moran. The party flew by Stratocruiser from Heathrow, with Eden giving Churchill an account of the Geneva Conference on the way.[31] In discussion with the President, Churchill at first thought he had committed him to agree to a meeting with Malenkov, but later Dulles persuaded Eisenhower to change his mind.[32] Instead, the two leaders at Eisenhower's suggestion drafted a joint Declaration along the lines of the Atlantic Charter of 1941. Like the earlier document, it was of little real value, but as in 1941 its terms were referred to the Cabinet in London, where the mention of 'the right of self-determination' was queried on the grounds that it might cause trouble in the Colonies. The Cabinet preferred, and Eisenhower accepted, 'the principles of self-government'. A minor storm blew up over Guatemala, where an American-backed invasion force had attacked a Marxist regime. Pierson Dixon, the British permanent delegate to the United Nations Security Council, wished to vote in favour of the Council taking up the issue, but Churchill insisted, at Dulles' request, on ordering him to abstain in the vote, so that it could be referred to the (American-dominated) Organisation of American States.[33] Evan Luard, in his *History of the United Nations*, commented: 'There has perhaps been no episode in the organisation's history so discreditable to its reputation as this.'[34]

So far as Churchill was concerned, the results of the trip were rather negative. He paid a brief visit to Ottawa, where he was as usual warmly greeted, and then he and Eden boarded the *Queen Elizabeth* at New York for the return journey. While on board he planned precisely that 'solitary pilgrimage' to Moscow which Eisenhower had deplored the previous year, and he drafted a telegram to Molotov which he showed to Eden. Eden insisted on his passing the telegram to the Cabinet before it went to Moscow, but Churchill only agreed to do so if he could say that the message had Eden's approval in principle; Eden weakly agreed, which, as John Colville wrote, 'of course he does not'.[35] Eden was in fact travelling by sea only in the hope of extracting from Churchill a definite retirement date; according to Colville, Churchill 'tentatively fixed 21 September for the hand-over'.[36]

Churchill's message had been sent to Butler at the weekend when the members of the Cabinet were scattered, and it had been followed shortly by another message asking if it had yet been passed on. So Butler authorised its despatch to Moscow on 4 July, two days before the *Queen Elizabeth* reached Southampton. Next day, the 7th, an encouraging reply was received from Moscow, of which Churchill at once sent a copy to Eisenhower.[37] But when the Cabinet met that day under Churchill's chairmanship, Salisbury at once offered his resignation on the grounds that the Cabinet should have been properly consulted before the message was sent to Moscow.[38]

Churchill now began to retreat from his exposed position. At a further meeting of the Cabinet next day he said he would not go to Moscow to meet Malenkov, but only to Stockholm or Vienna or, as Eden suggested, Berne. Salisbury pressed the constitutional point:

> The message which the Prime Minister has sent to M. Molotov, although framed as a personal enquiry, is in my view an important act of foreign policy, and it would have been preferable that the Cabinet should have been given an opportunity to express their views on it before it was sent.

Crookshank agreed with Salisbury and said that he would have been against 'such an approach at the present time'. Eden pointed out that a draft had been sent to Butler before despatch to Moscow, but Butler said: 'There was nothing on the telegram to suggest that the views of the Cabinet were being invited.' Swinton then intervened to say that, although a Prime Minister was 'free to conduct unofficial correspondence with Heads of other Governments', the question was whether that correspondence committed the Cabinet. Salisbury said that he thought that in this instance 'the Cabinet's freedom of action had to some extent been limited.' Lyttleton, seeking to give Churchill an escape route, said that while he agreed with Swinton about the constitutional issue, 'it was still open to the Cabinet to decide not to proceed further with this project.' Churchill then adjourned the meeting, saying that he accepted that Eisenhower's reaction would be important in deciding whether to go ahead.[39] According to Crookshank, he was 'very shame faced. He knew he had been wrong.'[40]

Next day, 9 July another Cabinet meeting was held, and Churchill read out Eisenhower's reply. The President said:

> You did not allow any grass to grow under your feet... The fact that your message was sent so promptly after you left here is likely to give an impression more powerful than your cautionary words that in some way your plan was agreed at our meeting... In any event, I think you will agree that your program should be handled with the greatest delicacy to avoid giving either the misapprehension that we are in fact party to it, or the equally dangerous misapprehension that

your action in this matter reflects a sharp disagreement between our two countries.[41]

Churchill replied at once in a rather chastened tone:

> I hope you are not vexed with me for not submitting to you the text of my telegram to Molotov. I felt that as it was a private and personal enquiry which I had not brought officially before the Cabinet I had better bear the burden myself, and not involve you in any way. I have made it clear to Molotov that you were in no way committed... We shall keep you informed and I shall not seek any decision to make an official approach until I hear from you again.[42]

Churchill's retreat went further: at the Cabinet on the 9th, he said that he proposed to tell Eisenhower that he would expect the Russians to give:

> some definite proof of their sincerity, as a preliminary to a wider meeting – e.g. an undertaking to ratify the Austrian Treaty, and, perhaps, a promise to co-operate in the Atoms Bomb Plan. I shall urge the President to give his views on these specific proposals before the Cabinet is asked to decide whether a formal proposal for a two-Power meeting should be submitted to the Soviet Government.

Even this did not satisfy Salisbury, who said that he was 'opposed in principle to the idea of holding a high-level meeting with the Russians without participation of the United States.' He added that he had written to the Prime Minister to tell him this after his Commons speech on 11 May, 1953. The Prime Minister replied that the Cabinet would have to bear in mind Salisbury's views, and that he was not asking for a definite decision that day.[43]

The Cabinet did not meet again until the 13th, by which time Eden had returned to Geneva. Churchill again read a letter from Eisenhower, in which the President said that he would endeavour to 'mitigate any unfavourable reaction'. Churchill professed himself to be 'gratified' by this response, but indicated that he would not ask the Cabinet to reach any decision until after Eden's return from the Geneva Conference.[44] Eden was back by 23 July, and at Cabinet that day Churchill read out his letter to Eisenhower (agreed with

Eden) of 9 July suggesting a meeting at Stockholm, Vienna or
Berne, with a four-power conference to follow 'perhaps, as I
said to you, in London early in September'. But in addition:

> I should ask them for a Gesture or as better express, 'an Act
> of Faith'...an undertaking to ratify the Austrian Treaty on
> which *all* their conditions have been agreed, and to liberate
> Austria and Vienna from Russian domination. Surely it
> would be a help if they would accept your atomic theme
> which you told us about at Bermuda and afterwards pro-
> posed to United Nations.

Churchill also added a protest about the scare in the
American press to the effect that he and Eden had tried to
persuade the United States to recognise 'Red China'.[45]

Salisbury now explained that his view had been based on
the fear that the Americans might want to 'bring the
East/West issue to a head while they still have overwhelming
superiority in atomic weapons and are comparatively immune
from atomic attack by Russia.' He considered that during that
period our efforts 'should be to preserve the unity and coher-
ence of the Western Alliance'. Crookshank described this as a
'terrible Cabinet... Bobbety threatening to resign – also
Winston'.[46] Eden suggested that the decision should at least
be postponed until after the Soviet reaction to the Geneva
Conference was known, and this was agreed.[47]

On 24 July the Soviet Government circulated a new proposal – to hold a meeting of all the European powers, together
with the United States, to discuss European security.[48] This
note solved the British Cabinet crisis, for Churchill acknowledged that it 'created a new situation'. Churchill undertook
to send a personal message to this effect to Molotov. The same
Cabinet committed its members to the manufacture of a hydrogen bomb, so as to 'enable us to play our part in deterring
a potential aggressor from embarking on major war'.[49]

The final stages of the Geneva Conference were enacted in
mid-July. Although Dulles was unwilling to return to the
Conference table, at a meeting in Paris on 13 July he was persuaded by Eden and Mendès-France to send back his Under-
Secretary, Bedell Smith. The breakthrough came just in time
to meet Mendès-France's deadline: on 20 July he and the

Vietminh Foreign Minister agreed on a demarcation line between North and South Vietnam at the 17th Parallel. With India, Canada and Poland providing the supervisory commissions for the three countries, the agreements could be finally signed on 21 July. The Americans did not participate, but two days later and rather grudgingly Dulles declared that the United States 'noted' the results, and 'said that, in accordance with the United Nations Charter, we would not seek by force to overthrow the settlement.'[50]

It was only after the Geneva Conference was over that Eden was prepared to go ahead with the formation of a South-East Asia Treaty. A study group in Washington had devised a plan for this and on Eden's insistence the 'Colombo Powers' – India, Pakistan, Ceylon, Burma and Indonesia – were invited to associate themselves with it. In fact only Pakistan did so, but the other powers welcomed the fact that they had been consulted. The conference, which established the treaty, met at Manila on 6 September, and Britain was represented there not by Eden, who was too busy with European affairs, but by the Marquis of Reading, who was his second Minister of State.[51]

Eden received much praise for his skill in achieving a peaceful solution at Geneva. But there were reservations about the French losses.

A *Times* leader was entitled 'The Price of Peace'. It said:

> There is cause for deep thankfulness in the agreement on Indo-China. There cannot be joy... The result has been gained by ten weeks of unremitting imaginative skill on the part of the British Foreign Secretary, mainly in private talks with Mr Molotov and Mr Chou En-lai, often when the chances of success seemed nil. It has been clinched in the last month by the frankness with which M. Mendès-France looked facts in the face... Yet the losses...remain heavy.

And when Eden gave an account of the final stages of the conference to the Commons, the *Times* parliamentary correspondent commented:

> Judging from the volume of cheering, there seemed to be a certain reserve, at any rate on his side of the House, in the reception which members offered today to Mr Eden's statement on Indo-China.[52]

As we have seen, it was the hydrogen bomb which finally convinced Churchill that he could agree to the Egyptian terms for
British withdrawal from Suez – namely, the removal of all
British troops and the maintenance of the base by civilians
only. On 23 July the Cabinet agreed that Antony Head, the
Secretary of State for War, should go out to Cairo to clinch the
deal, which would involve a seven-year agreement for the base
to be maintained by British civilian contractors and a withdrawal of all troops within a 20-month period. Head travelled
out next day, and on 28 July Eden was able to announce the
agreement to the Commons. It was debated on the last full day
of the parliamentary session, and carried by 257 votes to 26,
the minority being the remnants of the Suez Group who had
survived a strong appeal from Churchill to give way on this
issue.[53] The Labour Party decided to abstain from the vote,
and largely did so. Crossman commented in his diary:

> [C]an one blame the unfortunate Tea Room men who can't
> make out what is really Conservatism and what is really
> Socialism, after a Conservative Government signs the treaty
> with China and Russia against the will of America and evacu-
> ates Suez, policies which were considered Bevanite by the
> right wing of the Labour Party only twelve months ago?[54]

After the resumption of diplomatic relations with Iran,
which as we have seen took place during the Bermuda
Conference, it remained to settle the dispute between the
Iranian Government and the Anglo-Iranian Oil Company.
Eden reported to the Cabinet in January 1954 that the new
Iranian Government, although keen to come to an agreement, were not willing to tolerate the resumption of control at
Abadan by the Anglo-Iranian Oil Company, but would accept
the idea of a consortium of companies to undertake the marketing, while the Iranians themselves would undertake the ex-
traction and refining. There would be compensation for the
AIOC for the loss of its assets. The Cabinet agreed to negotiate
on this basis.[55] In obtaining agreement to these terms, Eden
had difficulty not only in persuading his Cabinet colleagues
but also the chairman of the company to cut their losses. In
his diary he described the latter, Sir William Fraser, as having a
'limited Glasgow accountant's outlook and all that that entailed'.[56] The agreement allowed American companies to take

40 per cent of the consortium, and the AIOC was reduced to the same proportion, with the remaining 20 per cent divided between Royal Dutch/Shell and the Compagnie Française des Petroles.[57] The British company also received substantial compensation for its loss, both from the other companies and from the Iranian Government.[58] The agreement was concluded at the end of July, and Eden sent Dulles a telegram of thanks for the 'generous help' of the US Government, and especially 'the unfailing cooperation of Mr [Loy] Henderson the United States Ambassador'.[59]

Meanwhile, secret negotiations were proceeding in London to enable the withdrawal of the Anglo-American occupation force in Trieste. This was in Zone A of the territory, including the port itself. Zone B was already occupied by the Yugoslav Army. The British and American Governments had proposed on 8 October 1953 that their occupation force should be replaced by the Italian Army, and that the zonal boundary should henceforth be the international boundary.[60] This created a storm of hostility in both countries, as each claimed the entire territory. But in 1954 private talks took place in London, and the Yugoslavs were eventually persuaded to accept the solution which Dulles and Eden had originally proposed – together with a *douceur* of $20 million and £2 million. Eden described this in his memoirs as 'a classic example of the true function of diplomacy, an open agreement secretly arrived at'.[61] The agreement was initialled in London on 5 October 1954.[62]

In mid-August Eden and Clarissa took a short holiday in an Austrian castle, where he found 'it is still raining but at least there is no direct line to F.O. or Chartwell.'[63] Meanwhile Mendès-France was grappling with the problem of the EDC, and how to secure its ratification by the French Assembly. Although he himself favoured it in principle, some of his colleagues in the French Cabinet, especially the Gaullists, were opposed. He therefore sought to secure amendment of the treaty by means of 'protocols', which were put before the other five powers for approval. A conference met at Brussels to consider the proposed changes, but the other five powers were unanimous in rejecting them. On his way back to Paris Mendès-France elected to fly to Biggin Hill in Kent for a brief visit to Churchill, who with Eden (now hastily back from Austria) met him at Chartwell. Mendès, when pressed to put EDC in its original form to the French Assembly, said that 'he could not make it a question of confidence without destroying his Cabinet.'[64] All the same, he did put the Treaty to the Assembly at the end of the month, and it was defeated by 319 votes to 264.[65] Even before this occurred, the British Cabinet were considering ways of admitting Germany to NATO, and Macmillan suggested to Eden that it should be done by means of using the Brussels Treaty of 1948, although that was originally devised to resist any renewed German aggression.[66]

When the Cabinet met on 8 September, Eden said that he would make a tour of the capitals of the six countries of Western Europe. He said that he would probably have to offer to guarantee to keep four divisions on the Continent to ensure agreement, but Churchill thought that this should not be accorded without a corresponding commitment by the United States, so the issue was left in abeyance.[67] When the Cabinet met a week later Eden had already been to Brussels (for Benelux), Bonn, Rome and Paris. It was only in Paris that the discussions proved difficult, but Mendès-France agreed in the end to Germany's admission to NATO. Eden proposed to hold an early conference of the nine powers most directly involved – including the United States and Canada as well as Britain. Churchill and the Cabinet congratulated him on the success of his tour, but the Prime Minister warned that any British guarantee of a Continental commitment should be carefully timed and 'should, if possible, be accompanied by similar undertakings by the United States Government.'[68]

Eden presided over the nine-Power conference which was duly held in London from 27 September. When Dulles arrived he complained privately to Eden that the new proposals had no 'supranational features'.[69] But in public he spoke of Eden's 'brilliant and statesmanlike initiative', and duly promised to recommend to the President a renewal of 'a pledge comparable to that which was offered in connection with the European Defense Community Treaty'. This was immediately followed by Eden's commitment to retain on the Continent the four divisions already there, or their equivalent, and the tactical air force – subject only to withdrawal in the event of 'an acute overseas emergency'.[70] Harold Macmillan, who dined at the

French Embassy on the following evening, described the atmosphere as 'elated', and Mendès-France implied to him that he was 'now determined to make the Conference succeed'.[71]

But there were still difficulties to be overcome with the French Assembly. The decisions were confirmed at a further Conference in Paris at the end of October, and the European members of the revised Brussels Treaty organisation, now including Germany and Italy, were constituted as the 'Western European Union', with headquarters in London. When Mendès-France put the agreements to the French Assembly for ratification just before Christmas, however, they were rejected by 280 votes to 258. That evening, Eden issued a statement from the Foreign Office pointing out that if there were no ratification, the British commitment to the Continent would lapse, and on 29 December the French Assembly changed its mind and ratified the Treaty.[72]

This was the crowning achievement of Eden's *annus mirabilis*, as it was called by a member of his own staff.[73] Churchill had told the Conservative Party Conference in Blackpool in October:

> Without his energy and boldness the London conference would not have taken place, and without his knowledge, experience, tact, and skill it could never have reached its favourable conclusion.[74]

And on 20 October Eden received the Order of the Garter from the Queen – an honour which he had been offered in 1945 but had then, like Churchill, refused.[75]

It was frustrating for Eden that just at the time of his greatest successes in foreign policy he was constantly deprived of the greatest prize of all, the premiership which he had expected for so long and which had been virtually promised to him for September 1954. On 10 August, on the eve of his holiday, he wrote to Churchill pointing out:

> If there isn't sufficient time for the new Government to make its own name for itself in advance of the general election, then it will have no chance of survival. It will be hard enough anyway. But at least a year, beginning with a Party Conference, seems to me the minimum.

This would have meant Churchill retiring before the Party Conference of 1954, as it was generally agreed that 1956 would be too late for a General Election in view of the expected impact of rating valuations. Eden went on to add: 'I hope you won't hesitate to talk to any of our colleagues about it while I am away.'[76]

Churchill consulted Butler about his reply, and also explained his desire to stay on to Macmillan. It was only Macmillan, apparently, who told him that he really ought to go; Butler allowed himself to be impressed by Churchill's argument about the poor outlook for 'fag-end' governments.[77] Finally Churchill wrote to Eden on 24 August to say that he was staying on for the time being:

> Fag-end Administrations have not usually been triumphant. I can remember Rosebery after Gladstone and AJB [Balfour] after Salisbury. Both were brushed aside in spite of their ability, experience and charm. …One thing stands forth. There must be a thorough reconstruction of the Government.[78]

Eden visited Churchill at No. 10 on 27 August. Before doing so, he had a talk with Butler and Macmillan. According to Eden's diary, both were agreed that Churchill should go. On meeting Churchill, Eden said, again according to his diary:

> If I was not fit to stand on my own feet & choose an administration now, I should probably be less so a year from now. The Govt was not functioning well & this was putting a heavy strain on all his senior Ministers. These were able men but there was no co-ordination. …I added that I envied Oliver [Lyttelton], who was retiring to return to the City & would like to do as he had done. He replied that the Party would never forgive me if I did, that they were counting on me, etc. I was young. It would all be mine before sixty. Why was I in such a hurry? Anyway if I felt like it he would be ready for me to take over Leadership of the House and home front. I showed no enthusiasm and felt none.

Then Churchill suggested that Eden might lead a revolt of five or six Cabinet Ministers, but Eden said 'he knew perfectly well that I was the last person to want to do this after our many years of work together. Then there was some emotion…' So they parted cordially, in spite of Eden's disappointment.[79]

On 7 September Butler and Eden dined with the Prime Minister to discuss Cabinet changes. Butler reported to the Chief Whip next day:

> The one constructive idea which emerged was that AE might become Minister of Defence, that he might have a secretariat to help him with home front problems, & that he might or might not take Chair of the Home Affairs Ctee. He would probably take over Philip [Swinton]'s Press Relations and help with the Party. He would not try to lead the House. The reason why the Ministry of Defence came up was because AE did not know how his duties as Deputy PM – free ranging – would be explained. Nor does he wish to give the world the impression that he is leaving the world scene & its terrible problems for what might be described as Party issues. Moreover the Ministry of Defence is not a heavy post & would give him time for other things. Besides he feels that as future PM the experience in Min Defence would be invaluable.

Butler added about the wider changes:

> The PM is somewhat lethargic about Reconstruction. While quite ready to make any changes necessary, he did not seem to have grasped the need for exhibiting to the Elector new men & measures. …The PM said that the vacancies in the Cabinet were likely to be Defence, Ld Chancellor, plus the transference at the Foreign Office. To this AE added Education & perhaps changes at Bd of Trade & C'wealth Relations… The PM said there were 2 candidates for the Cabinet Sandys & Eccles. AE is unhappy about the latter. The junior posts were hardly considered & conveniently left to you…[80]

Thoughts of reconstruction were put off until after the Conservative Party Conference, which met at Blackpool early in October. Churchill, buoyed up by one of Lord Moran's pills, was in vigorous form. After praising Eden's work in concluding the London Conference, he said:

He and I are very good friends and we have a family rela-
tionship which I value very much. There is quite enough for
both of us to do at the present time. You may be quite sure
that we shall settle our affairs in the future between ourselves, governed only by what we believe to be the greatest
interest of the public service and also the fortunes of our
party.[81]

The *Times* correspondent commented:

So far from indicating any intention of putting off the
harness, the old warrior dominated a big occasion with
consummate ease and delivered a speech of great range
and power in one of his most sparkling platform
performances.[82]

It was not until a week later that Churchill's Cabinet recon-
struction was announced. Eden had decided against a move
for himself, but Lord Simonds, the Lord Chancellor, and Lord
Alexander, the Minister of Defence, retired. Their replace-
ments were, respectively, David Maxwell Fyfe, the Home
Secretary, and (unexpectedly, to those not in the know)
Harold Macmillan. Duncan Sandys replaced Macmillan at the
Ministry of Housing and Local Government, and David Eccles
took Miss Horsbrugh's place as Minister of Education. Gwilym
Lloyd George, the Minister of Food, whose Ministry had
almost disappeared, succeeded Maxwell Fyfe at the Home
Office, and the remnants of the Ministry of Food were transferred to the Ministry of Agriculture, now headed by
Heathcoat Amory. Osbert Peake, the Minister of Pensions, was
promoted to the Cabinet, and, outside the Cabinet still,
Selwyn Lloyd became Minister of Supply in succession to
Sandys. Maxwell Fyfe on his promotion to be Lord Chancellor
took the title of Lord Kilmuir. *The Times* reported that the
changes reduced the average age of the Cabinet by two and a
half years; this was much less than Salisbury and others had
hoped for.[83]

10 Setting the People Free

If Eden was the undisputed number two in the Cabinet, by 1954 Butler had become the undisputed number three. When Eden was ill in America he had acknowledged Eden's priority above himself,[1] but his own achievement as acting Premier while both Churchill and Eden were disabled earned him the respect of both his own colleagues and of the wider public.[2] When in January 1954 he arrived in Sydney, Australia, for the opening of the Commonwealth Economic Conference, at which he led the British delegation, it was announced that he had been appointed a Companion of Honour.[3] During that year, largely owing to favourable terms of trade, the British economy continued to improve, and the Conservative objective of 'setting the people free' was gradually achieved by the ending of food rationing and the consequent reduction of the officialdom of the Ministry of Food. Tea, which came from within the sterling area, was freed of rationing in October 1952, followed in 1953 by chocolate and sweets, eggs and sugar. In May 1954 margarine, cooking fat, cheese and butter all came off the ration, and in July meat and bacon also.[4]

However, the pound sterling was still not convertible. The 'Collective Approach' to convertibility, to which Britain was pledged along with its sterling area partners, could not be realised until the American Administration committed itself to a more open policy, and although the Randall Report on External Monetary Policy, presented to Congress in January 1954, recommended various steps in this direction, it did not encourage an early return to convertibility for Britain; in fact it stated that 'Britain's reserves must be strengthened' before the move could be made.[5] Butler returned to England from Australia by way of India and Pakistan, but Robert Hall, now formally his Economic Adviser (and knighted in the New Year Honours), travelled by way of the United States where he talked to Treasury officials. He was reassured that the recession there would be 'shallow', but 'the Administration was still fairly weak and they were not doing any work on our Memorandum.'[6] Butler was evidently still worried about the fear of an American slump when he presented his Budget, which was notable for its absence of concessions to the tax-payer – even though Hall claimed to have 'managed to get the Chancellor to play down the loss of revenue expected because of a hypothetical U.S. slump.'[7] Although the *Economic Survey* published at the end of March showed a sterling area surplus of gold and dollar reserves for 1953 of £240 million, the budget which followed a few days later contained none of those 'rare and refreshing fruits' of which Gladstone had once spoken, the only important change being an increase of investment allowances for industry.[8]

But Butler was pleased by the comment of *The Economist* on 4 July: 'The miracle has happened – full employment without inflation, and this despite the heavy burden of defence, the rising burden of the social services, and some reduction in taxation.'

As he told his colleagues, however, 'the miracle must not be followed by disillusionment.' He therefore called for further cuts in expenditure in the immediate future.[9] He had warned the Prime Minister a day earlier that civil expenditure in 1955–56 would be £70 million higher, defence expenditure would be £200 million higher, and 'revenue will be less because Department trading receipts will be less.' The last point meant that stocks built up by the Ministries of Food and Materials would have been disposed of.[10]

The result was that Cabinet Committees were established to try to make the necessary economies. Swinton first of all took charge of the committee examining civil expenditure, and recommended an increase in prescription charges from one shilling per form to one shilling per item, and an increase in the charge for school milk from 7d per pupil per week to one shilling. He also recommended cuts in agricultural and food subsidies.[11] Meanwhile, a Defence Policy Review Committee had proposed not only to substantially reduce the expenditure on Civil Defence but also largely to disband the Anti-Aircraft Command, but this Committee, under Salisbury, had still not reduced the defence total to Butler's maximum of £1,500 million, for, including the costs of the British Army of the Rhine which the Treasury would now have to find without aid from West Germany, the bill still stood at £1,650 million. So the Prime Minister ordered a 'further scrutiny' of the estimates by 'a small group of Ministers'.[12]

This 'small group of Ministers' in fact consisted of Swinton once again, Duncan Sandys, the Minister of Supply, and in the absence of Alexander who was visiting North America, Nigel Birch, the Parliamentary Secretary of the Ministry of Defence. Its composition aroused the wrath of Alexander on his return in mid-August; he was particularly incensed by the role of Sandys in the affair, as the latter had long been advocating heavy cuts in the Army and Navy.[13] Alexander wrote rather tartly to the Prime Minister on 13 August: 'You will, I am sure, appreciate that it will be very difficult for me to serve you if I don't enjoy your confidence.'[14] Churchill replied emolliently:

> As you were away for a month the Cabinet felt you would not wish the scrutiny of the Service Estimates to be discontinued. Nigel Birch was at this small Committee on all occasions and to make sure that everything was in order I took the chair myself on the first occasion, thus making it a Cabinet Committee headed by the Prime Minister... The only reason why Duncan Sandys took part was because he has a lot of knowledge of the subject and is not committed to any one Service Department.[15]

Churchill also telephoned to Swinton warning him that Alexander was 'vexed at Duncan's intervention'.[16] A further sidelight on the feelings of all the Defence Ministers is provided by a letter from Jim Thomas, the First Lord, to Eden; he reported that at the first meeting of the Committee Antony Head, the Minister for War, turned up at No. 10 and gave the others '$\frac{1}{2}$ hour of the best and then swept out!' Thomas added: 'I hope you will mark this against Duncan who for some time now has constituted himself Minister of Defence. Actually he should be in the dock along with the rest of us not in the Judgment Seat...Bill [De L'Isle] is quite happy as Philip [Swinton] and Duncan are heavily biassed in favour of his bombers already!'[17] The bombers, it should be added, were designed to carry the country's ultimate deterrent, the atomic bomb.

The new Defence Review Committee did not present its report to the Cabinet until early November, by which time Alexander had been replaced by Harold Macmillan and Sandys by Selwyn Lloyd. At this meeting, Admiral Sir Rhoderick McGrigor, the First Sea Lord, objected to the naval economies, saying that more aircraft-carriers were needed to protect seaborne convoys, to act against 'the threat of Russian fleet activities' and for 'amphibious operations against Norway'. The Prime Minister, however, was in an economising mood: 'He was not convinced that the large and increasing resources which would be absorbed by the Fleet Air Arm were justified.' It was agreed that the withdrawal of forces from overseas stations – Suez and Korea in particular – should be expedited, with a view to bringing the 1955 defence estimates down to a total of £1,525 million.[18] A few days later Macmillan said that he would announce the reduction in Anti-Aircraft Command, the disbandment of several infantry battalions and the reorganisation of the Auxiliary Air Force in the debate on the Address.[19]

In his Budget speech in April, Butler had said that he was deferring increases in old age and disability pensions until the next session on the grounds that the issue had to await the report of the Committee under the chairmanship of Sir Thomas Phillips, a former Permanent Secretary of the Ministry of National Insurance. The Committee, which he had appointed in July 1953, was to look into the 'Economic and Financial Problems of Provision for Old Age'.[20] The issue raised serious actuarial problems, owing to the increasing number of old people and the consequent need for an increase in contributions. Osbert Peake, the Minister of Pensions and National Insurance who would have to undertake the legislation, was, as already noted, promoted to membership of the Cabinet in Churchill's mid-October changes.[21]

Meanwhile a Select Committee on Members' Expenses had reported to the Commons in February. Under the chairmanship of the Liberal leader, Clement Davies, it had unanimously recommended that, in order to keep up with inflation since 1946, when Members' salaries were last increased, they should be raised from the existing level of £1,000 to £1,500 a year.[22] Attlee wrote to *The Times* to support the proposal:

> In my time I have known members who either through sickness or infirmity were unable to perform their duties but, having no income in prospect, they hung on to their seats and no one had the heart to suggest that they should retire.

> Indeed, some of my most painful memories are of members
> of my own party who were obviously dying on their feet and
> yet appeared in the House because they could not afford to
> retire.[23]

But when the Cabinet came to discuss the issue in mid-March,
its members were given to understand that 'Conservative
opinion in Parliament and in the country was strongly against
the...proposal.' Conservative Members felt that their con-
stituents would be enraged if the Government was seen to be
raising MPs' salaries while doing nothing about old age pensioners. It was decided to have a Commons debate on the
question, without a division, to test the feeling of Members
generally.[24]

On 14 April Churchill told the Commons that although
the Select Committee's Report 'commands respect', the
Government had decided against a direct increase in salary. He
suggested that alternative schemes might be considered.[25]
Churchill's natural instinct was to be generous to Members,
but he was restrained by the feeling in the 1922 Committee,
which he had met on 7 April.[26] But the debate that took place
upon the adjournment on 13 May showed a sharp division
between the two parties, with Butler arguing in favour of a sub-
sistence allowance or a sum for expenses free of tax. He said:

> We shall have to take the decision on this matter in the light
> of views expressed by hon. Members themselves, and also of
> public opinion which is sensitive to the issue and which no
> hon. Member would be wise to neglect.[27]

Labour MPs were far from satisfied with this discussion which
had led to no vote, and later in the month, on 24 May, George
Thomas, one of the Cardiff Members, proposed a motion in
favour of the increase as suggested by the Select Committee.
He was seconded by the maverick Conservative Robert
Boothby, and the motion was carried by 280 votes to 166 – a
majority of 114.[28]

Caught between the emphatic free vote of the House and
the bitter hostility of the great majority of the Conservative
Party to any increase, the Cabinet remained in a quandary. On
1 June the 1922 Committee met again, and according to a
report secured by the Chief Whip:

Sir Robert Boothby and Mr Hugh Fraser defended their action in voting for the increase. Sir Robert Boothby was again very badly received. He stated that provided there was a free vote each Member was in a perfectly tenable position in his constituency, but this view was shouted down.[29]

On 2 June the Cabinet discussed the situation, and were told that 'five-sixths of their supporters in the House' had voted against the increase. The Prime Minister said that Butler must find some other way of 'improving the financial position of Members'.[30] Woolton sent a note to Eden enclosing a report by Stephen Pierssene, the General Director of Conservative Central Office, which declared:

> No subject has so stirred party feelings since the war, nor has the Party view been so overwhelmingly opposed to the proposed intentions of its own Government and of Parliament...There is no doubt that all the odium will be directed against the Government and that the Socialists will naturally make political capital out of it.[31]

Finally, the Prime Minister was authorised to make a statement on 24 June suggesting a discussion of allowances with the Opposition, to take the place of the proposed salary increase. He announced the Cabinet's agreed details on 8 July: £2 a day for any day on which the House was sitting, except for Fridays.[32] The only concession which the Opposition obtained was to have the allowances paid from 24 May – the date of the resolution calling for an increase.[33] The Labour Party was so affronted by the Government's attitude that it decided to refuse 'pairs' for Members absent on official duty.[34]

In the summer of 1954 the 1922 Committee was riding high, even at the expense of a Cabinet Minister's career. It not only carried through Independent Television and secured a limitation upon Members' salaries, it also forced the resignation of the Minister of Agriculture, Sir Thomas Dugdale, for failing to discipline civil servants of his Department over the Crichel Down affair.

Crichel Down in Dorset had been requisitioned before the war as a bombing range for the Royal Air Force. But in January 1950, as the RAF no longer required it, the land was turned over to the Ministry of Agriculture. In that year Lieutenant-Commander G.G. Marten, who had married the daughter and heiress of Lord Alington who had owned part of Crichel Down, applied to buy it back. But the Ministry placed the land in the charge of the Land Commission, with the intention of improving it and then letting it as a single unit. However, after the 1951 General Election Marten resumed his efforts to recover the land, which he thought was rightfully his, or rather his wife's. He took up the case with the local MP, R.F. Crouch, who was himself a farmer. Crouch first wrote on Marten's behalf to George Nugent, who was one of the two Parliamentary Secretaries of the Ministry of Agriculture. But the Ministry remained obdurate, and early in 1953 the land was transferred to Crown Lands and a tenant selected.

The Commissioner of Crown Lands, C.G. Eastwood, was new to his job, having just been transferred from the Colonial Office. Faced with the problem of applications for the tenancy which had been submitted before the one already selected was chosen, he wrote that it would be necessary 'at least to appear to implement the promises made to them'. An Under-Secretary at the Ministry agreed: 'We can consider whether there is anything that can be done with a view, at any rate, to appear to be implementing past promises.' In September the Crown Lands' tenant was installed. At that point, after several further approaches to the Ministry had been turned down, Marten formed a 'Crichel Down Protest Committee' and sent to Whitehall a petition with numerous signatures.

On 20 October the Food and Agriculture Committee of the 1922 Committee discussed the question, and Dugdale was invited to attend. Shortly afterwards he at last saw Marten personally and told him that he would institute a Public Inquiry. A Cabinet Committee chaired by Maxwell Fyfe concluded early in 1954 that a previous owner should at least have 'an opportunity of buying it...in competition with other prospective purchasers'.[35] The Inquiry, which was held at Blandford, heard witnesses for a week at the end of April and the Officer appointed, Sir Andrew Clark QC, submitted his report to the Minister in mid-May.[36] It was published as a White Paper on 15 June. *The Times* said that the report 'has thrown disquieting light on how bureaucracy, left to itself, is capable of acting.' It added:

The only crumb of comfort for the citizen in Sir Andrew's findings is that all concerned are entirely acquitted of suspicion of bribery or corruption... What is needed to clear the air is an assurance from the Front Bench that the Government are resolved...to give dispossessed owners of land most favoured treatment – and further, to take every step to see that, within the narrowest limits of national necessity, acquired land is released, fairly and promptly, from State control.[37]

Dugdale, in an interim Commons statement on Sir Andrew's report, said of the civil servants who were censured: 'I am satisfied that no further action by me in relation to them is necessary.'[38] But when he met the Food and Agriculture Committee of the party a few days before the promised Crichel Down debate, *The Times* found that feeling was running high against him:

> Many took the view that by his interim statement on the report the Minister had committed himself to the shielding of civil servants who should be disciplined, and that unless he is prepared to take some further action – which would now be difficult – he should resign.[39]

Robert Carr, Eden's Parliamentary Private Secretary, wrote to him to give him the current news, and included this account of the backbenchers' meeting:

> The Party is still feeling strongly on this matter and David M-F [Maxwell Fyfe] quite failed to allay the fears. Tommy Dugdale is far too popular personally for it to be a case of hunting him to death. But I am sure the majority feel he must resign on the issue, and several speakers said this at the meeting. There is a sad feeling about him – no one wants to hurt him but having condoned instead of condemned the mistakes (and worse) of his Civil Servants, his own resignation seems to many people the only way out.[40]

The Prime Minister appointed a small committee of three – two retired civil servants and a businessman – to advise on the transfer of the five men found most culpable by Sir Andrew Clark. This report was circulated to the Cabinet on 19 July. Eastwood was returned to the Colonial Office and three of the four others were assigned to different duties within the Ministry of Agriculture.[41] The debate on Crichel Down finally took place on 20 July. It was opened by the Minister himself. He gave a detailed account of the Crichel Down story, and announced that 'it is our policy progressively to get rid of emergency powers which permit private interests in land to be overridden.' He indicated that disciplinary action was being taken after all against those who had been censured in the report. He then concluded, to the surprise of the House:

> Having now had this opportunity of rendering account to Parliament of the actions which I thought fit to take, I have, as the Minister responsible during the period, tendered my resignation to the Prime Minister, who is submitting it to the Queen.

He had in fact resigned on the previous day at an interview with the Prime Minister.[42]

Norman Chester, a wartime civil servant turned academic, reflected on the case in the journal *Public Administration*. He wrote:

> Primarily Crichel Down was a failure of political sensitivity. It would appear that the Minister of Agriculture continued, with little or no change, the policy of his predecessor notwithstanding that the Conservative Government had come to power avowedly to handle government controls rather differently and with much greater regard for individual interests.

He added also that 'Crichel Down revealed failures in the Civil Service process. For one thing there was undoubtedly a fair amount of sheer inefficiency.' He pointed out that there was no one person fully in charge, and inaccuracies in detail occurred. As for the attitude of civil servants to the public in general, he quoted the telling circular which Edward Bridges, the Permanent Secretary to the Treasury, despatched to them all afterwards:

> The circumstances that led up to this report have brought forcibly to their Lordships' attention, as to that of the country as a whole, the need for constant vigilance to ensure respect for the rights and feelings of individual

members of the community who may be affected by the work of Departments. The confidence of the public in the administration of Government Departments depends upon this vigilance.[43]

As for Dugdale, Churchill described his resignation, in a letter immediately published, as 'chivalrous in a high degree', and Oliver Lyttelton, in a private letter to Eden, remarked acidly that 'The Party...are not the Gents they used to be but have such a large percentage of 30/- suits in search of portfolios.'[44]

At the end of July Churchill had to replace two of his Cabinet Ministers – Oliver Lyttelton, who was retiring from the Colonial Office in order to return to business and make some money before his old age, and Dugdale. Eden was particularly upset by Lyttelton's departure; he regarded him as an important ally in the Cabinet who had sent him many friendly letters full of gossip during his illness. Lyttelton had survived two major parliamentary challenges to his Colonial policy in 1953: one in October in British Guiana where he authorised the Governor, Sir Alfred Savage, to suspend the constitution after an unduly partisan ministry was formed; the other in November, when he allowed Sir Andrew Cohen, the Governor of Uganda to impose a sentence of exile on the Kabaka of Buganda, a hereditary ruler who feared the impact of an East African Federation. On both issues Lyttelton defended his position with considerable success.[45] On his retirement his post was taken by Alan Lennox-Boyd, who had been Minister of Transport outside the Cabinet; Dugdale's place was taken by Derick Heathcoat Amory. The new Minister of Transport was John Boyd-Carpenter, who had been Financial Secretary to the Treasury. This was not a major reconstruction of the Government, and, as *The Times* said, 'The feeling must persist that this can only be a prelude to the more far-reaching changes in structure and in personalities which the Government need after their nearly three years in office.'[46]

In July Butler presided over a meeting of the Organisation for European Economic Co-operation, to discuss the prospects for convertibility. The meeting, held at Church House, Westminster, produced no communiqué, and this was because, as Butler indicated afterwards, the American representatives (who were there only as observers) were unable to promise any action by the United States to implement the Randall Report.[47] President Eisenhower had attempted to persuade Congress that year to pursue 'good creditor' policies, and it was true that in 1953 and 1954 there had been extensive 'offshore' purchases by the American Defense Department. But with Congress's desire for economy in the future, the prospect for 1955 onwards was bleak, and Butler probably also feared that with a British General Election on the horizon there was danger of a 'run' on sterling.[48]

In late September Butler crossed the Atlantic to represent Britain at the annual meeting of the World Bank and the International Monetary Fund. He went a few days early to visit Canada and stay with the Governor-General, Vincent Massey, whom he had known during his eleven years as High Commissioner in London. Butler's own son, Adam, was one of the Governor-General's two aides-de-camp, and one object of Butler's visit to Canada was to tell his son that his mother was slowly dying of cancer of the jaw. He had warned Massey beforehand: 'I am the prey of one of the greatest enemies of mankind, so I do not know if there might not be last minute adjustments.'[49] In the end, his wife, after much suffering, died in December.

When Butler reached Washington, all that George Humphrey, the American Treasury Secretary, could do was to assure him that Eisenhower would 'press vigorously for the enactment of the Administration's trade liberalisation program' when the new Congress met in January 1955.[50] So Butler's hopes of early United States tariff reduction and simplification and elimination of 'Buy American' clauses in American legislation were doomed to failure, as were the hopes of early convertibility of the pound.[51] He told reporters:

> If the United States placed 1.5 per cent of its national income in fresh investment overseas – the British figure – that would mean that $5,000 millions a year would become available to strengthen world trade. A further one per cent of the American market in manufactured goods...would mean much to Britain and the entire sterling area.[52]

In spite of the delay in the return to convertibility, Butler was justified in taking an optimistic view of the British economy. As G.D.N. Worswick, an Oxford economist by no means friendly to the Conservative Party, wrote at the end of the decade:

> Industrial production and gross national product were rising strongly, and exports began to rise again at the end of 1953...[R]etail prices ...did indeed rise, first, because of the subsidy cuts and later as a result of decontrol (meat and tea for example), but for the majority of people the rise in money incomes was as great or greater than the rise in prices. Employment rose and unemployment fell, from 450,000 at the beginning of 1953 to 280,000 at the end of 1954. To the layman, at any rate, the claim that 'Conservative freedom' worked might not seem to lack foundation.[53]

The only clear weakness of Government policy had been the concentration – as the result of an election pledge – upon housing at the expense of industrial investment. But the investment allowances triggered in the 1954 Budget did initiate what Worswick called an 'investment boom'. And there was a corresponding boom in consumer goods – 'motor cars, refrigerators, washing machines, television sets, vacuum cleaners and other domestic appliances', encouraged by the removal of hire-purchase restrictions in August 1953.[54]

It was not surprising, therefore, that at the Trades Union Congress at Brighton in September 1954 the policy of wage restraint was upheld by a majority of three to two, and that Richard Crossman could say of the ensuing Labour Party Conference that 'there wasn't a single home issue on which there was a spark of interest.'[55] Even on German Rearmament, where there was a fierce conflict, in the end the Conference decided to back the Government line. The internecine warfare within the Labour Party, between the Bevanite intellectuals and the more moderate right-wing leadership, was much more prominent than any disagreement with the Government.

Butler arrived back in England as the Conservative Party Conference was assembling, and he hardly had time to prepare his speech to the delegates before he made it. This was the first time that a party conference had been televised, and the cameras naturally concentrated on the chairman,

Anthony Eden, it still being the practice for the Leader of the
Party – Churchill – to make his appearance only for a closing
speech. Butler spoke on the Friday (8 October), and offered
the slogan 'Invest in Success'. But the sentence in his speech
which really roused the delegates was his comment: 'I see no
reason why, in the next quarter of a century, if we run our
policy properly and soundly, we should not double our standard of living in this country.'[56]

A week later, the more drastic Cabinet changes which had
already been forecast were announced. Lord Simonds retired
from the Woolsack to be replaced by Sir David Maxwell Fyfe,
and the latter's successor as Home Secretary was Major Gwilym
Lloyd George, whose post as Minister of Food was amalga-
mated with that of the Minister of Agriculture. Lord Alexander
also retired, to be succeeded by Harold Macmillan. The latter
was replaced as Housing Minister by Duncan Sandys, the
Minister of Supply. The new Minister of Supply was to be
Selwyn Lloyd, and Nigel Birch became Minister of Works, both
still outside the Cabinet. Florence Horsbrugh, the Minister of
Education gave up her post and left the Cabinet, being created
a Dame, and her successor was Sir David Eccles, formerly
Minister of Works. *The Times* remained concerned about 'the
date of the change-over' – that is to say from Churchill to Eden
– and it queried the amalgamation of Food with Agriculture: 'It
is asking too much of any Minister to be able to hold the
balance fairly between the interests of the consumer and the
powerful agricultural interest.'[57] The latter point was echoed
next day in Parliament when Attlee remarked: 'Is not the amalgamation rather like that of the young lady and the tiger?'[58]
Neither commented on the departure of the only woman in
the Cabinet, but she was not thought to have been a success, at
any rate by the Chief Whip.[59]

Attlee's comment had been made on the reassembly of
Parliament for the fag-end of the Session. *The Times* noted that
there were 'fewer apparent issues dividing the parties than
there were three years ago.'[60] And Churchill, addressing
the Lord Mayor's Banquet at the Guildhall, said that the
Government had:

> found a strong measure of responsibility among many of the
> leaders of the Opposition and among the strongest – I do

not say the loudest – elements in their rank and file. This, and the sober, stable view of the great trade unions, have aided Her Majesty's Government in the conduct of foreign affairs, and given the feeling that a government in this ancient kingdom has a stature and substance considerably above the ordinary ins and outs of party politics.[61]

Meanwhile the Government had already given much thought to the legislative programme for the 1954–55 Session, as it was expected to be the last before a General Election. In April Woolton and other senior Ministers had discussed the timing of the next election with Churchill and attempted to persuade him that, owing to the danger of the increase of unemployment which might be the result of the expected American recession, it was desirable to go to the country sooner rather than later.[62] On 5 May the Cabinet appointed a Cabinet Committee under Crookshank's chairmanship to consider what measures might be put forward for legislation in 1954–55, and also invited the Home Secretary – still David Maxwell Fyfe – to consider how the remaining Defence Regulations could be dismantled.[63] Crookshank's committee reported in late July with a series of necessary bills – economy bills, bills to abolish emergency powers and 'social welfare and other useful bills' – of which he hoped an 'essential minimum' would be included in the Queen's Speech.[64] Next day, Maxwell Fyfe submitted a paper pointing out that, out of 215 regulations which the Government had inherited in 1951, only 60 would remain by the end of 1954. And certain regulations would have to be kept, for instance that sustaining exchange control, that maintaining the Industrial Disputes Tribunal and that allowing open-cast mining. But it would be possible, by legislation, to extinguish the comprehensive powers of economic control at present available under Defence Regulation 55 and related regulations. It would thus ensure that another Government could not reintroduce economic control without fresh parliamentary authority.[65]

Iain Macleod, the Minister of Health, wrote to Eden to suggest that the abolition of controls should go into the election manifesto rather than in the programme for the next Session. He argued that 'Defence Regulation 55 sounds very terrifying when declaimed, but the people of this country don't believe and won't believe that Attlee's Socialist party is hellbent on expropriation of all property.' He himself preferred to 'give effect to the various Gowers Reports on Health, Welfare and Safety.' Sir Ernest Gowers had chaired a committee appointed in 1945 to deal with the closing-hours of shops and to 'make recommendations regarding the statutory regulations regarding the health, welfare and safety of those employed and...the hours of employment of young persons.'[66] Although the committee had made various reports, the first as early as 1947, they had never been followed by legislation, and even now Butler thought that 'we must be very careful':

> The bill on Agriculture, for example...includes a series of rather silly regulations about washing places, clean towels, etc., which though kind hearted, might be regarded by farmers and workers as ridiculous, especially after the severe economic strain imposed by the present disastrous weather... The same consideration applies to Industry... The best bet under Gowers...would therefore seem to be the Shops Bill.[67]

Late in October the Cabinet appointed a committee under Butler's chairmanship to draft the Queen's Speeches on the Prorogation and at the Opening of the new Parliament, which was not to be until 30 November.[68] There was no sign of any Gowers Bill in the final draft, nor of any legislation to dismantle Defence Regulations. The emphasis was put on old age pensions; the removal of 'wartime powers and regulations' and the enactment of legislation based on the Gowers Reports duly appeared in the manifesto for the next election.

Churchill was already conscious that MPs of all parties were going to make a special celebration of his eightieth birthday on 30 November, which was also the day of the State Opening of Parliament. At the request of a committee of Members of both Houses, he gave a number of sittings to the distinguished portrait painter Graham Sutherland. One week before his birthday, he went to Woodford, his constituency in Essex, to attend the presentation of a portrait to his wife Clementine. He made an extemporary speech on this occasion in which he claimed:

Even before the war had ended...I telegraphed to Lord Montgomery directing him to be careful in collecting German arms, to stack them so that they could easily be issued to the German soldiers whom we should have to work with if the Soviet advance continued.[69]

A *Times* leader-writer reproved him:

Why? What on earth made him say it? It certainly will not help to convince the Russians that the Western Powers are straightforward in their declarations of peace today. Nor, by suggesting that we were ready to use Nazi-indoctrinated troops in 1945, will it help the cause of West German rearmament now... The idea was unrealistic at the time; it is unwise to come out with it now.[70]

On 1 December Shinwell asked him for an explanation in the Debate on the Address, and Churchill apologised, admitting that no such telegram could be found.[71] The debate took place in the friendly atmosphere engendered by the celebration of Churchill's birthday on the preceding day.

The presentation of his own portrait took place in Westminster Hall immediately after the State opening of Parliament. The hall was crowded, and Churchill and Clementine were greeted at midday by the members of the committee who organised the occasion, including political opponents, notably Jennie Lee, who was there with her husband Aneurin Bevan. Winston and Clementine took their seats on either side of the Speaker, and Attlee then made a felicitous speech recalling the episodes of Churchill's life, including the Dardanelles campaign, in which (although he did not say so) he himself had taken part: 'I wish that you had had full power to carry it to success.' He concluded his speech with a quotation from Tennyson's *Ulysses*:

Old age hath yet his honour and his toil... Some work of noble note may yet be done.[72]

The portrait was then unveiled, and Churchill, who had already seen it and disliked it owing to Sutherland's rather cruel depiction of himself, nevertheless made an acceptance speech which conveyed, with much good humour, his sense of the honour which Parliament had conferred upon him:

I am most grateful to Mr Attlee for the agreeable words he has used about me this morning, and for the magnanimous appraisal that he has given of my variegated career. I must confess, however, that this ceremony and all its charm and splendour may well be found to have seriously affected my controversial value as a party politician. However, perhaps with suitable assistance I shall get over this reaction and come round after a bit.[73]

The Father of the House, Dai Grenfell, had presented the Prime Minister with a volume containing the signature of all but 26 MPs – and some of the latter, who had been away or ill, added their signatures later. Lord Salisbury then paid a tribute on behalf of the members of the House of Lords, and finally Churchill with Clementine went out down the aisle of the Hall, to receive another ovation from a crowd assembled outside in New Palace Yard.

In his reply to Attlee, Churchill had said of the portrait that it was 'a remarkable example of modern art', and his comment drew 'prolonged applause and laughter'. He added: 'It certainly combines force with candour. These are qualities which no active member of either House can do without or should fear to meet.' This comment drew further laughter.[74] But his true reaction to the portrait was expressed in a comment to his doctor, Lord Moran, to whom he said: 'You can't look a gift horse in the mouth.' It preyed on his mind so much that after a few months Clementine secretly destroyed it.[75]

11 The Last Session

Members of the Cabinet were conscious that in late 1954 they were entering the last Session of the existing Parliament. Having completed the great bulk of their election programme, they now sought to satisfy the most powerful of the external pressure groups, the old age pensioners. Osbert Peake, the Minister of Pensions and National Insurance, told Parliament on 1 December when he presented the National Insurance Bill that pensions would rise by about half as much again as they had been set by the Labour Government in 1946. For a single man the weekly payment, which had been 26 shillings, would now rise to 40 shillings; for a couple it would rise from 42 shillings to 65. This was, if anything, somewhat ahead of the cost of living, which had risen in the period by 44 per cent. But insurance payments were also to go up by one shilling each for employer and employee.[1] The Minister had in fact agreed these changes with the Chancellor in mid-November. At that time he reckoned that the Bill could be passed by mid-February.[2] But the Cabinet, while accepting the proposals, insisted that the legislation should be carried before Christmas, although asserting that: 'There is no evidence of any widespread hardship among old age pensioners.[3]

On 3 December the Phillips Report was at last published. It pointed to the actuarial problem, which it summed up as follows:

Today the number of men and women of pensionable age is just under seven million, or about 2 in 15 of the population..... In 1979 the proportion is likely to be nearly 3 in 15.

The Report therefore recommended that the pensionable age should be raised from 65 to 68 for men, and from 60 to 63 for women. But there were memoranda of dissent from three members of the Committee – the two trade union members, who were against any alteration in the date of retirement, and Dame Janet Vaughan, the only woman, who recommended 'parity between pension ages for men and women'.[4]

Moving the Second Reading of the Bill on 8 December, the Minister indicated that the Government had rejected the main recommendation of the Phillips Report of raising the age of entitlement, which would certainly have been seized upon by the Opposition as an issue of controversy. Dr Edith Summerskill, for Labour, did not quarrel with the new rates, which were not ungenerous, but deplored the fact that they would not operate until April or May when the new books were ready. She also maintained that the Exchequer grant, which had been a component of all old age pension schemes since their introduction in 1909, was inadequate. It had been one-fifth of the total sum in 1946; now it was to be only one-seventh.[5] As Douglas Jay stated on the second day of the debate, the Labour Party had decided not to divide the House on the Bill,[6] but the General Council of the TUC sent a delegation to see the Minister about this a few days later; he did not give way.[7] The National Insurance Bill was duly enacted before the Christmas Recess.[8]

An issue which came to the fore in the later months of 1954 was that of 'coloured [i.e. black]' immigration, especially from the West Indies. In early February Churchill had warned the Cabinet that:

> .....the rapid improvement of communications was likely to lead to a continuing increase in the number of coloured people coming to this country, and their presence would sooner or later come to be resented by large sections of the British people.

But he added:

> It might well be true, however, that the problem has not yet assumed sufficient proportions to enable the Government to take adequate counter-measures.

Meanwhile the Commonwealth and Colonial Secretaries were asked to find out what powers other Governments possessed to deport British subjects.[9]

The upshot of the enquiries was instructive. All the white dominions except New Zealand had powers to deport 'indigent immigrants as well as criminals and undesirables'. In the Colonies, 'powers to restrict immigration are generally invoked in order to protect indigenous peoples against undesirable Europeans.'[10]

In late November the Home Secretary reported to the Cabinet that the rate of coloured immigration was now about 10,000 a year; he thought that a Departmental Committee should be appointed to frame legislation, and the Cabinet agreed.[11] But Swinton, while agreeing that the Dominions had nothing to complain about, pointed out that if preferential treatment were given to citizens of the Irish Republic, they would have grounds for complaint.[12] Early in December Lennox-Boyd, the now Colonial Secretary, put in a paper saying 'we should strenuously avoid doing or saying anything now which could be interpeted as favouring racially discriminatory action.'[13] He was invited by the Cabinet to join the Home Secretary in drawing up draft legislation.[14] In mid-January the Home Secretary reported that 'the preparation of a bill is now in hand.'[15]

Ministers were still in two minds about what action should be taken. Harold Macmillan thought that the problem should be 'ventilated'. He concluded that 'legislation is hopeless unless it is agreed between all parties.'[16] When the Cabinet discussed the matter again at the end of January, they were told that Cyril Osborne, a Tory backbencher, had been proposing to introduce a Bill under the ten-minute rule, but had been persuaded not to by a meeting of the Conservative Commonwealth Affairs Committee. The Cabinet thought that this was no bad thing in view of Princess Margaret's forthcoming visit to the West Indies 'and the recent election in Jamaica of a government whose future policy was unpredictable.'[17]

The only further development before the spring was that the Cabinet received the draft of a White Paper detailing the immigration controls of the members of the Commonwealth and Colonies.[18] Norman Brook, the Cabinet Secretary, warned the Prime Minister that its publication 'may provoke a lot of awkward questions.' He doubted if it was wise 'to give unnecessary advertisement to this'.[19]

No legislation was enacted until 1961.

At the Blackpool Conference of the Conservative Party in October 1954, Monckton emphasised the main principle of the Government's attitude to the trade unions: 'For myself I would say that the less party politics come into industrial relations the better for every one of us.' And he added:

Throughout my term of office, I must say how impressed I
have been – in what is not the easiest job of my life – by the
wisdom, moderation, and sense of responsibility of the great
bulk of the trade union movement, and of its members, certainly of the TUC itself.[20]

Nevertheless the unions were increasingly getting involved
in demarcation disputes, in spite of the TUC's own
Bridlington Agreement of 1939, whereby the unions bound
themselves not to 'poach' members from each other. One
major conflict of this sort arose in the docks, where the
Transport and General Workers' virtual monopoly was challenged by the National Union of Stevedores and Dockers. In
August 1954 the Stevedores and Dockers took advantage of a
dispute at Hull to recruit members there.[21] Then in October,
using the London dockers' grievance about compulsory overtime, they precipitated a major strike on the Thames which
already by the 7th left 130 ships idle, with 17,000 dockers on
strike.[22] By the 20th the strike had spread to Merseyside and
Southampton and 288 ships were reported held up.[23]
Monckton had told the Commons on the 19th that he was appointing a Court of Inquiry, as the strike was:

having a serious effect on the country's export trade, it is
endangering food supplies, and it threatens to cause unemployment in other industries.[24]

Meanwhile a Cabinet Committee on Emergencies was
meeting, but it was reluctant to introduce military labour, and
Monckton informed the Committee on the 27th that the same
view was taken by the employers, the Port of London
Authority, and the Transport and General Workers:

They feared that its introduction would halt any drift back
to work, spread the strike to Smithfield Market, road transport workers and other workers and in fact precipitate a
miniature general strike.[25]

On the same day the Court of Inquiry which Monckton had
set up under Lord Evershed presented an interim report
which recognised the need to require 'reasonable overtime'
in the docks.[26] After Monckton had seen the various parties to
the dispute at the Ministry of Labour, the men returned to

work on 1 November. *The Times* bemoaned the damage to trade involved in establishing that overtime was 'voluntary but necessary',[27] but the Stevedores and Dockers had cause to celebrate the success of their inroads into the membership of the rival union.

A few weeks later it was the National Union of Railwaymen who were threatening another strike. The conflict was the result of an award by the Railway Staffs National Tribunal to engine drivers and firemen, the skilled element of the industry.[28] General Sir Brian Robertson, who had left the Army and was now Chairman of the British Transport Commission, asked the Minister of Transport if the Government would assist him to provide a pay increase, but when the Cabinet discussed the issue, Monckton opposed it on the ground that it would have a knock-on effect on other industries. Robertson was therefore told that there was no money available. The railwaymen reacted by calling a strike for 9 January.[29] Monckton responded by his now familiar technique of appointing a Court of Inquiry, this time under Sir John Cameron QC.[30]

But Monckton was taken aback to find himself under pressure from Churchill to somehow find money for the railwaymen. He turned to Eden for support. According to the latter's diary:

> He was sure we must stand firm, the whole Ministry of L[abour], the trade unionists of the Deakin etc variety, the employer and a minority of the N.U.R. [Railwaymen] were agreed. W[inston] on the other hand was very weak and eager for compromise and RAB was surprisingly in line with him. I expressed my surprise whereupon Walter said that he was afraid RAB was 'just sucking up to the old man.'[31]

The issue was still being debated at the first Cabinets of 1955. Eden noted on 6 January:

> W[inston] and I had rather a sharp altercation at Cabinet. He attacked me for being bellicose from the start and added 'You'll get your strike all right.' I countered that he had chucked his reins on the horse's neck and said I agreed with Times and M. Guardian leaders this morning.[32]

Both *The Times* and the *Guardian* had opposed pay increases without substantial concessions from the union in respect of more flexible working.

The conflict was resolved, however, in the union's favour by the interim Report of the Cameron Court of Inquiry. It said that: 'Having willed the end, the nation must will the means.' This implied that the railwaymen's demands, which Robertson agreed were not excessive, must somehow be met. *The Times* commented that the report was 'unhelpful' and that the union ought to make 'concessions' in return, that is to say, by improving working practices and eliminating 'feather-bedding'.[33] But the Cabinet, in the light of the report, gave the Transport Commission authority to accept the railwaymen's demands, and the strike was at once called off. The men secured an extra six shillings on their basic rates.

The Times now warned:

> It is in the nature of floods to advance when the dykes are down... It is very easy to arrange for large sums of money to change hands if those concerned have virtually been told that they do not need to worry where the money is coming from.[34]

But it also helped that Butler, perhaps prodded by Churchill, had been willing to provide the rationale for the Cabinet to abandon the strict policy of nationalised industries that they should balance their accounts 'taking one year with another'. He told the Cabinet on 4 January that:

> Their plans for modernising the railways, the promise of greater flexibility in freight charges and the economies to be secured by a redeployment of railway manpower, taken together, afford us prospects of making the railways profitable in the long term which would justify us in accepting an increased deficit for a further period.[35]

But James Stuart, who returned to Forres near Elgin after the Cabinet meetings, wrote a wry letter to Butler afterwards:

> Your remark to WSC about being as bad as Campbell of the N.U.R. amused me and was very true. He wanted 'Peace in (his) time' at almost any price. John Cameron Q.C. opened up an awkward issue but no doubt you are watching that. Apparently the tax-payer is under an obligation to foot the bill of any nationalised industry whether they work and try to put their house in order – or not. The Act of nationalisation said the opposite – to my mind.[36]

In mid–January Monckton's doctor ordered him to take a rest for some weeks. He went off to Sicily. On the day he went it was reported that the Transport Commission had reached full agreement with the railwaymen, but that the locomotive engineers were discontented, as they felt that their differential was being eroded.[37] At the end of January a British Railways development plan was announced, covering a 15-year period, involving the phasing out of steam locomotives and their replacement by diesel or electrification: it was to cost £1,200 million over the period.[38]

There was no great surge of wage demands after the railway settlement as *The Times* feared, but when Monckton returned to work in March he was faced with a strike that secured high visibility. The maintenance men on the London newspaper presses belonged to the Engineering Union or to the Electrical Trades Union, and on 25 March they struck against the newspaper proprietors in order to obtain direct representation, which they had not previously had. The news blackout, so far as the London papers were concerned, continued until 19 April, and thus readers missed the most notable of government changes – the retirement of the Prime Minister himself.

In late September 1954 the Cabinet agreed to hold a London Conference of Commonwealth Prime Ministers in late January and early February. An important issue of principle had to be discussed, namely that occasioned by the advance of the Gold Coast (later renamed Ghana) towards independence. Should African ex-colonies be admitted on a basis of equality with the existing members, or should there be a two-tier Commonwealth?[39] The matter had already been discussed in the Commonwealth Office and the Cabinet, Swinton having put up a paper to his colleagues which said: 'The only safe assumption is that the offer of anything short of full membership would be unacceptable.'[40] But the upshot of the meeting was that Swinton was appointed Chairman of a Cabinet Committee to consider the matter further. A paper was drafted expressing Swinton's views, and circulated to the Prime Ministers of Canada, Australia and New Zealand. (South Africa was not consulted at this stage: it was assumed that, in spite of the introduction of *apartheid*, her Prime Minister would agree to go along with the majority.) Late in

October 1954, Swinton visited Canada and broached the topic directly with St Laurent, the Prime Minister. He said that:

> The Gold Coast was likely to be the first and this was not likely to happen for three years. But it was felt we ought to be looking ahead and that we should have the opportunity of informal talks with some of the Commonwealth Prime Ministers....[W]hen a new country attained what we used to call 'Dominion Status' that country would almost certainly ask to be accepted as a full sovereign Member of the Commonwealth....We had considered whether anything in the nature of a two-tier system was practicable.... We had come to the conclusion that this would be impossible, and if it were attempted it would probably lead to a country, which we were anxious to retain in the Commonwealth, seceding.

Swinton added, however:

> This would not prevent our dealing differently on a number of matters with new Members. As the Prime Minister was aware, there were already matters on which we and the old Commonwealth countries exchanged complete information and ideas, which were not so fully shared with others.

St Laurent said that 'he felt that the conclusion we had come to was right.'[41]

It was particularly on defence matters that the Government sought consultation with the 'old' Commonwealth. Macmillan prepared for them a paper on defence strategy which was approved at a Cabinet in late December.[42] The upshot was that Australia and New Zealand both maintained commitments in Malaya.[43] Both countries also accepted Swinton's view of the future of Commonwealth membership: he listed the Central African Federation, the Gold Coast, the Malayan Federation, Nigeria and the West Indies Federation as likely candidates for admission 'within the next ten or twenty years'; but the development of Kenya, Tanganyika, Uganda and Sierra Leone he regarded as 'uncertain'. Menzies of Australia expressed his nostalgia for the old grouping of four, the 'white dominions' of Canada, Australia, New Zealand and South Africa: '[A]lready the number of second reading speeches made at these meetings is reducing their value, and affecting the old intimate association.' But he accepted that 'the separate meetings that we have had on defence at this Conference and which have become a recognised feature which all Commonwealth Governments accept is a useful precedent.' He did not think that South Africa would try to veto the admission of the Gold Coast, as her government 'is anxious not to be alone.'[44]

Meanwhile Eden and Churchill both recognised the importance of India in relation to international affairs. According to Shuckburgh, the Prime Minister said that he had told Nehru that 'he should be the light of Asia. to show all those millions how they can shine out, instead of accepting the doctrines of Communism.'[45] Nehru and Eden were both guests of the Mountbattens on the weekend of 5 and 6 February, but Eden found it difficult to talk politics because 'Edwina [Mountbatten] was so left-wing and hostile to Pakistan.'[46] Pakistan had decided to become a republic, which nevertheless the Conference agreed should not affect its status as a Member of the Commonwealth.[47]

The focus of British foreign policy was still the Far East, owing to the tension between China and the United States. On 2 December the Americans signed a mutual defence treaty with the Chinese Nationalists under Chiang Kai-shek, guaranteeing the island of Formosa (now known as Taiwan) and the Pescadores. The territories concerned were all at least 70 miles off the coast of mainland China, but Chiang's forces also occupied a few islands which were very close to the mainland – Quemoy, Matsu and the Tachens: these latter could be and were being bombarded from the mainland. Early in January Chiang agreed to evacuate the Tachen Islands, but he clung on to Quemoy and Matsu, which as *The Times* said 'have little strategic importance at all, except for picador kinds of raids.'[48]

When the Cabinet discussed the issue in February, it accepted Eden's view that 'large sections of world opinion' would disagree with the American Government if it publicly committed itself to the defence of the offshore islands; the Prime Minister agreed with this. 'The United States Government would be falling into an obvious trap if they made a public declaration' to that effect.[49] He wrote to Eisenhower to warn him:

You know how Anthony and I have tried to keep in step with you and how much we wish to continue to do so. But a war to keep the coastal islands for Chiang would not be defensible here.[50]

The President replied quickly to say that he could not control Chiang's actions over Quemoy and Matsu, but that the American guarantee extended only to Formosa itself and the Pescadores, and that Chiang had agreed not to undertake offensive operations against the mainland. He added, however:

It would surely not be popular in this country if we became involved in possible hostilies on account of Hong Kong or Malaya, which our people look upon as 'colonies' – which to us is a naughty word. Nevertheless I do not doubt that, if the issue were ever framed in this way, we would be at your side.[51]

On hearing this reply, the Cabinet were 'impressed' by the firmness with which the President had stated the considerations underlying the policy of the United States Administration in respect of the islands off the China coast;[52] Macmillan described it in his memoirs as 'a powerful, well-argued and persuasive document'.[53]

Meanwhile on 17 February Eden left London by air for the first meeting of the South East Asia Treaty Organisation at Bangkok. He was accompanied by a sizeable delegation: the party included Sir Anthony Rumbold, his Principal Private Secretary, and two other Private Secretaries, A.W. Graham and Robert Carr MP. The other Foreign Office members of the party were Sir Harold Caccia, a Deputy Under Secretary of State, W.D. (later Sir Denis) Allen and D.T. Holland, a legal adviser. Eden was also accompanied by his wife Clarissa, and by Field Marshal Sir John Harding, the Chief of the Imperial General Staff; they were joined by Malcolm MacDonald, the British Commissioner-General in South-East Asia.[54] On the way out he stopped briefly in Cairo, and met the Egyptian dictator Colonel Nasser, with whom he was photographed – to his subsequent embarrassment – shaking hands.[55] The meeting of the South East Asia Treaty Council lasted only three days, but it enabled Eden to discuss the problem of Formosa with Dulles. As he reported to the Commons, the Americans 'have effectively restrained the Chinese Nationalists in recent weeks from initiating attacks against the Chinese mainland.'[56]

On the way home Eden went to Singapore, where he discussed policy with British representatives in Vietnam, Cambodia and Laos, and he paid brief visits to Rangoon and to Delhi, where he again talked to Nehru. But his most important stop was at Baghdad, where he negotiated the framework of a new agreement with Iraq to replace the existing treaty on a basis of equality. He returned by way of Rome and was able to attend a Cabinet on 7 March; the treaty with Iraq was finalised by the end of the month.[57] Eden planned to visit Turkey for three days before then, but was prevented by influenza.[58]

As the results of the Defence Review emerged, Lord De L'Isle, the Air Minister, wrote to Harold Macmillan, the new Minister of Defence, to suggest that they should only be revealed very discreetly to the public:

> Like alcohol new ideas are best absorbed slowly into the system. Reliance on deterrents rather than defence won't be too palatable to the public.

Macmillan's comment on the letter was 'To use the modern debased vernacular, "I couldn't agree with you more".'[59] In the event the principal changes – the reliance on deterrents and the abolition of the Anti-Aircraft Command – were indicated by the Prime Minister in his speech on the Address on 1 December, but attention was diverted from them by his attempt to explain his gaffe at Woodford on 23 November when he said that at the time of the German surrender he had telegraphed Montgomery to stockpile German arms so that they could easily be issued to German troops again if necessary.[60]

The Defence White Paper was published on 17 February. Its most notable feature was that it stated clearly that Britain would manufacture 'thermo-nuclear bombs', commonly known as hydrogen bombs. The withdrawal of troops from Suez and Trieste and the reduction of those in Korea from divisional to brigade strength would allow a military strategic reserve to be created in the United Kingdom; however, although the Anti-Aircraft Command would be abolished, anti-aircraft defence would still be needed 'in the field and for the local defence of certain vital targets'. Fighter Command would still have major responsibilities, and a 'Mobile Defence Corps' would be formed 'as part of the R.A.F. reserve forces'. As for the Navy, it would contribute heavy carriers to the NATO fleet, and would also complete three cruisers with 'advanced artillery'.[61]

Churchill himself moved the Motion to approve the White Paper on 1 March. He pointed out that it was on Attlee's initiative that Britain had begun to make atomic weapons:

> Confronted with the hydrogen bomb, I have tried to live up to the right hon. Gentleman's standard. We have started to make that one, too. It is this grave decision which forms the core of the Defence Paper which we are discussing this afternoon.

And he added:

> There is no absolute defence against the hydrogen bomb, nor is any method in sight by which any nation, or any country, can be completely guaranteed against the devastating injury which even a score of them might inflict on wide regions.

He pointed out that now 'continents are vulnerable as well as islands' and argued that in these conditions 'safety will be the sturdy child of terror, and survival the twin brother of annihilation.' He referred only briefly to NATO and the role of conventional forces, and concluded:

> Mercifully, there is time and hope if we combine patience and courage. All deterrents will improve and gain authority during the next ten years. By that time, the deterrent may well reach its acme and reap its final reward. The day may dawn when fair play, love for one's fellow men, respect for justice and freedom, will enable tormented generations to march forth serene and triumphant from the hideous epoch in which we have had to dwell. Meanwhile never fear, never flinch, never weary, never despair.[62]

The *Times* parliamentary correspondent reported that:

> For all that Mr Shinwell [moving the Labour amendment] complained that there was nothing original in the Prime

Minister's speech opening the two-day defence debate...the crowded House found enough to hold it in almost utter silence.Sir Winston Churchill himself shattered the stillness when, slapping each side of the despatch box, he declared that a quantity of plutonium probably less than would fill it would suffice to produce weapons that would give unassailable world domination to any great Power which was the only one to have it.[63]

Shinwell had moved an amendment to the White Paper on behalf of the Opposition accepting the need for the 'deterrent', but deploring the failure to reorganise the Forces and Civil Defence, or to 'explain the grave and admitted deficiencies' in their existing weaponry.[64]

The debate continued for a second day, and Churchill interrupted a speech by Aneurin Bevan to explain that he had been 'struck down by a sudden illness which paralysed me completely, physically', and this had prevented him from persuading Eisenhower to agree to a meeting with Malenkov.[65] This was a dramatic statement, as he had never previously admitted in public that he had had a serious stroke; but more drama was to follow, when Bevan stated his disagreement with his own Front Bench:

> Do they mean that nuclear weapons would be used with the support of the British Labour Movement against any sort of aggression? I want to know the answer. If my right hon. Friend the Leader of the Opposition says that is the interpretation of the Amendment, then I do not propose to vote for it this evening.

And later he interrupted Attlee's own speech, saying:

> What I want to know is whether the use of the words to which I have referred in our Amendment associates us with the statement that we should use thermo-nuclear weapons in circumstances of hostilities, although they were not used against us.

Attlee replied bluntly 'deterrents, by the possession of thermo-nuclear weapons, are the best way of preventing another war.'[66] This resulted in a substantial revolt of the Parliamentary Labour Party: although a three-line Whip had been issued, 61 MPs abstained from the vote, and the *Evening Standard* declared that:

> Not for the first time, Mr Bevan has proved one of the Tory party's greatest electoral assets.[67]

The Parliamentary Party voted to withdraw the Whip from him, but the National Executive by a narrow majority allowed him to offer a pledge of loyalty and thus avoid expulsion from the Party.[68]

At the time of Churchill's reshuffle of Ministers in October, *The Times* in a leader headed 'Penultimate?' hinted that the change of Premier was imminent:

> Even though Sir Winston Churchill's peacetime administration may have been the turning point in Britain's post-war fortunes, the electorate will be thinking not of that but of the new men. They themselves will do better if they have time to find their feet. Above all, if the Conservatives are to retain their present impetus they should have some idea of the date of the change-over.[69]

Crookshank for one thought the 'change-over' was overdue. Churchill had offered him the Home Office in place of Maxwell Fyfe who went to the Woolsack, but he refused, and asked to continue as Lord Privy Seal and Leader of the House. He wrote to Eden (with copies to Salisbury, Butler and Macmillan):

> I feel very strongly about the whole affair, but as I gather you have agreed to carry on with him as Prime Minister, it would be absurd to be more royal than the Prince of Wales, and stage a private one-man abstention. If therefore he does ask me to stay on in the administration in my present post, I shall do so rather than rock the boat: but we are all I think taking upon ourselves very great responsibilities, for we all know that he is not fit to carry on … We have a duty to the nation which we neglect at our and its peril.[70]

Macmillan had suggested privately to Churchill that Eden should be given a clear and definite understanding about the handover. 'He must have this and have a fair run on his own before the election.'[71] But the birthday celebrations gave

Churchill confidence to say he could carry on until the summer of 1955.[72] This stung Eden into action a few days before Christmas. He wrote Churchill a letter painting a gloomy picture of the party's prospects of winning another election if the date was delayed:

> I find it diff[icult] to see in wh[at] sphere we c[oul]d add to our rep[utation] in the next few months. I can see many in which we might down it. The industrial outlook is serious. Apart from the Railways we have already been warned that the miners and the engineers have also demands to put forward. A gov[ernmen]t that is awaiting a gen[eral] election can be open to blackmail in these matters. A succession of strikes will be deeply damaging, the Comm[unist]s know this full well.

Perhaps he did not realise that nearly always strikes at election time hurt the Labour Party more than the Conservatives. But Eden found the outlook unprepossessing in other directions too:

> In housing, we have the point that Duncan rightly mentioned to us, to say nothing of rents. In Trade, the probs of GATT, Jap competition etc will become more severe.

Duncan Sandys had pointed out that fewer houses were now being completed for local authorities to rent. 'Against all this', Eden added 'it is true that the Chancellor may be able to introduce a popular Budget, but we all know how ephemeral is pop gratitude for taxes remitted.' As for foreign affairs:

> I see little to hope for immed[iately] except ratification of the Paris treaties. I think the Russians will cool off after a while but they are not likely to be negociable for some time after the ratification. Meanwhile the Far Eastern scene will continue dangerous the threat to Indo China greater still.

He then suggested that an election as early as February or March might be desirable, for 'I fear increasing diff[iculties] falling prestige as the New Year unfolds.'[73]

He concluded by asking the Prime Minister for an early talk with 'some of us'. The meeting was duly held at 3 p.m. on 22 December, with Crookshank, Butler, James Stuart and Woolton present as well as Churchill himself and Eden.

Churchill first of all read out Eden's letter, and Woolton at once pointed out that a new register came into force in mid-February, but an election would be possible in March if the Chancellor would agree to postpone his Budget. Butler did not like this, but acknowledged that it could be done. Woolton then had a brief conversation with Pierssené, the General Director of Central Office, presumably by telephone, and said that rather than wait until October – which he had maintained was the best time for the Conservative Party to go to the country – there would be a possibility in May 'concurrently with the borough elections'. Eden then argued that for him to wait to take over the government until June or July would be 'impossible'; as Woolton put it in his diary:

> Eden ... said that he found it impossible to accept the idea that he should take over at the end of June or July and be in the position of having to get a new Government for a very short time, without meeting Parliament and with all the uncertainties and inconveniences such a course would entail. He was definite that he would not accept this suggestion.

Churchill then said:

> I know you are trying to get rid of me and it is up to me to go to the Queen and hand her my resignation and yours, but I won't do it; but if you feel strongly about it you can force my hand by a sufficiently large number of Ministers handing in their resignations, in which case an election will be inevitable; but if this happens I shall not be in favour of it and I shall tell the country so.

Eden replied by saying he thought the Prime Minister had been 'very hard' in his language to them. The meeting broke up with the issue unresolved.[74]

It was early in January that Macmillan lunched with Lord Moran, the Prime Minister's doctor, and told him that he thought Churchill should retire. This was a surprise for Moran; as he put it, 'Winston called him the Captain of the Pretorian Guard.' As Prime Minister, Churchill presided over the sessions of the Commonwealth Conference, but found it very hard work, saying 'The work in unceasing, two meetings every day, five hours altogether, and I am in the Chair the whole time.' In mid-February he told his doctor:

I've made up my mind that I shall go in April. But I'm not telling anyone. I want it to come as a surprise. So I'm spreading the gospel the other way that there is no reason why I should not carry on.[75]

What had happened was related in Eden's diary for 1 February:

> After consultations with Rab, Harold and Bobbety [Butler, Macmillan and Salisbury] all of whom agreed situation must be cleared up, I asked to see W at 5 p.m. All very quiet and smooth. After discussion of my plans I asked for his. At my suggestion he sent for calendar. He admitted he could not carry on and after discussion said I could base my plans on his departing last week of session before Easter. I told Rab who confessed later that he had spoken to him in similar terms.[76]

Eden thus went to the Far East with the expectation that the Premiership was at last within his grasp. On his return in March he conferred with Woolton, who had not as yet had the retirement date confirmed to him, about the idea of holding an election in May, partly to capitalise on Labour disunity following the split over the hydrogen bomb. 'We agreed that the announcement of the election should be made on the 15th April, immediately before the Budget.'[77] Churchill meanwhile had invited the Queen and the Duke of Edinburgh to dine with him at No. 10 Downing Street on 4 April.

There was, however, a hitch in the arrangements, as so often before. On 10 March Sir Roger Makins sent a telegram to the Foreign Office reporting a conversation that he had just had with Dulles. The President was prepared to visit Paris on 8 May, the tenth anniversary of the armistice in Europe, in order to exchange ratifications of the Paris Agreements with President Coty of France, Dr Adenauer of Germany and Sir Winston Churchill. This was seen as a method of putting pressure on the French – whose upper house, the Conseil de la République, had still not confirmed the Assembly's vote – and also agreeing proposals (to be prepared by a prior conference of Foreign Ministers) to be put before the Russians.[78] Eden passed the telegram to Churchill with the comment that it was 'woolly' and that, so far from encouraging the French Senators to ratify, it might put their backs up. Also, Eden told

Churchill, 'in May there is a possibility of our own domestic affairs reaching a critical phase and that our international activities may well be hampered just then by developments at home.'[79]

But Churchill reacted much more warmly to the telegram, which he took to mean that Eisenhower was now willing to agree to an early four-power meeting. He wrote: 'The proposal of a meeting of Heads of Government which he would attend himself must be regarded as creating a new situation which will affect our personal plans and time-tables.' He added pointedly:

> It also complicates the question of a May election to which I gather you are inclining. Your proposed last sentence.... might be dangerous as it seems to suggest that the Party politics of a snap Election to take advantage of Socialist disunity would be allowed to weigh against a meeting of the Heads of Government which would give a chance to the world of warding off its mortal peril. The British national reaction to this would not be favourable.[80]

Eden was stung by this remark, and at once replied very tartly:

> I have your message of today. I was not aware that anything I had done in my public life would justify the suggestion that I was putting Party before country or self before either.[81]

Churchill responded to this, again the same day:

> I am distressed that you should have read a personal implication, which I utterly repudiate, into a discussion of policy ... I am telling Norman Brook to summon the Cabinet for noon Monday.[82]

The minutes of the Cabinet meeting on the Monday morning (14 March), although as usual rather dry, indicated the conflict of views. Eden said that:

> The main question for the Cabinet to decide was whether an announcement of the plan outlined by Mr Dulles was likely to further our primary purpose of securing a fruitful Four-Power meeting with the Russians. I myself doubt whether it would improve the prospects of securing such a Meeting.

Churchill, on the other hand, said:

> I attach primary importance to the President's willingness to come to Europe for the purpose of making plans for a Four-Power Meeting with the Russians. This is a new and significant initiative, and we should welcome it.[83]

But the drama of the actual discussion was brought out by Woolton in his diary:

> Eden ... asked him whether the private arrangements at which they had both arrived were to be considered as still existing; Churchill replied that he must consider that, and the atmosphere became very tense, most people not knowing what we were talking about. Salisbury said it might be useful if the Cabinet were informed of what the private arrangements were, but we certainly could not go on in this election atmosphere.

Woolton's account continued:

> Eden said he must know where he stood in the matter. Churchill said there was no doubt about where anybody stood – it was his business to decide what he was going to do and if anybody didn't like it they could resign if they had no confidence in him. Eden replied that what Churchill was saying was that nobody had the competence to meet President Eisenhower except himself and he thought that he, after ten years as Foreign Secretary, might be considered to have some competence in the matter.[84]

The meeting was adjourned to the evening, and then to the next morning, when a draft reply composed in the Foreign Office and reflecting Eden's views was considered and approved. This was to the effect that although Eisenhower's proposal of visiting Europe, and if possible also London, was welcomed, 'precipitate action along the lines proposed by Mr Dulles was not likely to improve the prospects for a Four-Power Meeting with the Russians which might produce useful results.'[85] This seemed to be a rebuff for Churchill, and his hopes were finally dashed by another message from Makins, who reported that Dulles had told him that:

there had been some misinterpretation of what he and the President had in mind. They had contemplated that at a meeting in Paris, agreement might be reached on the terms of a note to the Russians proposing a Four-Power meeting in the autumn or winter of this year. It was not their intention that any such meeting with the Russians should be merged with, or follow soon after, the proposed meeting in Paris.[86]

The legacy of the clash between Churchill and Eden was, as Colville reported, that 'W. began to form a cold hatred of Eden who, he repeatedly said, had done more to thwart him and prevent him pursuing the policy he thought right than anybody else.' But, as Colville noticed, 'he was ageing month by month….More and more time was given to bezique and ever less to public business.' On 29 March he was again 'coldly determined not to go', and told the Queen at his audience that he thought of postponing his resignation, and did she mind? According to Colville 'she said no!' But that evening he and Clementine attended a farewell dinner party with the Edens. The party went well, as Eden behaved with great amiability, and so at 6.30 next day he saw Eden and Butler in the Cabinet Room and formally told them that his decision to resign now was final.[87] Eden and Butler then emerged from the room and solemnly shook hands.[88]

Churchill's last few days in office were not reported by the London press, owing to the newspaper strike, but *The Times*, which regarded itself as a journal of record, subsequently published summaries, and of course the provincial press and the radio were able to make much of the occasion. The strike had begun on 26 March and it only ended on 21 April; the actual departure date of Churchill was 5 April, and on the evening beforehand, as already arranged, he had entertained the Queen and the Duke of Edinburgh to a dinner at No. 10 Downing Street.

It was a glittering occasion, with about fifty guests.[89] Churchill did not invite all the Cabinet, but the senior members were there, with members of his own family, some of his personal staff and of the aristocracy and the leaders of the Opposition. Churchill seemed to have a special liking for duchesses. He himself proposed the toast of the Queen, recalling in a brief speech that he had drunk the toast of the Queen 'in the reign of your Majesty's great great grand-mother, Queen Victoria'.[90] Next day, 5 April, Churchill went to the Palace at 4.30 p.m. to resign his office. The Queen offered him a dukedom, but also ascertained beforehand that he would refuse it. [91]

Earlier that day he had presided over his last Cabinet at No. 10. His final remarks were that his own resignation would involve that of all his colleagues, but that they should continue at their posts until they heard otherwise. He concluded:

> It remains for me to wish my colleagues all good fortune in the difficult, but hopeful, situation which you have to face. I trust that you will be enabled to further the progress already made in rebuilding the domestic stability and economic strength of the United Kingdom and in weaving still more closely the threads which bind together the countries of the Commonwealth or, as I still prefer to call it, the Empire.

Eden then said that his Cabinet colleagues had asked him to speak on this occasion on behalf of them all:

> It therefore falls to me to express our sense of abiding affec-tion and esteem for you and our pride in the privilege of having served as your colleagues. I myself have enjoyed this privilege for sixteen years, others for varying shorter periods, but all, whatever the length of their service, have the same strong feelings of affection for you.

Eden's final words were:

> We shall always be grateful for your leadership, and for your friendship, over the years that have passed; and we will hope to enjoy in future your continuing interest and support in our endeavours.[92]

That evening Churchill entertained senior and junior Ministers at No. 10, to thank them personally for their service.[93] Now that Churchill was actually retiring, Ministers forgot their anxiety to remove him and felt only a sense of loss on his departure. As Macmillan put it in his diary, 'Now that he has really decided to go, we are all miserable.'[94]

Churchill had nevertheless been insistent that, in order to assert the Queen's prerogative, Eden should not be sent for until the following day.[95] It was therefore not until the morning of Wednesday, 6 April, that Eden drove from his official residence at No. 1 Carlton Gardens to receive the long-awaited Queen's mandate. That evening Churchill entertained his Downing Street and Chequers staff to a party before leaving shortly after 5 p.m. for Chartwell. On the 7th Eden made his first Cabinet appointments: Macmillan was to succeed him as Foreign Secretary and Selwyn Lloyd became Minister of Defence. Churchill had already arranged to fly off in the following week for a holiday at Syracuse. He took with him Lady Churchill, Lord Cherwell and Jock Colville. On the 5th the results of the Lancashire County Council elections became known: the council had reverted to Conservative control. This was the sign Woolton had been waiting for to confirm his expectation of a positive outcome for a General Election in May.[96]

12 Conclusion

Any assessment of the three-and-a-half years of the Churchill Government of the 1950s must start with a discussion of Churchill's own competence to hold the premiership. The issue was raised by his own doctor, Lord Moran, who, regardless of medical ethics, rushed into print with a substantial volume recounting his years of attending Churchill and accompanying him on trips abroad since 1941. As if to beg the question, he entitled the book *Churchill: The Struggle for Survival*, and argued that throughout the middle and later war years, as well as in the 1950s, old age was an enemy which was distorting and enfeebling his judgement. Shortly after the new Government was elected, in December 1951 he wrote of Churchill 'now struggling only with the humiliations of old age and with economic problems that are quite beyond his ken.' He revealed how, in June 1953 after his stroke, Butler and Salisbury had insisted on altering the medical bulletin that he and Russell Brain, the specialist he had brought in, had drawn up to make it sound reassuring, and on 6 April 1955, the day Churchill retired, he wrote 'This is the end of Winston's long struggle to keep his place in politics ... It has been a great effort for him to keep going; a drawn-out struggle with failing powers.'

The picture that Moran drew not only offended his family; it also drew a speedy response from the members of his 'Secret Circle' – the top-level civil servants of his day – who rapidly got together to present a series of essays depicting his vigour as a leader. With the almost equally misleading title of *Action This Day* – a label on documents which Churchill used during the war but never in peacetime – the essays were edited by Sir John Wheeler-Bennett, the historian. As Norman Brook, who was Cabinet Secretary in the early 1950s, put it:

> In the House of Commons, though his major speeches were not always successful, he continued to the end to be adroit and resourceful in answering Questions and dealing with Supplementaries...Towards the end of 1954 there were signs that he would not be able to carry on for very much

longer. He could still rise to the great occasion, by an effort
of will and a modest use of the stimulants prescribed by his
doctor. But in the daily round of his responsibilities he no
longer had the energy, mental and physical to give to papers
or to people the full attention which they demand.

John Colville admitted that 'Churchill's last year of office was
badly hit by ups and downs in his health.'

But Moran was to blame for not insisting on the integrity of
the medical bulletins on his patient. It is true that an honest
account would have precipitated a demand for his resignation,
but Colville at least was prepared for that, and, as he reported
to Eden, had recommended indirectly to the Queen that
Salisbury should be appointed acting Prime Minister. By following the course that he did, that is to say by concealing his
illness, Churchill – and Moran – took a gamble on a successful
outcome. That the gamble was successful can hardly have
eased the cares of the Queen at the time.

Whatever the state of the economy, international affairs
bulked large in Churchill's mind, and he assiduously courted
first Truman and then Eisenhower in order to maintain the
solidarity of the English-speaking peoples. His correspondence with Eisenhower took place regularly after the latter's
inauguration, and although Eisenhower may have resented
this constant pressure, he always took care to respond warmly
and courteously. They disagreed, of course, about the appro-
priateness of seeking an early 'summit' meeting, and on this
issue Churchill's own Foreign Secretary and the Foreign
Office as a whole were against him. But, like Gladstone in an
earlier epoch, Churchill was 'an old man in a hurry'. In the
event, in seeking to make what Eisenhower had called 'a solitary pilgrimage', he was opposed bitterly by members of his
own Cabinet, but saved from further humiliation by the clum-
siness of Soviet diplomacy.

Indeed, Churchill was not able to assume in this administration the powerful position he had held during the war. Then
he had been Minister of Defence and in constant liaison with
the Chiefs of Staff; now he had (from early in 1952) a separate
Minister of Defence and a Cabinet whose members were by no
means always amenable to his wishes. The most disgruntled of

them was Anthony Eden, his Foreign Secretary, who as we have seen disapproved of the policy of seeking an early *rap-prochement* with the Soviet Union. Churchill himself claimed that he and Eden saw eye to eye on nine-tenths of the issues with which they had to grapple; Eden would have put the figure much lower. Eden was also consumed by the ambition of succeeding to the premiership, which he originally thought had been promised to him shortly after the 1951 election. His diaries and also the memoirs of his Principal Private Secretary, Evelyn Shuckburgh, provide ample evidence of this. He was reluctant to move from the Foreign Office to another post where he could gain experience of home affairs, and re-mained Foreign Secretary throughout Churchill's premier-ship. At least this preserved him for what was described as the '*annus mirabilis*' of his diplomatic career, 1954.

In that year Eden, presiding jointly with Molotov at the Geneva Conference in the spring and early summer, suc-ceeded in extricating the French from their commitments in South East Asia, at a time when the Americans were prepared for a war with China, and perhaps with the Soviet Union as well. And then in the late summer, when the French Assembly finally rejected the European Community which their govern-ment had devised, he decided to refashion the Brussels Treaty into the Western European Union, after visiting all the capitals of Western Europe and drawing up a plan to bring West Germany into the North Atlantic Treaty. Like Churchill the year before, he was offered and accepted the Order of the Garter from a grateful monarch. Like Churchill, he had been offered it in 1945, but had then declined it.

Of the other Ministers, R.A. Butler made the most outstand-ing impression on the public. He was not only Chancellor of the Exchequer throughout the period; he had also carried the principal burden of administration during the illnesses of Churchill and Eden. But his reputation was in two major re-spects fortuitous. His acceptance of the Treasury scheme known as Robot, which was pressed on him early in 1952, and which would have entailed heavy unemployment, was only averted by the vigilance of Cherwell and Robert Hall, Butler's Economic Adviser, who eventually secured its defeat in the Cabinet. Equally important was the fact that, with the ending of hostilities in Korea, the terms of trade turned in Britain's favour, and it became possible to relax the whole apparatus of rationing and restrictions which had been inherited from the Labour Government. Butler's personal life, however, was unhappy: his wife Sydney died slowly in 1954 of cancer of the jaw.

Next to Butler in success as a Minister was Harold Macmillan, who as Minister of Housing achieved the target that the Party had promised in 1951, of 300,000 new houses a year. In this he had the full backing of the Prime Minister, who ensured that the necessary raw materials were made available, whatever the impact on other building programmes. Macmillan, unlike other Ministers, found time to write Cabinet Papers covering a wide range of topics, perhaps to the annoyance of his colleagues. But in the autumn of 1954 he won promotion to the post of Minister of Defence. Lord Salisbury was a Minister of scrupulous honesty, who even argued that it would not be worth while denationalising iron and steel if it were only to become a constant irritant of politics; he also frequently threatened to resign, taking a position of complete independence, much to Churchill's annoyance at times.

Of the other Ministers, a prominent feature was Churchill's attempt to use 'Overlords' – Cherwell, Leathers and Woolton – as co-ordinators of groups of Ministries. They were all wartime colleagues of the Prime Minister. Cherwell was his scientific adviser, and took responsibility for the development of the atomic bomb, which was tested and then exploded off the coast of Australia. He returned to his Oxford chair in 1953, but continued to retain an advisory role. Lord Leathers, who had the task of overseeing all transport policy, was not a success: his wartime experience had been limited to shipping. He had not wanted to take office again, and he also retired gratefully in 1953. The third 'Overlord' was Lord Woolton, who as the head of the Conservative Central Office was regarded as the architect of victory in 1951. He retained this post throughout Churchill's premiership, but he suffered a serious illness in late 1952 and was moved from the post of Lord President to that of Lord Privy Seal, where the obligations were less taxing. But he was at hand to advise Churchill about electoral prospects in late 1954 and early 1955.

The Cabinet contained two distinguished lawyers who had their eyes on promotion to high legal office, but had to postpone their ambitions to serve as work horses in civil posts. David Maxwell Fyfe had made a great reputation at the Nuremberg War Crimes Tribunal. He became Home Secretary, and piloted many of the Government's bills through the Commons, including commercial television, before succeeding Lord Simonds on the Woolsack in October 1954. Sir Walter Monckton, who had also hoped for a legal post, became Minister of Labour, with the task of keeping the peace with the trade unions. Although he succeeded well in his first two years, he found that 'appeasement' was becoming very difficult in the last year of Churchill's premiership.

One Minister who was not originally in the Cabinet, but forced his way in by sheer merit, was Lord Swinton, a veteran of the 1930s when he had held several Cabinet posts. He joined the Cabinet in 1953 as Secretary for Commonwealth Relations, and was also used by Churchill as a chairman of important Cabinet committees. Another colleague who commended himself to Churchill for his wit as well as his ability was Oliver Lyttelton, the Colonial Secretary until in late 1954 he finally withdrew in order to return to business and recoup his finances. He would have liked to have been Chancellor of the Exchequer, but Churchill denied him that post because of doubt about his ability as a speaker.

The Churchill Government was marked by a strong assertion of authority by the 1922 Committee, the backbenchers' organisation. The Prime Minister found himself at odds with the Committee over the desirability of commercial television almost immediately after taking office, and it was to his chagrin that a White Paper of May 1952 accepted the idea of 'some element of competition'. The issue was still being fiercely debated at the time of the Coronation early in June 1953. The broadcast and commentary won high praise for the BBC, but when the recording was shown in the United States it was interrupted by advertisements featuring a chimpanzee. This contretemps was immediately followed in Britain by the formation of the National Television Council, headed by Churchill's old friend Lady Violet Bonham-Carter. When the Cabinet debated the issue not long afterwards, the Chief Whip reported that if the Government proceeded with plans for commercial television 'the possibility of the Government's being defeated could not be excluded', and the Prime Minister said that 'to risk defeat over proposals which were unpalatable to respected elements both among Government supporters and in the country generally' would be folly: he favoured a free vote, which in view of Labour opposition would have killed the bill.

In the end the Cabinet delayed the issue until the following year (1954). The Television Bill which was then passed avoided sponsorship and created a new corporation, the Independent Television Authority. Churchill at least had the satisfaction that broadcasting by the new body did not begin until after his retirement.

The Suez Group differed from other revolts against Cabinet leadership in that it only involved a relatively small number of MPs – probably not more than forty, though for some time they had the tacit support of Churchill himself. It was a revolt against Eden's policy of seeking an accommodation with the Egyptian Government over British occupation of the Suez base. The rebels, led by Colonel Charles Waterhouse, in December 1953 tabled a motion to mark their disapproval of any concessions to what they regarded as an utterly untrustworthy Egyptian Government. However, when early in 1954 Churchill, accepting the vulnerability of the base to attack by an enemy armed with the hydrogen bomb, addressed its members in support of Eden's policy, the revolt collapsed and the treaty with Egypt was quickly concluded.

But 1954 also saw a Cabinet Minister forced out of office, largely by the pressure of the backbenchers, over the Crichel Down affair. Sir Thomas Dugdale, the Minister of Agriculture, failed to take sufficiently strong action against some of his civil servants who were found to have ridden roughshod over the rights of private individuals in a case of derequisitioned land. Although by no means unpopular as a Minister, he was forced to offer his resignation, which the Prime Minister felt bound to accept.

In the same year there was an astonishing refusal of the 1922 Committee to accept a pay rise for all members, in spite of an all-party recommendation in favour of making up for inflation since 1946. The backbenchers on the Conservative side would not allow the issue to be put to a free vote, fearing the wrath of the old age pensioners whose claims had been postponed to the 1954–55 Session. Butler as Chancellor was forced to bring in a scheme of expense allowances as a temporary alleviation.

It may have been a sign of weakening powers that before he left office Churchill failed to deal with the problem of rapidly increasing immigration from the Commonwealth and Colonies, the social consequences of which he clearly foresaw. The Government could easily have drafted and enacted a measure during that last session of the 1951 Parliament, which had relatively little other major business to occupy MPs, and the measure would have received plenty of support from the Opposition benches.

Nevertheless, so long as he chose to stay, there was never any doubt that Churchill himself was the linchpin of his ministry, and his carefully prepared set-piece speeches provided the keynote of government policy. By comparison the diplomatic successes of Eden, remarkable though they were, appeared somehow pedestrian. The signal of Churchill's speech of 11 May 1953, in spite of its unpopularity in the Foreign Offices of the West, pointed the way forward to the era of détente and summit meetings, although it had to follow Churchill's tenure of power rather than, as he would have dearly wished, crown his own career. But he had laid the foundations.

Appendix: Members of the Government, from 26 October 1951 to 5 April 1955

THE CABINET

Prime Minister
W.S. Churchill   (from 26 October 1951 to 5 April 1955 and Minister of Defence from 28 October 1951 to 1 March 1952)

Secretary of State for Foreign Affairs
R.A. Eden   (from 28 October 1951 to 6 April 1955 and Deputy Prime Minister)

Lord President of the Council
Lord Woolton   (from 28 October 1951)
Marquess of Salisbury   (from 24 November 1952)

Lord Privy Seal
Marquess of Salisbury   (from 28 October 1951)
H.F.C. Crookshank   (from 7 May 1952)

Lord Chancellor
Lord Simonds   (from 30 October 1951)
Viscount Kilmuir   (formerly Sir D. Maxwell Fyfe, from 18 October 1954)

Secretary of State, Home Office and Minister for Welsh Affairs
Sir D. Maxwell Fyfe   (from 28 October 1951)
Major G. Lloyd-George   (from 18 October 1954)

Chancellor of the Exchequer
R.A. Butler   (from 28 October 1951)

Secretary of State for Commonwealth Relations
Lord Ismay   (from 28 October 1951)
Marquess of Salisbury   (from 12 March 1952)
Viscount Swinton   (from 24 November 1952)

Secretary of State for the Colonies
O. Lyttelton   (from 28 October 1951)
A.T. Lennox-Boyd   (from 28 July 1954)

Secretary of State for Scotland
J.G. Stuart   (from 30 October 1951)

Minister of Defence
W.S. Churchill   (from 28 October 1951)
Earl Alexander of Tunis   (from 1 March 1952)
H. Macmillan   (from 18 October 1954)

Minister of Labour and National Service
Sir Walter Monckton   (from 28 October 1951)

Minister of Housing and Local Government
H. Macmillan   (from 30 October 1951)
D. Sandys   (from 18 October 1954)

President of the Board of Trade
G.E.P. Thorneycroft   (from 30 October 1951)

Secretary of State for Co-ordination of Transport, Fuel and Power
Lord Leathers   (from 30 October 1951)
                                     (*abolished 3 September 1953*)

Minister of Health (*ceases to be a Cabinet post, 7 May 1952*)
H.F.C. Crookshank   (from 30 October 1951 to 7 May 1952; also
                                     Leader, House of Commons)

Paymaster-General (*ceases to be a Cabinet post, 11 November 1953*)
Lord Cherwell   (from 30 October 1951 to 11 November
                                     1953)

Chancellor of the Duchy of Lancaster (*outside Cabinet 31 October 1951 to
                                     24 November 1952*)
Viscount Woolton   (from 24 November 1952; also Minister for
                                     Materials, 3 September 1953 to 16 August
                                     1954)

Minister of Agriculture and Fisheries (*outside Cabinet 31 October 1951 to
                                     3 September 1953*)
Sir T. Dugdale   (from 3 September 1953)
D. Heathcoat Amory   (from 28 July 1954, combined with Ministry
                                     of Food)

Minister for Education (*outside Cabinet, 2 November 1951 to 3 September 1953*)
Miss F. Horsbrugh   (from 3 September 1953)
Sir D. Eccles   (from 18 October 1954)

Minister of Food (*outside Cabinet 31 October 1951 to 3 September 1953*)
Major G. Lloyd-George   (from 3 September 1953)
D. Heathcoat Amory   (from 18 October 1954, combined with
                                     Ministry of Agriculture and Fisheries)

Minister for Pensions and National Insurance (*outside Cabinet from
                                     31 October 1951 to 18 October 1954*)
O. Peake   (from 18 October 1954)

MINISTERS OUTSIDE THE CABINET

First Lord of the Admiralty
J.P.L. Thomas   (from 31 October 1951)

Secretary of State for War
A.H. Head   (from 31 October 1951)

Secretary of State for Air
Lord De L'Isle and Dudley   (from 31 October 1951)

Minister of Transport (and Civil Aviation *from 1 October 1953)*
J.S. Maclay   (from 31 October 1951)
J. Boyd-Carpenter   (from 28 July 1952)

Minister of Supply
D. Sandys   (from 31 October 1951)
Selwyn Lloyd   (from 18 October 1954)

Minister of State
Selwyn Lloyd   (from 30 October 1951 to 18 October 1954)
Marquess of Reading   (from 11 November 1953)
A. Nutting   (from 18 October 1954)

Minister of State for Colonial Affairs
A.T. Lennox-Boyd   (from 2 November 1951)
H. Hopkinson   (from 7 May 1952)

Minister for Trade
D. Heathcoat Amory   (from 3 September 1953)
T. Low   (from 28 July 1954)

Minister for the Scottish Office
Earl of Home   (from 2 November 1951)

Postmaster-General
Earl De La Warr   (from 5 November 1951)

Minister of Works
D.M. Eccles   (from 1 November 1951)
N. Birch   (from 18 October 1954)

Minister of Fuel and Power
Geoffrey Lloyd   (from 31 October 1951)

Minister of Pensions
D. Heathcoat Amory   (from 5 November 1951 to 3 September 1953; combined with National Insurance, 1 September 1953)

Lord Advocate
J.L.M. Clyde   (from 2 November 1951)
W. Milligan   (from 30 December 1954)

Attorney-General
Sir L.F. Heald   (from 3 November 1951)
Sir R. Manningham-Buller   (from 18 October 1954)

Solicitor-General
Sir R. Manningham-Buller   (from 3 November 1951)
Sir H. Hylton-Foster   (from 18 October 1954)

Solicitor-General for Scotland
W.R. Milligan   (from 3 November 1951)
W. Grant   (from 10 January 1955)

Minister without Portfolio
Earl of Munster   (from 18 October 1954)

Chancellor of the Duchy of Lancaster *(becomes Cabinet post, 24 November 1952)*
Viscount Swinton   (from 31 October 1951 to 24 November 1952; and Minister of Materials in the Cabinet, 3 September 1953 to 15 July 1954 when post abolished)

Minister of Materials
Viscount Swinton   (from 31 October 1951 to 24 November 1952)
Sir A. Salter   (from 24 November 1952 to 1 September 1953; from 1 September 1953, combined with Duchy of Lancaster in the Cabinet; abolished 16 August 1954)

Minister of Food (*becomes Cabinet post, 3 September 1953*)
Major G. Lloyd-George   (from 31 October 1951 to 3 September 1953)

Minister of Agriculture and Fisheries *(becomes Cabinet post, 3 September 1953)*
Sir T. Dugdale   (from 31 October 1951 to 3 September 1953)

Minister of Education (*becomes Cabinet post, 3 September 1953*)
Miss F. Horsbrugh   (from 2 November 1951 to 3 September 1953

Minister of National Insurance (*becomes a Cabinet post, 18 October 1954*)
O. Peake   (from 31 October 1951; combined with Pensions from 18 October 1954)

Minister of Health *(Cabinet post, 30 October 1951 to 7 May 1952)*
I. Macleod   (from 7 May 1952)

Minister for Economic Affairs *(position abolished, 24 November 1952)*
Sir A. Salter   (from 31 October to 24 November 1952)

Notes

SPECIAL ABBREVIATIONS IN THE NOTES

AP	Avon Papers (Anthony Eden)
CC	Cabinet Conclusions (with year-date and number)
C/E	Chancellor of the Exchequer
CP	Cabinet Paper (with year-date and number)
D	Defence Committee
DDE	Dwight D. Eisenhower
FO	Foreign Office
FRUS	*Foreign Relations of the United States*
FS	Foreign Secretary
HL	House of Lords Debates
LP	Lord President
LPS	Lord Privy Seal
Min	Minister
MoD	Minister of Defence
MoL	Minister of Labour
PM	Prime Minister
PP	Parliamentary Papers
PREM 11	PM's Papers
RIIA	Royal Institute of International Affairs
SS	Secretary of State
SS for CR	SS for Commonwealth Relations
WSC	Winston S. Churchill

CHAPTER 1 THE LABOUR INTERLUDE

1. WSC, *Second World War*, vi, p. 583.
2. Macmillan, *Tides of Fortune*, p. 43.
3. Kilmuir, *Political Adventure*, p. 149.
4. Hoffman, *Conservative Party*, p. 249.
5. WSC, *Sinews of Peace*, pp. 93–105.
6. Gilbert, *WSC*, viii, p. 227.
7. Ibid., p. 244; James, *Eden*, p. 317.
8. Gilbert, op. cit., p. 227n.
9. Hoffman, *Conservative Party*, p. 81.
10. Goodhart, *1922*, p. 143.
11. Hoffman, *Conservative Party*, ch. V, pp. 137–66.
12. Stuart, *Within the Fringe*, pp. 145–6.
13. 145 HL Deb, 622 (13 Feb 1947).
14. Hoffman, *Conservative Party*, pp. 89–90.
15. Gilbert, *WSC*, viii, pp. 265–6.

16. WSC, *Europe Unite*, pp. 210–17.
17. Pelling, *Labour Governments*, p. 137.
18. Macmillan, *Tides of Fortune*, p. 165.
19. Ibid., p. 184.
20. Cook and Ramsden (eds), *By-Elections*, p. 376.
21. Goodhart, *1922*, pp. 146–8.
22. Nicholas, *General Election*, p. 70.
23. Ibid., p. 85.
24. *The Times House of Commons, 1950*, pp. 290–6.
25. Gilbert, *WSC*, viii, 510.
26. Nicholas, *General Election*, p. 286.
27. Ibid., p. 299.
28. Hoffman, *Conservative Party*, p. 251.
29. WSC, *In the Balance*, p. 352.
30. Hoffman, *Conservative Party*, p. 256.
31. Ibid., pp. 202–3.
32. Butler, *General Election*, p. 14.
33. Pimlott (ed.), *Dalton Diary*, p. 542 (11 May 1951).
34. On the Korean War, see Rees, *Korea*.
35. Butler, *General Election*, pp. 112ff.
36. Ibid., pp. 242f.

CHAPTER 2 CABINET MAKING

1. J.W. Wheeler-Bennett, *George VI*, p. 797.
2. R.A. Butler, *Art of the Possible*, p. 156.
3. Chandos, *Memoirs*, pp. 343–4; Lysaght, *Bracken*, p. 289.
4. Ismay, *Memoirs*, pp. 452–3.
5. Kilmuir, *Political Adventure*, p. 192.
6. Birkenhead, *Monckton*.
7. Bracken to Beaverbrook, 15 Jan 1952, in Bracken, *My Dear Max*, p. 129.
8. Shuckburgh, *Descent*, pp. 25–6 (17 Oct 1951).
9. Butler, *Art of the Possible*, pp. 116–17.
10. Colville, *Fringes*, pp. 631–2.
11. Macmillan, *Tides of Fortune*, p. 363.
12. Hansard, 493, cc12–15 (31 Oct 1951).
13. *The Times*, 29 Oct 1951.
14. Thorpe, *Selwyn Lloyd*, p. 153.
15. Macmillan, *Tides of Fortune*, p. 356.
16. WSC to Eden, 30 Oct 1951, FO 800/816.
17. Gilbert, *Churchill*, viii, p. 656.
18. Boyd-Carpenter, *Way of Life*, pp. 87–8.
19. Ibid., p. 87.
20. *The Times*, 31 Oct 1951.
21. *Economist*, 3 Nov 1951.
22. CC (51) (30 Oct 1951).

23. *The Times,* 1 Nov 1951.
24. Crossman, *Diaries,* p. 30 (31 Oct 1951).
25. Ibid., p. 29.
26. Hansard, 493, c15 (31 Oct 1951).
27. CP (51) 1 (31 Oct 1951) C/E, 'The Economic Position:. Analysis and Remedies', CC (51) 2, 3 and 4 (1,2, and 5 Nov 1951).
28. Hansard, 493, cc67–79 (6 Nov 1951).
29. Hansard, 493, cc191–208 (7 Nov 1951).
30. Hansard, 493, c184 (7 Nov 1951).
31. RIIA, *Documents,* 1951 pp. 344–8.
32. Hansard, 493, c1176 (15 Nov 1951).
33. Hansard, 494, cc34–53 (19 Nov 1951).
34. Boothby, *Recollections,* p. 220.
35. Kilmuir, *Political Adventure,* p. 187.
36. D.M. Pitblado to PM, 7 Dec 1951, PREM 11/214.
37. Boothby, ibid., pp. 221–2.
38. WSC, *Stemming the Tide,* p. 204 (6 Dec 1951).
39. Hansard, 494, c2491.
40. Buchan-Hepburn to PM, 1 Dec 1951, PREM 11/241.
41. Washington to FO, 'Weekly Political Summary', 5 Jan 1952, FO 371/97588.
42. Acheson, *Present at the Creation,* p. 597.
43. SS, 'Memorandum of a Dinner Meeting at the British Embassy, 6 Jan 1952, *FRUS 1952–1954,* vi, 745–6.
44. *The Times,* 10 Jan 1952.
45. Ibid., 11 Jan 1952.
46. CC (52) 3 (14 Jan 1952).
47. Washington to FO 'Weekly Political Summary', FO 371/97580.
48. Richard Strout, *Christian Science Monitor,* quoted Washington to FO, 23 Jan 1952, 'Summary of Reactions of the Press and Radio to Mr Churchill's Address to the Joint Session of Congress...' FO 371/97593.
49. Franks to FS, 27 Jan 1952, FO 371/97593.
50. Communiqué on the Agreement reached between President Truman and British Prime Minister....on the Appointment of a Supreme Commander for the Atlantic, Washington, 18 Jan 1952, RIIA, *Documents,* 1952, p. 1.
51. *The Times,* 29 Jan 1952.
52. WSC, *Stemming the Tide,* pp. 237–40.
53. Bradford, *George VI,* p. 462.

CHAPTER 3 ROBOT AND AFTER

1. CC (52) 9 (29 Jan 1952).
2. Hansard, 495, c6 (29 Jan 1952).
3. Ibid., c210 (30 Jan 1952) C (52) (28 Jan 1952).
4. Hansard, ibid., c224.

5. R.W.B. Clarke, 'Convertibility', 25 Jan 1952, T 236/3240.
6. Plowden, *Industrialist*, p. 143. But for 'another theory', see MacDougall, *Don and Mandarin*, p. 86.
7. Bolton memo, 16 Feb 1952, T 236/3240.
8. C/E to PM, 20 Feb 1952, ibid.
9. Bridges to Plowden, 22 Feb 1952, ibid.
10. Plowden, p. 146; McDougall, p. 89.
11. PM to FS, 21 Feb 1952, Avon Papers 20/16/28.
12. Hall to Plowden, 22 Feb 1952, T 236/3240.
13. Plowden, *Industrialist*, p. 147.
14. FS to PM, 23 Feb 1952, PREM 11/138.
15. Cherwell to PM, 26 Feb 1952, Cherwell Papers.
16. Hall, *Diaries*, vol I, p. 206.
17. CC (52) 23, 24 and 25 (28 and 29 Feb 1952), T 236/3242.
18. Shuckburgh to FS, 31 Dec 1952, Avon Papers 20/16/33.
19. C/E to FS, 1 Mar 1952, Avon Papers 20/16/30.
20. Salisbury to C/E, 4 Mar 1952, Butler Papers E4.
21. Hansard, 497, cc1269–1301 (11 Mar 1952).
22. *Daily Telegraph*, 12 Mar 1952.
23. *Manchester Guardian*, 12 Mar 1952.
24. *News Chronicle*, 12 Mar 1952.
25. *Daily Mirror*, 13 Mar 1952.
26. *Economist*, 15 Mar 1952.
27. Hansard, 497, c1407 (12 Mar 1952).
28. PM to LP, 21 Mar 1952, Woolton Papers 25/45.
29. MacDougall, *Don and Mandarin*, p. 101.
30. Ibid., p. 102.
31. Hall, *Diaries*, vol I, p. 212 (21 Mar 1952).
32. Cherwell to PM, 'Setting the Pound Free', 18 Mar 1952, PREM 11/137.
33. PM to C/E, 20 Mar 1952, ibid.
34. CP (52) 111, C/E, 'The Balance of Payments Position' (9 Apr 1952).
35. CC (52) 57 (29 May 1952).
36. CC (52) 62 (17 Jun 1952).
37. WSC, *Stemming the Tide*, p. 298 (11 Jun 1952).
38. Hansard, 502, c407 (12 Jun 1952).
39. Hall, *Diaries*, vol I, p. 232.
40. MacDougall, *Don and Mandarin*, p. 102.
41. Ibid.
42. Butler Papers G24; Butler, *Art of the Possible*, p. 160.
43. CP (52) 226, MHLG, 'The Great Debate: Financial and Economic Policy' (4 July 1952).
44. Cherwell to PM, 'Housing', 16 July 1952, PREM 11/688.
45. Hansard, 503, c2149–50 (16 Jul 1952).
46. Hall, *Diaries*, vol I, p. 241.
47. Hansard, 504, c1275–6 (29 Jul 1952).
48. Ibid., 1290.
49. LP to PM, 21 Jul 1952, Cherwell Papers.
50. Cherwell to PM, 23 Jul 1952, ibid.

51. Hall, *Diaries,* vol I, p. 245.
52. CP (52) 376, FS, 'Commonwealth Economic Conference' (31 Oct 1952).
53. Cherwell to PM, 31 Oct 1952, Cherwell Papers.
54. CC (52) 92 (3 Nov 1952).
55. CC (52) 103 (8 Dec 1952).
56. CC (53) 6 (3 Feb 1953).
57. CP (53) 22, FS and C/E, 'The Collective Approach to Freer Trade and Currencies' (21 Jan 1953).
58. Hansard, 510, c1684 (3 Feb 1953).
59. Plowden, *Industrialist,* p. 158.
60. *The Times,* 27 Feb 1953.
61. Eden diary, 4 Mar 1953, Avon Papers 20/1/29.
62. C/E to PM, 7 Mar 1953, in Washington to FO, Cherwell Papers.
63. Plowden, *Industrialist,* p. 158.
64. Hansard, 514, c62 (14 Apr 1953).
65. Hansard, 514, c216 (15 Apr 1953).
66. *The Times,* 15 May 1953.

CHAPTER 4 KOREA AND COLONIAL PROBLEMS

1. Rees, *Korea,* p. 269.
2. WSC to FS, 16 Nov 1951, PREM 11/112.
3. WSC to FS, 13 Dec 1951, ibid.
4. Selwyn Lloyd to Eden, 16 Jun 1952, Avon Papers 20/15/10.
5. Attlee, Hansard, 502, c2038–9 (24 Jun 1952).
6. Selwyn Lloyd, Hansard, 503, c250 (1 Jul 1952).
7. Sir E. Dening (Tokyo) to FO, 2 Jul 1952, PREM 11/111.
8. WSC to Sir W. Strang, 3 Jul 1952, ibid.
9. WSC to FS, 21 Jul 1952, ibid.
10. FS to PM, 21 Jul 1952, ibid.
11. CC (52) 71, 22 Jul 1952.
12. CC (52) 47, 29 Apr 1952.
13. WSC to Strang, 12 Jul 1952, PREM 11/116.
14. For the text, see RIIA, *Documents,* 1952, pp. 446–9.
15. CP (52) 441, FS, 'Proceedings of the 7th General Session of the U.N.', 15 Dec 1952.
16. Shuckburgh to Franks, 22 Nov 1952, Avon Papers 20/18/18A.
17. Franks to Shuckburgh, 26 Nov 1952, ibid., 20/18/18B.
18. Eden, Hansard, 510, c1672 (3 Feb 1953).
19. Dulles, 'Memo of Conversation with P.M. Nehru, 21 May 1953', *FRUS 1952–1954,* xv, 1086.
20. Declaration of Sixteen Nations, 27 Jul 1953, RIIA, *Documents, 1953,* pp. 407–8.
21. Rees, *Korea,* pp. 460–1.
22. SS for the Colonies, 'The Colonial Territories, 1952–53', PP. *1951–52,* xxiii, 11.

23. CC (51) 10, 22 Nov 1951.
24. CP (51) 26, SS for the Colonies, 'The Situation in Malaya', 20 Nov 1951.
25. CC (52) 3, 14 Jan 1952.
26. Lyttelton, Hansard, 503, c2380 (17 Jul 1952).
27. SS for the Colonies, 'The Colonial Territories, 1951–52', PP. *1951–52*, xxiv, 37.
28. SS for the Colonies, 'The Colonial Territories, 1952–53', PP. *1952–53*, xxiii, 33–4.
29. CAB 131/12 Defence Committee, 8, 9 Jul 1952.
30. B. Berman, *Colonial Kenya*, p. 349.
31. SS for the Colonies, 'The Colonial Territories, 1952–53', PP. *1952–53*, xxiii, 26.
32. Chandos, *Memoirs*, p. 382.
33. SS for the colonies, 'The Colonial Territories, 1951–52', PP. *1951–52*, xxiv, 39.
34. CC (52) 16, 12 Feb 1952.
35. Chandos, *Memoirs*, p. 409.
36. R. Hyam, 'The Political Consequences of Seretse Khama', *Historical Journal*, 29, 4 (1986).
37. Hyam, ibid., pp. 934 and 936.
38. R. Hyam, 'Britain, Rhodesia and South Africa 1948–1953', *Historical Journal*, 30, 1 (1987).
39. Goldsworthy, *Colonial Issues*, pp. 217, 219.
40. CP (52) 445, LP, SS for Commonwealth Relations and SS for the Colonies, 'Proposed Federation of Southern Rhodesia, Northern Rhodesia and Nyasaland', (16 Dec 1952).
41. CC (52) 107, 22 Dec 1952.
42. Hyam, *Historical Journal*, 30, 168; SS for the Colonies, 'The Colonial Territories, 1953–54', PP. *1953–54*, xxv,
43. Head to Eden, 11 Sept 1952, AP 20/15/17.
44. CP (51) 40, FS, 'Egypt' (6 Dec 1951).
45. CC (51) 18, 19 Dec 1951.
46. CC (51) 22, 29 Dec 1951.
47. *The Times*, 26 Jan 1952.
48. CC (52) 8, 28 Jan 1952.
49. CC (52) 17, 14 Feb 1952.
50. CP (52) 63, FS, 'Egypt', 5 Mar 1952.
51. CC (52) 29, 12 Mar 1952.
52. Acheson to Gifford, 22 and 28 Mar 1952, *FRUS 1952–1954*, ix, 1778–82 and 1784–6.
53. CP (52) 202, FS, 'British Overseas Obligations' (18 Jun 1952).
54. Stevenson to FO, 29 Jul 1952; WSC to FS, 30 Jul 1952, PREM 11/392.
55. WSC to FS, 7 Aug 1952; FS to PM, 9 Aug 1952, PREM 11/392. 'Ducker' was the Harrow swimming pool.
56. WSC to Min. of State, 19 Aug 1952, ibid.
57. CP (52) 369, FS, 'Egypt', 27 Oct 1952.
58. CC (52) 91, 29 Oct 1952.
59. *The Times*, 22 Sept 1952.

60. Ibid., 17 Oct 1952.
61. Eden in Hansard, 505, c1014 (22 Oct 1952).
62. Eden, *Full Circle*, p. 245.
63. CC (53) 9 (11 Feb 1953).
64. Eden in Hansard, 511, cc602–6 (12 Feb 1953).
65. Gifford to Dept of State, 3 Jan 1953, *FRUS 1952–1954*, ix, 1939–41.
66. Shuckburgh, *Descent*, p. 75 (29 Jan 1953).
67. WSC to DDE, 19 Feb 1953, *FRUS 1952–1954*, ix, 1989–91.
68. Memo of Conversation by SS, 4 Mar 1953, ibid., p. 2008.
69. DDE to Eden, 16 Mar 1953, ibid., pp. 2020–1.
70. WSC to Eisenhower, 18 Mar 1953, ibid., pp. 2026–7.
71. Hankey memo, 22 May 1953, quoted Louis, 'The Anglo-Egyptian Settlement of 1954', Louis and Owen (eds), *Suez*, p. 54.

CHAPTER 5 THE EUROPEAN DEFENCE COMMUNITY

1. RIIA, *Documents, 1949–50*, pp. 326–31.
2. Attlee, Hansard, 484, c67 (12 Feb 1951).
3. Dockrill, *West German Rearmament*, p. 67.
4. Kilmuir, *Political Adventure*, p. 187.
5. Reynaud, RIIA, *Documents, 1951*, pp. 146–8.
6. CP (51) 32, PM, 'United Europe' (29 Nov 1951).
7. Giles, *Locust Years*, p. 140.
8. Boothby, *Recollections*, pp. 221–2.
9. DDE to Eden, 8 Dec 1951, AP 20/15/1.
10. Communiqué, Anglo-French talks, Paris, 18 Dec 1951, RIIA, *Documents, 1951*, pp. 141–2.
11. Macmillan to Eden, 21 Dec 1951, AP 20/15/2.
12. Pitblado to PM, 7 Dec 1951, PREM 11/214.
13. Spaak, *Continuing Battle*, p. 222.
14. CC (52) 17, 14 Feb 1952; Communiqué of Foreign Ministers' Meeting, 19 Feb 1952, RIIA, *Documents, 1952*, p. 83.
15. Eden diary, 4 Mar 1952, AP 20/1/28.
16. Ismay, *Memoirs*, pp. 461–2.
17. Fisher, *Macleod*, pp. 80–5.
18. Alexander to PM, 4 Apr 1952, PREM 11/373.
19. D (52) 28, 'Cooperation with European Defence Forces' (23 Jun 1952).
20. Montgomery to PM, 10 Dec 1952, PREM 11/373.
21. Colville to Montgomery, 14 Dec 1952.
22. CP (52) 434, FS, 'EDC and Alternative Plans' (10 Dec 1952).
23. CC (52) 29, 12 Mar 1952.
24. For the text of both notes, see RIIA, *Documents, 1952*, pp. 86–91.
25. Schumacher to Adenauer, 22 Apr 1952, ibid., p. 95.
26. Eden diary, 3 May 1952, AP 20/1/28.
27. CC (52) 43, 16 Apr 1952.
28. RIIA, *Documents ,1952*, pp. 96–100.
29. Ibid., pp. 247–52.

30. *FRUS 1952–54,* vii, 256. For the text of the agreements, see RIIA, *Documents, 1952,* pp. 105–65.
31. SS to Embassy in UK, 12 Jun 1952, *FRUS, 1952–54,* vii, 267.
32. McCloy to State Dept, 8 Jul 1952, ibid., p. 287.
33. US Govt to USSR, 10 Jul 1952. RIIA, *Documents, 1952,* pp. 175–7.
34. USSR to US Govt, 23 Aug 1952, ibid., pp. 186–92; USSR to US Govt, ibid., pp. 195–7.
35. FO 371/101741, quoted Dockrill, op. cit., p. 106.
36. Giles, *Locust Years,* pp. 178–9.
37. Shinwell, Hansard, 504, c1725 (31 Jul 1952).
38. Pimlott, Dalton, p. 613; Campbell, Bevan, p. 289.
39. *The Times,* 2 Aug 1952. See also Crossman, *Diaries,* p. 133.
40. Hansard, 504, c1350 (1 Aug 1952).
41. Giles, *Locust Years,* p. 178.
42. Ibid., p. 177.
43. Note by WSC on FS to PM, 'Joint Military Planning with the EDC', 23 Feb 1953, PREM 11/373.
44. Eden diary 4 Mar 1953, AP 29/1/29.
45. Ibid., 3 Apr 1953.
46. Ibid., 4 Apr 1953; *The Times,* 6 Apr 1953.

CHAPTER 6 PRIVATISATION

1. *Manifesto of the Conservative and Unionist Party,* 1951.
2. See above, p. 21.
3. CC (51) 1 (30 Oct 1951).
4. CC (51) 2 (1 Nov 1951).
5. CC (51) 6 (12 Nov 1951); Hansard, 493, c670–1 (12 Nov 1951).
6. CC (51) 10 (22 Nov 1951).
7. CC (52) 22 (27 Feb 1952).
8. CC (52) 24 (29 Feb 1952).
9. CC (52) 27 (9 Mar 1952).
10. CC (52) 3 (18 Mar 1952).
11. *The Times,* 4, 7, 9 and 10 Apr 1952.
12. Ibid., 5 Apr 1952.
13. *Economist,* 8 Mar 1952.
14. Hansard, 498, c2731–2 (9 Apr 1952).
15. CC (52) 42 (10 Apr 1952).
16. *The Times,* 17 Apr 1952.
17. *Economist,* 19 Apr 1952.
18. Crossman, *Diaries,* p. 108 (16 Jun 1952).
19. *The Times,* 8 May 1952.
20. Ibid., 9 May 1952.
21. *Economist,* 17 May 1952.
22. Nicolson, *Diaries and Letters,* p. 224 (22 May 1952).
23. CC (52) 50 (7 May 1952).
24. 'Transport Policy', PP. *1951–2,* xxv, 821–4.

25. *The Times,* 9 May 1952.
26. *Economist,* 17 May 1952.
27. Hansard, 501, c517 (21 May 1952).
28. Ibid., c528.
29. PM to Leathers, 28 Sep 1952, PREM 11/559.
30. CC (52) 84 (7 Oct 1952).
31. PM to Leathers, 16 Oct 1952, PREM 11/559.
32. CC (52) 91 (29 Oct 1952).
33. CP (54) 215, Min of Tpt, 'Road Haulage Disposals' (2 Jul 1954).
34. CP (55) 59, Min of Tpt, 'Road Haulage Disposals' (28 Feb 1955).
35. *The Times,* 18 Aug 1955.
36. Hansard, 501, c528 (21 May 1952).
37. TUC, *Annual Report, 1950,* pp. 564–575.
38. Kent, *In On The Act,* p. 236.
39. CC (52) 65 (3 Jul 1952).
40. CC (52) 68 (14 Jul 1952).
41. CC (52) 69 (15 Jul 1952).
42. Crookshank diary, 15 Jul 1952, p. 76.
43. Salisbury to Swinton, nd, Swinton Papers 174/6/3.
44. Eden diary, 15 July 1952, Avon Papers 20/1/28.
45. Hansard, 504, cc1282, 1313 (29 Jul 1952).
46. *Economist,* 2 Aug 1952.
47. Hansard, 508, c266 (27 Nov 1952).
48. Burn, *Steel Industry,* p. 374.
49. TUC, *Annual Report, 1953,* pp. 411–20.
50. Burk, *First Privatisation,* p. 2.
51. Woolton to PM, 22 Mar 1954, PREM 11/711.
52. Butler to PM, 13 Apr 1954, ibid.
53. Crookshank to PM, 25 May 1954, ibid.
54. CC (54) 44 (29 June 1954); Hansard, 530, cc279–81 (13 Jul 1954).
55. Burk, *First Privatisation,* p. 140.
56. Ibid., p. 141.
57. Ibid., p. 142.
58. CC (52) 36 (3 Apr 1952).
59. Norman Brook to PM, 22 Apr 1952, PREM 11/1213.
60. Walker-Smith to PM, 13 May 1952, ibid.
61. CC (52) 52 (13 May 1952).
62. 'Broadcasting: Memorandum', PP. *1951–2,* xxv, 27.
63. *The Times,* 16 May 1952.
64. HL Deb, 176, c1288 (22 May 1952).
65. Ibid., c1313.
66. Ibid., c1448 (26 May 1952).
67. Hansard, 502, c277 (11 Jun 1952).
68. Ibid., c1561 (19 Jun 1952).
69. *The Times,* 25 Nov 1952.
70. Shuckburgh, *Descent to Suez,* p. 57 (22 Nov 1952).
71. *The Times,* 21 Feb 1953.
72. CC (53) 16 (3 Mar 1953).
73. Briggs, *Sound and Vision,* p. 472.

74. *The Times,* 4 Jun 1953.
75. Briggs, p. 904.
76. CC (53) 35 (17 Jun 1953).
77. CP (53) 171, Cab Sec, 'Television Development' (17 Jun 1953).
78. Briggs, p. 915.
79. *The Times,* 31 Aug 1953.
80. 'Broadcasting: Memorandum on Television Policy', PP. *1953–4,* xxvi, 339–51.
81. Hansard, HL Deb, 184, cc511–748 (25 and 26 Nov 1953).
82. Hansard, 522, cc44–520 (14,15 and 16 Dec 1953).
83. Hansard, 525, cc1440–554 (25 Mar 1954).
84. Sendall, *Independent Television,* vol i, pp. 34, 59, 92.

CHAPTER 7 THE STRUGGLE AGAINST ILLNESS

1. Strang to Moscow, 28 Mar 1953, AP 20/16/10.
2. FS, to Moscow, 30 Mar 1953, AP 20/16/10A.
3. Eden diary, 3 Apr 1953, AP 20/1/29.
4. Eden diary, 4 Apr 1953, Ibid.
5. Pethybridge, *Post-war Russia,* p. 125.
6. *The Times,* 6 Apr 1953.
7. WSC to DDE 6 Apr 1953, PREM 11/1074. This file contains the private exchanges of the Prime Minister and President throughout the period.
8. *The Times,* 8 Apr 1953.
9. Ibid., 13 Apr 1953.
10. WSC to DDE, 9 Apr 1953.
11. WSC to DDE, 10 Apr 1953.
12. DDE to WSC, 11 Apr 1953.
13. 'Address by President Eisenhower on the Prospects for World Peace', 16 Apr 1953, RIIA, *Documents, 1953,* pp. 48–50.
14. Hansard, 514, cc655–6 (20 Apr 1953); WSC to DDE, 21 Apr 1953.
15. DDE to WSC, 25 Apr 1953.
16. WSC to DDE, 4 May 1953.
17. DDE to WSC, 5 May 1953.
18. WSC to DDE, 6 May 1953.
19. WSC, *Unwritten Alliance,* pp. 52–4.
20. *The Times,* 12 May 1953.
21. Colville, *Fringes,* p. 367.
22. DDE to WSC, 22 May 1953.
23. WSC to DDE, 24 May 1953.
24. DDE to WSC, 20 Jun 1953, and WSC to DDE, 20 Jun 1953.
25. Giles, *Locust Years,* p. 388.
26. *The Times,* 6 Jun 1953; Eden, *Full Circle,* pp. 51–2.
27. Butler, 'Note, June 1953', Butler Papers G 26.
28. Soames, *Clementine,* p. 434.
29. Moran, *Struggle for Survival,* p. 408 (24 Jun 1953).

30. Butler to Eden, 27 Jun 1953, AP 20/16/124; Macmillan, *Tides of Fortune*, p. 516.
31. *The Times*, 27 Jun 1953.
32. Colville, *Fringes*, pp. 668–9.
33. Colville to Clarissa Eden, 26 Jun 1953, AP 220/16/123.
34. *The Times*, 27 Jun 1953.
35. Jane Portal to Butler, 28 Jun 1953, Butler Papers G 26.
36. *The Times*, 29 Jun 1953.
37. Butler to Eden, 27 Jun 1953, AP 20/16/124.
38. Moran, *Struggle*, p. 411 (28 Jun 1953).
39. *The Times*, 30 Jun 1953.
40. WSC to DDE, 1 Jul 1953.
41. CC (53) 39 (6 Jul 1953).
42. CC (53) 42 (13 Jul 1953).
43. WSC to DDE, 17 Jul 1953.
44. DDE to WSC, 22 Jul 1953.
45. RIIA, *Documents, 1953*, pp. 77–8.
46. Ibid., pp. 78–81.
47. Colville, *Fringes*, p. 672.
48. Thomas to Eden, 14 Jul 1953, AP 20/16/141.
49. H of L, Deb, 183 cC1023, 1042 (29 Jul 1953).
50. CC (53) 48 (10 Aug 1953).
51. *The Times*, 10 Aug 1953.
52. WSC to Eden, 30 Aug 1953, AP 20/16/144.
53. *The Times*, 4 Sep 1953.
54. *The Times*, 9 Sep 1953.
55. Jane Portal to Butler, 23 Sep 1953, Butler Papers G 26.
56. Eden diary, 1 Oct 1953, AP 20/1/29.
57. *The Times*, 9 Oct 1953; for the Soviet note of 28 September, see RIIA, *Documents, 1953*, pp. 91–5.
58. WSC, *Unwritten Alliance*, p. 58.
59. Ibid., p. 67.
60. *The Times*, 12 Oct 1953.
61. Moran, *Struggle*, p. 477.
62. Colville, *Fringes*, p. 679.

CHAPTER 8 BERMUDA AND BERLIN

1. Hailes Papers, HAIS 4/12, nd.
2. AP 20/16/146, nd.
3. CC (53) 52 (16 Sep 1953).
4. WSC, *Unwritten Alliance*, p. 71.
5. Moran, *Struggle*, p. 488 (3 Nov 1953).
6. James (ed.), *Chips*, p. 479 (3 Nov 1953).
7. Macmillan, Hansard, 520, cc171–94 (4 Nov 1953).
8. Eden, Hansard, 520, cc308–21 (5 Nov 1953).

9. *The Times,* 5 Nov 1953.
10. Dugdale, Hansard, 520, cc620–9 (9 Nov 1953).
11. For communiqué, 18 Oct 1953, see RIIA, *Documents, 1953* , pp. 97–8.
12. WSC to DDE, 5 Nov 1953, PREM 11/1074.
13. DDE to WSC, 7 Nov 1953, ibid.
14. WSC to DDE, 7 Nov 1953, ibid.
15. For this and later quotations from Conference proceedings, see *FRUS, 1952–4,* v, 1737–837.
16. Colville, *Fringes,* p. 683.
17. Soviet note to Western Powers, 26 Nov 1953, and reply, 8 Dec 1953. RIIA, *Documents, 1953,* pp. 107–12.
18. Selwyn Lloyd to Eden, 3 Dec 1953, FO 800/697.
19. Ambrose, *Eisenhower,* p. 129.
20. RIIA, *Documents, 1953,* p. 356.
21. Ibid., pp. 110–11.
22. Eden to WSC, 30 Nov 1953, AP 20/16/158.
23. Shuckburgh, *Descent,* p. 178.
24. CC (53) 79 (15 Dec 1953).
25. Moran, *Struggle,* p. 513.
26. *The Times,* 16 Dec 1953.
27. Ibid., 17 Dec 1953.
28. WSC, *Unwritten Alliance,* pp. 94, 98.
29. Hansard, 522, c690 (17 Dec 1953).
30. RIIA, *Documents, 1953,* p. 112.
31. CC (54) 3 (18 Jan 1954).
32. CC (54) 10 (22 Feb 1954).
33. CC (53) 78 (14 Dec 1953).
34. Worswick and Ady, *British Economy,* p. 536.
35. CC (53) 79 (15 Dec 1953).
36. *Economist,* 19 Dec 1953.
37. CP (53) 363, MoL, 'Industrial Disputes' (29 Dec 1953).
38. *The Times,* 1 Jan 1954.
39. Ibid., 9 Jan 1954.
40. Ibid., 22 Jan 1954.
41. TUC, *Report, 1954,* pp. 239–40.
42. *The Times,* 1 Apr 1954.
43. Ibid., 12 Feb 1954.
44. CP (54) 32, MoD et al., 'Pay of the Armed Forces' (29 Jan 1954).
45. Hansard, 524, c1024 (2 Mar 1954).
46. Ibid., 523, c204 (2 Feb 1954).
47. CC (54) 14 (3 Mar 1954).
48. CC (54) 24 (31 Mar 1954).
49. Hansard, 526, cc195ff (6 Apr 1954).
50. *The Times,* 7 Apr 1954.
51. *Manchester Guardian,* 7 Apr 1954.
52. Ibid., 9 Apr 1954.
53. *Sheffield Telegraph,* 12 Apr 1954.

CHAPTER 9 THE H-BOMB AND EDEN'S DIPLOMACY

1. *Punch,* 3 Feb 1954.
2. Shuckburgh, *Descent,* p. 141 (4 Mar 1954).
3. Ibid., p. 145 (11 Mar 1954).
4. Note by Butler, 12 Mar 1954, Butler Papers G 27.
5. WSC, *Unwritten Alliance,* p. 157 (12 Jul 1954).
6. *The Times,* 26 Mar 1954.
7. WSC to DDE, 24 Mar 1954.
8. DDE to WSC, 28 Mar 1954.
9. Hansard, 526, c36 (5 Apr 1954).
10. Ibid., cc36–43.
11. Ibid., c54. These exchanges were omitted from the version of the speech printed in WSC, *Unwritten Alliance,* pp. 127–36.
12. *The Times,* 6 Apr 1954.
13. Crookshank, diary, p. 126.
14. Crossman, *Diaries,* p. 306 (6 Apr 1954).
15. *The Times,* 8 Apr 1954.
16. DDE to WSC, 8 Apr 1954.
17. *The Times,* 13 Apr 1954.
18. Hansard, 526, c969 (12 Apr 1954).
19. CP (54) 134 FS, 'Indo-China' (7 Apr 1954).
20. Crossman, *Diaries,* p. 312 (21 Apr 1954, but referring to 14 Apr).
21. Hansard, 526, c1795 (29 Apr 1954).
22. CP (54) 155 Cab Sec, 'Indo-China' (27 Apr 1954).
23. CC (54) 30 (28 Apr 1954).
24. *FRUS 1952–1954,* xvi, 627.
25. Shuckburgh, *Descent,* p. 193 (5 May 1954).
26. Eden, *Full Circle,* p. 121 (quoting note of 20 May 1954).
27. Makins to Eden, 21 May and 18 Jun 1954, AP 20/17/18 A and 19.
28. CC (54) 43 (22 Jun 1954).
29. WSC to DDE, 21 Jun 1954.
30. WSC to DDE, 21 Jun 1954.
31. Moran, *Struggle,* p. 558.
32. Ibid., p. 562; Colville, *Fringes,* p. 693.
33. Moran, *Struggle,* pp. 567–8 (28 Jun 1954).
34. Luard, *United Nations,* i, 300.
35. Colville, *Fringes,* p. 698.
36. Ibid., p. 697.
37. WSC to DDE, 7 Jul 1954.
38. CC (54) 47 (7 Jul 1954).
39. CC (54) 48 (8 Jul 1954), c.a.
40. Crookshank diary, p. 133 (8 July 1954).
41. DDE to WSC, 7 Jul 1954.
42. WSC to DDE, 8 Jul 1954.
43. CC (54) 49 (9 Jul 1954).
44. CC (54) 50 (13 Jul 1954).
45. WSC to DDE, 9 Jul 1954.

46. Crookshank diary, p. 134.
47. CC (54) 52 (23 Jul 1954).
48. Soviet note, 24 Jul 1954, RIIA, *Documents, 1954*, pp. 46–51.
49. CC (54) 53 (26 Jul 1954), c.a.
50. Statement by SS, 23 July 1954, *FRUS 1952–1954*, xvi, 1550.
51. For the text of the treaty signed 8 Sep 1954, see RIIA, *Documents, 1954*, pp. 153–6.
52. *The Times*, 21 and 23 Jul 1954.
53. Hansard, 531, c820 (29 Jul 1954).
54. Crossman, *Diaries*, p. 340 (30 Jul 1954).
55. CC (54) 1 (7 Jan 1954).
56. Eden diary, 17 Dec 1954, AP 20/1/30.
57. FO to Teheran, 1 Apr 1954, PREM 11/726.
58. Yergin, *Prize*, p. 477.
59. FO to Washington, 5 Aug 1954, PREM 11/726.
60. RIIA, *Documents, 1953*, pp. 290–1.
61. Eden, *Full Circle*, p. 188.
62. *The Times*, 6 Oct 1954.
63. Eden to Lyttelton, 10 Aug 1954, AP 20/17/173.
64. 'Conversations at Chartwell with M Mendès-France, 23 Aug 1954', PREM 11/672; Giles, *Locust Years*, p. 226.
65. Giles, *Locust Years*, p. 228.
66. CC (54) 57 (27 Aug 1954).
67. CC (54) 59 (8 Sep 1954).
68. CC (54) 60 (17 Sep 1954).
69. Eden, *Full Circle*, p. 162.
70. RIIA, *Documents, 1954*, pp. 24 (Dulles) and 26 (Eden), 29 Sep 1954.
71. Macmillan to Eden, 30 Sep 1954, AP 20/17/6.
72. Eden, *Full Circle*, p. 162.
73. James, *Eden*, p. 389.
74. WSC, *Unwritten Alliance*, p. 188 (9 Oct 1954).
75. *The Times*, 21 Oct 1954.
76. Eden to WSC, 10 Aug 1954, quoted Gilbert, *Churchill*, viii, 1046.
77. Macmillan, *Tides of Fortune*, p. 541; Butler to WSC, 18 Aug 1954, Butler Papers.
78. WSC to Eden, 24 Aug 1954, AP 20/17/179.
79. Eden diary, 27 Aug 1954, AP 20/1/30.
80. Butler to Buchan-Hepburn, 8 Sep 1954, HAIS/4/8.
81. *The Times*, 11 Oct 1954.
82. Ibid.
83. Ibid., 18 Oct 1954.

CHAPTER 10 SETTING THE PEOPLE FREE

1. Butler to Eden, 27 Jun 1953, AP/16/124.
2. See, e.g., *Daily Mirror*, 15 Dec 1953.
3. *The Times*, 7 Jan 1954.

4. For details of derationing, see Worswick and Ady, *British Economy*, p. 439.
5. Quoted in CR Schenk, 'The Sterling Area and British Policy Alternatives', *Contemporary Record*, vi (1992), 283.
6. Hall, *Diaries*, vol ii, p. 7 (8 Apr 1954).
7. Ibid., p. 8.
8. *The Times*, 31 Mar 1954; Hansard, 526, c224 (6 Apr 1954).
9. CP (54) 252, C/E, 'Report of the Committee on Civil Expenditure' (23 Jul 1954).
10. C/E to PM, 22 Jul 1954, PREM 11/657.
11. CC (54) 51 (20 Jul 1954).
12. CC (54) 54 (27 Jul 1954).
13. See, e.g., Min of Supply, 'Defence Policy and Expenditure' (20 Nov 1953), Sandys papers, 4/1/1. This was submitted to the Ministerial Committee on Defence Policy as DP (M)(3)15.
14. Alexander to PM, 13 Aug 1954, PREM 11/701.
15. PM to Alexander, 15 Aug 1954, ibid.
16. Copy of telephone message from PM to Swinton, 19 Aug 1954, ibid.
17. Thomas to Eden, 1 Aug 1954, AP 20/17/170.
18. CC (54) 73 (5 Nov 1954).
19. CC (54) 75 (11 Nov 1954).
20. Hansard, 526, c211 (6 Apr 1954).
21. *The Times*, 18 Oct 1954.
22. Ibid., 17 Feb 1954.
23. Ibid., 18 Feb 1954.
24. CC (54) 18 (15 Mar 1954).
25. WSC in Hansard, 526, c1150 (14 Apr 1954).
26. Goodhart, p. 168.
27. WSC in Hansard, 527, c1495–6 (13 May 1954).
28. Hansard, 528, c30ff.
29. Chief Whip's Report, 'Special Meeting of the 1922 Committee', 1 Jun 1954, AP 20/17/123.
30. CC (54) 38 (2 Jun 1954).
31. Note, 'M.P.s salaries: View from the Areas', enclosed in Woolton to Eden, 3 Jun 1954, AP 20/17/128.
32. WSC in Hansard, 529, c515 (8 Jul 1954).
33. CC (54) 50 (13 Jul 1954).
34. Goodhart, p. 169; Crossman, p. 334 (8 Jul 1954).
35. CC (54) 3 (18 Jan 1954); R.D. Brown, *Crichel Down*, for more details.
36. For the Report, see PP. *1953–4*, xi, 203ff.
37. *The Times*, 16 Jun 1954.
38. Dugdale in Hansard, 528, c1759 (15 Jun 1954).
39. *The Times*, 16 Jul 1954.
40. Carr to Eden, 16 Jul 1954, AP 20/17/145.
41. CP (54) 238, Cab Sec, 'Crichel Down' (19 July 1954).
42. Crookshank Diary, 19 July 1954; Hansard, 530, c1194 (20 Jul 1954).
43. D.N. Chester, 'The Crichel Down Case', *Public Administration*, xxxii (1954), 390–7.
44. *The Times*, 21 Jul 1954; Lyttelton to Eden, nd, Aug 1954, AP 20/17/174.

45. *Manchester Guardian,* 17 Dec 1953, quoted Goldsworthy, *Colonial Issues,* pp. 245f.
46. *The Times,* 29 Jul 1954.
47. Ibid., 17 Jul 1954.
48. *New York Times,* 17 Jul 1954 and 24 Sep 1954.
49. Butler to Massey, 24 Aug 1954, Butler Papers G 27.
50. *Journal of Commerce* (New York), 23 Sep 1954.
51. *Wall Street Journal* (New York), 27 Sep 1954.
52. *Manchester Guardian,* 1 Oct 1954.
53. Worswick in Worswick and Ady, *British Economy,* p. 30.
54. Ibid., p. 32.
55. Crossman, *Diaries,* p. 350 (1 Oct 1954).
56. *The Times,* 9 Oct 1954.
57. Ibid., 18 Oct 1954.
58. Attlee in Hansard, 531, c1032 (19 Oct 1954).
59. Buchan-Hepburn to Butler, 7 Sep 1954, Butler Papers G 27.
60. *The Times,* 19 Oct 1954.
61. WSC, *Unwritten Alliance,* p. 193 (9 Nov 1954).
62. Woolton Diary, 14 Apr 1954, Woolton Papers.
63. CC (54) 32 (5 May 1954).
64. CP (54) 246, LPS, 'Legislative Programme: 1954–55 Session' (22 Jul 1954).
65. CP(54) 247, Home Sec, 'Legislation to Complete the Dismantling of Defence Regulations' (23 Jul 1954).
66. Macleod to Eden, 30 Jul 1954, Butler Papers G 27.
67. Butler to Eden, 24 Aug 1954, AP 20/17/184.
68. CC (54) 68 (20 Oct 1954).
69. WSC, *Unwritten Alliance,* p. 198 (23 Nov 1954).
70. *The Times,* 25 Nov 1954.
71. WSC, *Unwritten Alliance,* pp. 204–20 (1 Dec 1954).
72. *The Times,* 1 Dec 1954.
73. WSC, *Unwritten Alliance,* p. 201–3 (30 Nov 1954).
74. Audience reaction reported in *The Times,* 1 Dec 1954.
75. Moran, *Struggle,* p. 616; Soames, *Clementine,* pp. 712–13.

CHAPTER 11 THE LAST SESSION

1. Hansard, 535, c146ff (1 Dec 1954).
2. CP (54) 337, Min of Pensions & NI, 'Timetable for Review of War Pensions and NI Pensions Benefits' (8 Nov 1954).
3. CC (54) 75 (11 Nov 1954).
4. 'Report of the Ctee on the Economic and Financial Problems for the Provision for Old Age', PP. *1954–55,* vi, 589–712.
5. Hansard, 535, c494 (8 Dec 1954).
6. Ibid., c1121 (9 Dec 1954).
7. TUC, *Report 1955,* p. 155.
8. Hansard, 535, c2772 (22 Dec 1954).

9. CC (54) 7 (3 Feb 1954).
10. CP (54) SS for CR, 'Deportation of British Subjects: Power of Commonwealth Governments' (21 Feb 1954); CP (54) 85 SS for the Colonies, 'Deportation of British Subjects: Power of Colonial Governments (3 Mar 1954).
11. C (54) 234, Home Sec, 'Colonial Immigrants' (22 Nov 1954); CC (54) 78 (24 Nov 1954).
12. CP (54) 236, SS for CR, 'Colonial Immigrants' (23 Nov 1954).
13. CP (54) 379, SS for the Colonies, 'Colonial Immigrants (6 Dec 1954).
14. CC (54) 82 (6 Dec 1954).
15. C (55) 5 (11 Jan 1955).
16. Macmillan to Eden, 14 Jan 1955, PREM 11/824.
17. CC (55) 8 (31 Jan 1955).
18. CC (55) 15 (17 Feb 1955).
19. Norman Brook to PM, 17 Feb 1955, PREM 11/824.
20. *The Times,* 11 Oct 1954.
21. TUC, *Report 1955,* p. 106.
22. *The Times,* 8 Oct 1954.
23. Ibid., 21 Oct 1954.
24. Hansard, 531, cc1035–6 (19 Oct 1954).
25. Ministerial Ctee on Emergencies, 27 Oct 1954, PREM 11/1035.
26. *The Times,* 28 Oct 1954.
27. Ibid., 1 Nov 1954.
28. Ibid., 17 Nov 1954.
29. CC (54) 85 (13 Dec 1954).
30. Monckton to PM, 24 Dec 1954, PREM 11/1026.
31. Eden diary, 23 Dec 1954, AP 20/1/30.
32. Ibid., 6 Jan 1955, AP 20/1/31.
33. *The Times,* 6 Jan 1955.
34. Ibid., 7 Jan 1955.
35. CC (55) 1 (4 Jan 1955).
36. Stuart to Butler, 9 Jan 1955, Butler Papers G46/8.
37. *The Times,* 20 Jan 1955.
38. Ibid., 25 Jan 1955.
39. CC (54) 61 (21 Sep 1954).
40. CP (53) 122, SS for CR, 'The Colonial Territories and Commonwealth Membership' (8 Apr 1953).
41. SS for CR, 'Report on Visit to Canada' (18 Oct 1954), Swinton Papers 6/4.
42. CC (54) 92, Conclusions (22 Dec 1954).
43. J.D.B. Miller, *Survey,* p. 67.
44. CP (55) 43, SS for CR, 'Commonwealth Membership' (11 Feb 1955).
45. Shuckburgh, *Descent,* p. 251 (18 Feb 1955).
46. Eden diary, 6 Feb 1955, AP 20/1/31.
47. Mansergh, *Documents and Speeches,* pp. 290–1.
48. *The Times,* 31 Jan 1955.
49. CC (55) 13 (15 Feb 1955).
50. WSC to DDE, 15 Feb 1955, PREM 11/1074.
51. DDE to WSC, 19 Feb 1955, loc. cit.

52. CC (55) 16 (22 Feb 1955).
53. Macmillan, *Tides of Fortune*, p. 553.
54. *The Times*, 16 Feb 1955.
55. Eden, *Full Circle*, p. 221.
56. Hansard, 536, cc157–60 (8 Mar 1955).
57. Hansard, 539, cc379–83 (30 Mar 1955).
58. *The Times*, 16 Mar 1955.
59. De L'Isle to Macmillan and reply, both 17 Nov 1954, F 800/116.
60. WSC, *Unwritten Alliance*, pp. 196–7 (23 Nov 1954) and pp. 204–24 (1 Dec 1954).
61. MoD, 'Statement on Defence, 1955', PP. *1954–55*, x, 475–504.
62. WSC, *Unwritten Alliance*, p. 234 (1 March 1955).
63. *The Times*, 2 Mar 1955.
64. Hansard, 537, c1905 (1 Mar 1955).
65. Ibid., c2116 (2 Mar 1955).
66. Ibid., cc2118, 2176.
67. *Evening Standard*, 3 Mar 1955, quoted Jackson, *Rebels and Whips*, p. 127.
68. Jackson, p. 130.
69. *The Times*, 18 Oct 1954.
70. Crookshank to Eden, 12 Oct 1954, AP 20/17/208.
71. Macmillan to WSC (copy to Eden), 2 Oct 1954, AP 20/17/202A.
72. Moran, *Struggle*, p. 623.
73. Eden to WSC, ? Dec 1954, AP 20/17/218.
74. Woolton diary, 22 Dec 1954.
75. Moran, *Struggle*, pp. 626–8, 630.
76. Eden diary, 1 Feb 1955, AP 20/1/31.
77. Woolton diary, 11 Mar 1955.
78. Washington to FO, 10 Mar 1955, AP 20/18/70.
79. Eden to PM, 11 Mar 1955, AP 20/18/1.
80. WSC to FS, 12 Mar 1955, AP 20/18/5.
81. Eden to PM, 12 Mar 1955, AP/18/5A.
82. WSC to FS, 12 Mar 1955, AP 20/18/6.
83. CC (55) 23 (14 Mar 1955).
84. Woolton diary, 14 Mar 1955.
85. FO to Washington, 15 Mar 1955, AP 20/18/8.
86. Washington to FO, 15 Mar 1955, AP 20/18/10.
87. Colville *Fringes*, pp. 706–8.
88. Butler, *Art of the Possible*, p. 177.
89. Soames, *Clementine*, p. 642.
90. *The Times*, 21 Apr 1955.
91. Colville, *Fringes*, p. 709.
92. CC (55) 28 (5 Apr 1955).
93. *Manchester Guardian*, 6 Apr 1955.
94. Macmillan, *Tides of Fortune*, p. 558.
95. WSC to Eden, 2 Apr 1955, AP 20/18/57.
96. *Manchester Guardian*, 6 Apr 1955.

Bibliography

UNPUBLISHED SOURCES

Public Record Office

Cabinet Minutes
Cabinet Papers
Foreign Office Papers – FO371; FO800
Prime Minister's Papers PREM 11

Private Papers

Avon Papers, Birmingham University Library
Butler Papers, Trinity College, Cambridge
Cherwell Papers, Nuffield College Library, Oxford
Crookshank Diary, Bodleian Library, Oxford
Hailes Papers, Churchill College, Cambridge (Buchan-Hepburn)
Sandys Papers, Churchill College, Cambridge
Swinton Papers, Churchill College, Cambridge
Woolton Papers, Bodleian Library, Oxford

PUBLISHED SOURCES

Acheson, D., *Present at the Creation* (1970).
Ambrose, S.E., *Eisenhower the President* (New York, 1991).
Avon, Earl of, *Full Circle: the Memoirs of the Rt Hon. Sir Anthony Eden (The Eden Memoirs, Vol. 3) (1960)*.
Berman, B., *Control and Crisis in Colonial Kenya: The Dialectic of Domination* (1990).
Birkenhead, Lord, *Walter Monckton* (1969).
Boothby, Lord, *Recollections of a Rebel* (1978).
Boyd-Carpenter, J., *Way of Life: The Memoirs of John Boyd-Carpenter* (1980).
Bracken, Brendan, *My Dear Max: Letters to Lord Beaverbrook, 1925 to 1958* (1990).
Bradford, S., *King George VI* (1989).
Briggs, Asa, *The History of Broadcasting in the United Kingdom, Vol. 4, Sound and Vision* (Oxford, 1979).
Brown, R.D., *The Battle of Crichel Down* (1955).
Burk, K., *The First Privatisation: The Politicians, the City and the Denationalisation of Steel* (1991).
Burn, D., *The Steel Industry, 1939–59* (Cambridge, 1961).
Butler, D.E., *British General Election of 1951* (1952).

Butler, R.A., *The Art of the Possible* (1971).

Campbell, J., *Nye Bevan and the Mirage of British Socialism* (1987).

Chandos, Lord, *The Memoirs of Lord Chandos* (1962).

Churchill, W.S., *The Sinews of Peace* (1948).

Churchill, W.S., *Europe Unite* (1950).

Churchill, W.S., *In the Balance* (1951).

Churchill, W.S., *The Second World War*, Vol. VI (1954).

Churchill, W.S., *Stemming the Tide* (1953).

Churchill, W.S., *The Unwritten Alliance* (1961).

Colville, J., *The Fringes of Power, Downing Street Diaries, 1939–1955* (1986).

Cook, C. and Ramsden, J (eds), *By-Elections in British Politics* (1973).

Crossman, R., *Diaries: The Backbench Diaries of Richard Crossman* (ed. J. Morgan, 1981).

Dockrill, S., *Britain's Policy for West German Rearmament, 1950–1955* (Cambridge, 1991).

Fisher, N., *Iain Macleod* (1973).

Foreign Relations of the United States (Washington, DC).

Gilbert, Martin, *Winston S. Churchill*, Vol. VIII: *'Never Despair', 1945–1965* (1988).

Giles, F., *The Locust Years: The Story of the Fourth French Republic* (1991).

Goldsworthy, D., *Colonial Issues in British Politics*, 1945–1961 (Oxford, 1971).

Goodhart, Philip (with Ursula Branston), *The 1922: The Story of the Conservative Backbenchers' Parliamentary Committee* (1973).

Hall, *Diaries*: see Roberthall.

Hoffman, J.D., *The Conservative Party in Opposition, 1945–51* (Cambridge, 1964).

Ismay, Lord, *Memoirs of General the Lord Ismay* (1960).

Jackson, R., *Rebels and Whips* (1968).

James, Robert Rhodes (ed.) *Chips: The Diaries of Sir Henry Channon* (1967).

James, Robert Rhodes, *Anthony Eden* (1986).

Kent, Sir H.S., *In On the Act: Memoirs of a Lawmaker* (1979).

Kilmuir, Lord, *Political Adventure: The Memoirs of the Earl of Kilmuir* (1964).

Louis, W.R. and Owen, R. (eds), *Suez: The Crisis and Its Consequences* (Oxford, 1989).

Luard, E., *A History of the United Nations: the Years of Western Domination, 1945–1955* (1982).

Lysaght, C.E., *Brendan Bracken* (1979).

MacDougall, D., *Don and Mandarin: Memoirs of an Economist* (1987).

Macmillan, Harold, *Tides of Fortune 1945–1955* (1969).

Mansergh, N., *Documents and Speeches on Commonwealth Affairs, 1952–62* (1963).

Millar, J.D.B., *Survey of Commonwealth Affairs, 1953–1969* (1974).

Moran, Lord, *Churchill, the Struggle for Survival, 1940–65* (1966).

Nicholas, H.G., *British General Election of 1950* (1951).

Nicolson, H., *Diaries and Letters, 1945–62, Vol. 3* (1968).

Pelling, H., *The Labour Governments, 1945–51* (1984).

Pethybridge, R.W., *History of Post-war Russia* (1966).

Pimlott, B., *Hugh Dalton* (1985).

Pimlott, B., (ed.), *Political Diary of Hugh Dalton* (1986).

Plowden, E., *An Industrialist in the Treasury, the Post-War Years* (1987).

Rees, D., *Korea: The Limited War* (1964).

Roberthall, Lord, *Diaries* (two vols, 1989 and 1991)

Royal Institute of International Affairs, *Documents on International Affairs, 1949–1954* (1953–57).

Sendall, B., *Independent Television in Britain, Vol. I: Origin and Foundation, 1946–62* (1982).

Shuckburgh, Evelyn, *Descent to Suez: Diaries, 1951–56* (1986).

Soames, Mary, *Clementine Churchill* (1979).

Spaak, P.H., *The Continuing Battle* (1971).

Stuart, J., *Within the Fringe* (1967).

Thorpe, D.R., *Selwyn Lloyd* (1989).

Wheeler-Bennett, J.W., *King George VI* (1958).

Worswick, G.D.N. and Ady, P.H., *The British Economy in the 1950s* (Oxford, 1962).

Yergin, D., *The Prize: The Epic Quest for Oil, Money, and Power* (New York, 1991).

Index

209